SERMON SUBSTANCE

SERMON SUBSTANCE

by

Ralph G. Turnbull

BAKER BOOK HOUSE
Grand Rapids 6, Michigan
1958

Library of Congress Catalog Card Number: 58-59824

Copyright 1958, by Baker Book House

Printed in the United States of America

DEDICATED

to my brother

ROLAND

who has been Pastor, Professor, College President,

yet always a Preacher

and

a discriminating judge of building a sermon

"There was *a clearing-house* in his soul where all impulses were ordered and adjusted, and this response gave him happiness."

JOHN BUCHAN, *Sir Walter Scott*

"Then said *the Interpreter,* 'Come in; I will show thee that which will be profitable to thee.' "

JOHN BUNYAN, *The Pilgrim's Progress*

"I shall light *a candle of understanding* in thine heart, which shall not be put out, till the things be performed which thou shalt begin to write."

THE APOCRYPHA, II ESDRAS 14:25

"When indisposed to reading and study, to read of my own remarks, the fruit of my studying divinity, &c., *to set me agoing again.*"

JONATHAN EDWARDS, *Commonplace Book*

Introduction

The task of sermon preparation is a delight when the busy pastor knows what to prepare. But there are days when there is no stirring of the wind, and he feels like a ship becalmed. What then? Is it a denial of faith to lift a top sail in the hope and expectation that the wind will blow again? Here it is that sermon substance has a place of stimulus and suggestion. No man is original, and the writer makes no such claim.

How are sermons born? Where do the ideas come from? A casual glance at a magazine, the reading of a book, talking with a friend, listening to another speaker or preacher, delighting in the music which is wafted through the air, the confidence of someone to whom you minister in sickness or in need, the illumination of Scripture as you pray: all these and many other ways are the media through which the divine Spirit brings to birth the message.

This book is a modest attempt to set down some valid and tried ways of interpretation in preaching. There are suggestions for each Sunday of the year. No attempt is made to give the sermons in full or with much illustration. This is substance, the core to build the whole. There are topical, textual, expository, doctrinal, pastoral, and biographical ideas with the Bible reading and other forms of structure. The texts are quoted from the King James Version; but other versions and translations should be consulted.

It is the conviction of the writer that the true art of homiletics is not an invention but a discovery. Coming to the study of the Scriptures, guidance is sought in prayer and meditation. As the Holy Spirit illumines what He inspired, interpretation is given and understanding begins. Grammar, literary forms, exegesis and criticism are thus utilized in the willing obedience to truth as it is found in Jesus Christ.

These selections do not specially touch on what is known as "life-situation" preaching or the essay-sermon type. The reason is that we are in a day of the revival of biblical preaching, and these are so based. But, when preached, each message with doctrinal emphasis is and should be applied to life with its needs and demands. With this in mind, these emphases would deal with the larger context of the church year and find unity within variety.

> "O! many a shaft, at random sent,
> Finds mark the archer little meant!
> And many a word, at random spoken,
> May soothe or wound a heart that's broken."

SIR WALTER SCOTT, *The Lord of the Isles.*

Here's to *a shaft at random* and much stimulus to every reader, the layman within the church in devotion and the pastor who has the divine passion to preach!

RALPH G. TURNBULL

THE FIRST PRESBYTERIAN CHURCH
SEATTLE, WASHINGTON

Contents

1. At the Threshold

"My presence shall go with thee...."—Exodus 33:14

We are "at the gate of the year." When George VI was King of Great Britain, one of his last acts before his death was a broadcast to the empire. In that message to his people he quoted these appealing words:

"I said to the man who
stood at the gate of the year,
'Give me a light that I may
tread safely into the unknown.'
And he replied:
'Go out into the darkness
and put your hand into the hand of God,
That shall be to you better
than light, and safer than a known way.' "

These words remind us that we are at the threshold of another year. We are looking out upon an untried pathway, a future all unknown. How shall we know the way? Many have asked that question. The answer is in the text. Moses was given this eternal word for his people when they stood at the threshold.

The Hebrew nation desired to know the pathway: God promised His presence. They asked for a charted course: He gave them a convoy through the trackless spaces. They wished a map of the journey in advance: He brought them a Word of assurance. As they sought for light in the darkness, God put out His hand to lead them. Is not this the right way of faith? If we walk by faith, we must trust and venture, nothing doubting God's presence for the new year.

I. *Enriching and Enabling.* With God by our side is the assurance of *rest*: not the cessation from toil and labor, but a poise and calm in the midst of work. John Ruskin has it that there is no music in a rest, but there is the making of music. This is true when we lean on God. When the Israelites entered the Promised Land after the wilderness wandering, there was no complete and final rest. To possess the land they had to overcome giants and walled cities. Possessing their possessions enabled them to enter into the rest of reward. There is a rest remaining for God's people in Jesus Christ, the Rest-Giver, who takes the loads under His yoke to rest the weary.

Moreover, there is *peace* for those who find God's presence. The New Testament makes much of this. It is the absence of worry, hurry, and flurry. It is freedom from carking care and anxiety

13

which frets. This mastery of circumstances is the promise of God to His people in every age. Yesterday may have exposed you to danger and defeat. Today opens up the possibility of an enriching experience of God's strength available. It is enriching through His presence and enabling because of the grace He proffers.

II. *Conditional and Decisive.* Someone might ask concerning the ways and means of entering into this blessed life. The promise of God's presence is not given to all without exception. It is offered to all, and yet there are those who have no knowledge of this because they do not accept God's basis of partnership. One who is not a Christian believer and disciple has no assurance of this life. He gropes in the darkness of uncertainty. Trust in God through Christ brings the basis of security and cancels despair.

"If thy presence go not with me, carry us not up hence" (Exod. 33:15), so Moses pleaded. How dare men venture without the *guide?* This is decisive and definite. It is common sense! How pitiful the home where death has entered when there is no acquaintance with the God of all comfort. It is dark and tragic for hearts without anchorage of faith.

To face the demand and hazards of the unknown year is a fearful thing without God and His promises. It is going out into the darkness without a light. It is groping with an outstretched hand that never touches the hand of God. If we are to possess our possession in the land of tomorrow, if we are to enjoy *rest* and *peace,* then we must fight the giants of lust, greed, and mammon, and we must subdue the walled cities of jealousy, covetousness, and pride. Truly we shall need the presence of the Captain of the Lord's hosts with us. He stands with drawn sword to fight our battles and enlist us in the ranks of those who live and move and have their being in God. (Acts 17:28).

> ... Who dares to say, "I know
> What waits us in the year to be"?
> God, Who art over sword and plow,
> Whose ends our wisest cannot guess,
> Whatever waits us, temper Thou
> Our spirits to Thy purposes!
> Not our immunity to pray;
> Give us but strength to tread the way
> That opens to us day by day
> With high and holy readiness.

At the beginning, there is the practice of the presence.

2. The Bow in the Cloud

"I do set my bow in the cloud, and it shall be for a token of a covenant between me and the earth."—Genesis 9:13

The idea of the covenant is familiar in these days of international relationships. Men enter into covenants or pacts one with another. From the Bible we are given examples of how God makes and keeps His covenants. Abraham received one with the sign of circumcision. Noah was given one with the sign of the rainbow. It was no light thing to enter into a covenant relationship. Man has often failed with man, but God has always kept His covenant and oath. At the beginning of a new year or as we venture into something new, let us recall this agelong covenant and its message.

I. *The Promise of a New Beginning.* The flood came to that early period of man's life. It came as judgment upon sin. Geologist and archaeologist testify. Beyond the catastrophe was this pledge of a fresh start for the race. Was any stability possible in the future? God's answer to the disturbed mind was in the rainbow sign. Many suffer today in rude shock and bitter disappointment. Tragedy and failure are all around. Here is the divine answer to all such. God offers hope for tomorrow.

II. *A Silver Lining in the Dark Cloud.* To survive a flood experience is not to lose fear and anxiety. The terrible darkness of the storm had passed, but is there a gleam of light that tells of another day dawning? Noah found that God had provided something better for him and his family. When the cross was mentioned long ago, it was thought of as a death of shame because of the ignominy of crucifixion. But in it there was a silver lining to transform the world of sin!

III. *God's Faithfulness in the Midst of Change.* Is there anything like a changeful cloud? Vapors flit across the sky. How transient and brief is our life! (cf. James 4:14.) It is strange that God wrote His message in the changing tablet of the skies. What is the enduring word? There is no caprice with God. The recurring seasons are tokens of that fidelity. "Change and decay in all around I see; O Thou who changest not, abide with me." God has no variableness neither shadow cast by turning.

IV. *In the Mysterious Is Found Mercy.* The flood and the clouds spoke of mystery, although Noah had been warned by God. The rainbow expressed mercy in the midst of judgment. The clouds were God's pavilion. In the thick darkness is the eternal throne.

Out of the cloud comes the voice divine. We ask, "Why does God permit sin, suffering, disease, temptation, death?" The mystery baffles the soul until we see the covenant sign of the suffering God who reconciles all things in the final mystery of the cross. The last word is not with evil but with righteousness.

V. *In the Familiar Is Seen an Expression of God's Love.* The rainbow was not seen for the first time by Noah. Here the stress is not on the creation of a rainbow but upon its message and use. Thus God speaks to us in the old and not the new. It is easy to neglect the familiar in looking for the unusual. Yet God speaks in the still small voice and may pass by the fire, the wind, and the earthquake (I Kings 19:12). The old tune, the familiar word, the native speech and accent, the past associations of earlier days are made alive as a sign once again. Thus Jesus took familiar bread and wine of the common meal and the annual Passover feast to symbolize a richer covenant of redemption as His pledge of undying love to sinners.

VI. *Know That God Is Looking and Remembering.* Sometimes the rainbow cannot be seen because clouds are hiding the sun. Like George Matheson, the blind poet-preacher in the Presbyterian Church, Edinburgh, Scotland, we may *"climb* the rainbow" as well as sing "trace the rainbow through the rain." We think not merely of the rainbow itself, but we are mindful that it is a sign that God is keeping His promise for ever. The rest of the hymn is, "And feel the promise is not vain, That morn shall tearless be." In God's everlasting mercy we find the covenant in Christ to be strong and reassuring. In Him we may rest for salvation and safety.

The *bow in the cloud* of Genesis is matched by the *rainbow around the throne* of Revelation 4:3. Mercy with majesty intertwine.

>"Our rainbow arch, Thy mercy's sign,
>All, save the clouds of sin, are Thine."

3. God's Call to Preach

"Now in the fifteenth year of the reign of Tiberius Caesar, Pontius Pilate being governor of Judea and Herod being tetrarch of Galilee, and his brother Philip tetrarch of Ituraea and of the region of Trachonitis, and Lysanias the tetrarch of Abilene, Annas and Caiaphas being the high priests, the word of God came unto John the son of Zacharias in the wilderness. And he came into all the country about Jordan, preaching...."—Luke 3:1-3

When God plans to advance His kingdom, He begins by selecting men who will be instruments of His grace and power. With amazing audacity and magnificent irony the historian Luke narrates one of these providential occasions. As God's ways are not man's ways, so here we trace the divine activity in the affairs of men. Behind the outward events of the time, God is also working His will in the lives of chosen individuals. Some may not be aware of what He is doing, but one man becomes conscious of the divine power at work in his life.

I. *In biblical times* the call of God came to John, who was chosen in an unusual manner. One emperor, one governor, three provincial rulers, and two high priests were passed by as insignificant persons in the scale of history, whereas this one man of the desert was preferred before them. Man's method of writing history is to bring the "great" and the important leaders into focus as the events of the age are related. God's method is to uncover the greater events and the most important person behind the acts of history.

When history is rewritten by God, the desert is more important than the Temple, the humble home is greater than the Palace, and the common man is mightier than the potentate. Neither the emperor of Rome nor the populace of Jerusalem took notice of John. They knew nothing of the coming of the word of God to him. In John the Baptist the courses of the ages were turned.

As in the days of the herdsman Amos of Tekoa and of the shepherd David of Bethlehem, so the New Testament abounds in this witness. God lays His hands upon the seemingly weak and obscure channel to wield His power. The treasure is always in an earthen vessel that the glory should belong to God alone.

II. *In medieval years* the call of God came to similar "Johns." They, too, were used to turn the world upside down. During the reign of Emperor Charles V, Elector Frederick of Saxony, and when Leo X was Pope, the word of God came to the son of a

17

miner at Erfurt in Germany, Martin Luther by name. In the reign
of Henry VIII of England, the Earl of Arran being Regent of
Scotland, and Beaton Cardinal at St. Andrews, the word of God
came to John Knox, a student and sometime galley slave.

Church history indicates the recurring strain of this divinely
appointed way of recruiting men for the sacred ministry. Whitefield the bartender, Wesley the university tutor, Carey the cobbler,
Finney the lawyer, Moody the salesman, Bunyan the tinker, and
Edwards the philosopher are examples among a host of the sovereign variety of divine choice. "Ye have not chosen me, but I
have chosen you, and ordained (appointed, R.V.) you ..." (John
15:16).

III. *In modern days* the call of God comes in the same way.
The need to recruit men for the sacred calling is urgent and insistent. Vast multitudes are not only unchurched but unevangelized.
Those who are to serve God and this generation are to be found in
our congregations and also in our communities.

When the history of our era is written, what will it be like?
What will be the most important events recorded of this tem-
pestuous age? Man will likely record the discovery of atomic energy,
the hydrogen bomb, the conquest of Mount Everest, the crossing
of the snowy wastes of the Poles, the upreach of the guided missiles
and Sputnik. But how will God write it? Perhaps God will write
again through some chronicler thus: "In the second term of the
Presidency of Dwight D. Eisenhower; when the young Queen
Elizabeth led the British Commonwealth; in the time when new
dictators arose in Russia; when men's hearts hoped for peace and
yet were filled with fear, the word of God came to...."

Somewhere in a Sunday school class, perhaps in an obscure
home in the country, possibly in a college classroom, or by a steel
mill furnace, or flying a jet plane, the word of God comes to some
John. As God passed by a Pharaoh for Moses, a Saul for David,
an Eli for Samuel, a Nebuchadnezzar for Daniel, a Haman for
Esther, an Uzziah for Isaiah so in His sovereign wisdom He may
lay hands on the unnoticed and unlikely life.

Whoever hears that call can never be the same again. There is
an imperative constraint of the divine Spirit and an insistent
voice which must be obeyed.

4. The Gospel Ministry

"The minister of Jesus Christ ... ministering the gospel of God...."—Romans 15:16

When men are called of God into the gospel ministry, there are standards to be observed. In the history of the church there are many examples of the ways and means God uses in the appointment and service of His servants. Paul here tells of his hopes and aspirations in the work of Jesus Christ.

I. *The Minister.* Several names or titles are given to those who are called into the work of God. *Servant, slave, herald, teacher, shepherd, ambassador, pastor, evangelist,* and others might be cited. A profitable line of study is suggested by scrutiny of the New Testament words thus selected among many.

The text, however, uses the word for "servant" which has its root idea of *"one who discharges a public office."* The office and the man are vitally linked together. There are religious groups in the world who would say that the office sanctifies the man and the man's character and conduct do not matter finally. In the Protestant tradition there is a high ideal that the man sanctifies the office and character counts.

The thought in this interpretation of the servant, then, is that of one who engages in public office and service on behalf of others. This stresses the minister as engaged in a *priestly* concern for others. Even as the Hebrew priests of the Tabernacle and Temple carried the names of the twelve tribes on their breasts, so the Christian minister carries in and through *prayer* the people to whom and for whom he ministers in the holy place.

The minister is engaged in the noblest and most glorious calling to which a man can give himself. Thomas Goodwin, Chaplain to Oliver Cromwell, said: "God had but one Son and He was a preacher." The public servant is a "minister *of Jesus Christ.*"

II. *The Ministry.* The work has been suggested in the office above — "minister of Jesus Christ ... *ministering* the gospel of God." What is this "ministering"? Again the word is significant. It has the idea of *"performing sacred rites or priestly service."*

Thus, in this service we present man to God. The minister stands in the community as a sign that God has not left that place alone. His representative carries the people, whether they know it or not, to the throne of grace. Calvin spoke of "consecrating the gospel." Paul spoke, in Romans 12, of "presenting the body as

19

spiritual service." This priestly ministry is not Roman or sacerdotal but in the priesthood of believers.

In chapter 15, verse 20, Paul said, "I strive to preach." That was his ambition, his aim. The ministry needs a master-passion more than any other sphere of life. The fisherman seeks out rod and line to catch fish at every opportunity. The preacher or minister seeks out the opportunity to minister the gospel. Paul in the schoolhouse of Tyrannus at Ephesus (Acts 19:9) is an example of the true spirit as he "taught from eleven to four daily" (Moffatt). During the hottest time of the day, when some were resting, Paul labored to reach people.

We should not be tied to times and places, whether on a Sunday or a weekday. There are people to visit, souls to counsel, youth to instruct, adults to be trained, and the outsiders to be evangelized with the gospel. Ours is an unfinished task.

III. *The Methods.* The methods vary from New Testament accounts, but foundational are:

vss. 6, 18 — "The gospel of God ... by word and deed." Ministry must be biblical in essence.

vs. 19 — "By the power of the Spirit." Ministry should be spiritual and never secularized. We need Spirit anointing for the task.

vs. 29 — "In the fulness of the blessing of the gospel." Ministry must come out of our own experience. We need to know in our own hearts the truth we proclaim.

vs. 30 — "Strive together with me in your prayers." Struggle, contend with spiritual powers is the work of prayer by those who are in partnership with the man of God, even the congregation. A man may fail because the congregation does not uphold him in prayer.

Study the strategy of our spiritual warfare. The ministry is a partnership of God with a man and a people. The man is God's servant and then the servant of the people. The field is the world, even as Paul sought in verses 22 to 26. We begin where we are and reach out to all, preaching, teaching, praying, ministering the gospel.

5. Three Crosses

"With him they crucify two thieves...."—Mark 15:27

There is a magnetism in the cross of Christ as we survey its wonder and glory. It was there the young Prince of glory died. No one can climb the hill of Calvary and remain unmoved. There is not one cross but three crosses in view. Three persons were crucified that day. On "the green hill far away, outside a city wall," all men are divided. We stand on either side of the central cross. The thieves were "one on the right hand, and the other on the left." So we are related to the Christ of the central cross.

I. *The Unsaved.* The thief on the left is an object of tragedy and pity. Men are lost away from God. The soul that sins dies. The wages of sin is death. There is none righteous. All we like sheep have gone astray; we have turned every one to his own way. The terrible plight of this man lay, not in his wasted life alone, but in the solemn entrance upon eternal loss. To go out into the outer darkness without the knowledge of God's forgiving love is the greater loss. Sin brings its own nemesis and judgment.

Who was this man whose life was wasted in society and condemned in death? Was he a zealot who plundered? an anarchist who was lawless? The Scriptures do not tell us the names of the two thieves. Unnamed, they might well be representative of a vast multitude of lost men and women.

He was unrepentant and defiant. He cast the taunt of self-preservation in the face of Christ (Luke 23:39-41). He railed on Christ and was rebellious against God. He received his just reward of society's judgment. How terrible his end. Sin isolated, and sin brought him to ruin, an unsaved and lost soul.

II. *The Saved.* In contrast, "the dying thief rejoiced to see/That fountain in his day...." God's promise to forgive and pardon was believed by this poor man. The foulest life can be cleansed, the broken life can be mended, the enslaved life can be set free. We see in this man a soul passing from death to life, from darkness into light, from the power of Satan unto God. He moves from the path of hell to the gate of heaven.

We trace that sins of society are also sins against God. One seeking mercy finds it at once. As he looked away from self to the Saviour he saw that he and his companion were punished deservedly, but Jesus was innocent and guiltless. The judgment upon Jesus by the court, the mob shrieking, the disciples forsaking

21

— Jesus was left alone, except for this man. He reversed the judgment of the world concerning the Christ of God.

In his words with Jesus he became the first Christian believer
at the cross. He saw the kingdom of God beyond the tragedy.
Sudden conversion is genuine. All that precedes that holy hour is
preparation for the event in God's time.

III. *The Saviour.* The central cross and the most important is
that of Jesus the Saviour. He is in the midst of man's sin, touching
life where the need is greatest. Where sin abounds, grace much
more abounds. In the crucifixion three things are clear:

First, *Jesus was numbered with the transgressors.* The forecast
concerning His Passion included this terrible ordeal. The sinless
One shared the lot of the sinful. The just One knew the pangs of
the unjust. The perfect One experienced the agony of the marred
and the broken. In the Levitical Law the sin offering required
that the offerer place his hand upon the victim as a token of
identification. Jesus identified Himself with sinners and with sin.

Second, *Jesus was asked to save Himself and come down.* To
have done so would have made Him an example, a sublime
teacher, but not the Saviour. To bring Him down from the cross
is to deny His deity and power to redeem. A Christless cross would
be in vain and a crossless Christ would also be impotent. To save
others He could not come down. The Shepherd is smitten to save
the sheep.

Third, *Jesus was taunted that if He pleased the crowd they
would see and then believe.* How modern that sounds! See John
20:29 for the reply. The work is done. The sacrifice is complete.
Belief now rests in the Person of Christ. He is the one miracle and
His word and work are one in the cross and the resurrection.

Three crosses. We stand where the thieves were — on either side.
What are we saying and doing today? Look and listen at the cross
at the center. Do we join the saved or the unsaved?

6. Christ Is Able

"Believe ye that I am able to do this?"—Matthew 9:28

One of the New Testament affirmations is that Jesus Christ is able to do what no one else can. By every test and demand we find that He has the ability and the power to achieve the impossible. Many passages speak of this truth, and a selection is made to illustrate the many-sided strength of the Master, who is the Lord of all life.

I. *He is able to save to the uttermost.* "Wherefore he is able also to save them to the uttermost that come unto God by him, seeing he ever liveth to make intercession for them" (Heb. 7:25).

The word "uttermost" may suggest a time element or a horizon of farthest bounds, but primarily it means "utterly" or "completely." In Luke 13:11 there is a story of a woman who was helpless for eighteen years. She was altogether bowed down with her infirmity; she was utterly helpless. It is the same word used by the writer to Hebrews when he describes the power of Jesus. Our Lord's power to save is not partial or fragmentary but complete and final.

That is seen also in comparison to the ability of the Levitical priest of old, who had limited authority. Jesus saves from guilt, fear, despair, distress, sin, and death. There is no suggestion here of any priestly intervention of modern supposition, but, rather, the claim of an eternal priesthood by Jesus Christ. He lives to intercede. He alone is the Mediator. "He is able," cries Peter the denier. "He is able," cries the woman who was a sinner. "He is able," cries Zacchaeus the cheat. In all ages men have confessed that Christ is able to *save* completely and fully.

II. *He is able to succour them that are tempted.* "For in that he himself hath suffered being tempted, he is able to succour them that are tempted" (Heb. 2:18).

Although it is no sin to be tempted, the fact of temptation is inescapable. Jesus was tempted in the wilderness; through Peter; in the garden; all His life He faced it. The sinless one suffered through this. Sensitive personality without sin feels the brunt and shock of temptation acutely. His humanity was real, and His sympathy is for all.

To "succour" is the ability to run to help. Consider the compassion, fitness, right, and disposition of Jesus so to do. Bunyan, in *The Pilgrim's Progress*, shows Interpreter's house, with a man pouring water on a fire, but on the other side of the wall and the fire there is Another pouring on oil. Secret energy is given by Christ through the Holy Spirit. Christ succours those who seek Him. He never disappoints.

III. *He is able to satisfy the desires of the heart.* "I know whom I have believed, and am persuaded that he is able to keep that which I have committed unto him against that day" (II Tim. 1:12).

Paul speaks here of "guarding a deposit." Just as gold or money is deposited in a bank, so his life was lodged satisfactorily in Christ's keeping. He had committed his life. Christ has ability to guard against robbery or loss. "They shall never perish," said the divine Shepherd (John 10:28).

Such ability is the guarantee for the ministry of the gospel, for the body as an instrument of righteousness, for the advancement of character, and for life-work and vocation. The responsibility is transferred to Christ. To be safeguarded by Christ brings the secret of poise and peace. All our hopes and aspirations find their proper relationship in His will. Prayer, dedication, commitment — these find focus in this keeping power.

IV. *He is able to keep from stumbling.* "Now unto him that is able to keep you from falling, and to present you faultless before the presence of his glory with exceeding joy..." (Jude 24).

Consider the dangers of the way and the weaknesses of life. Look only to God, who can transform all things. We become sure-footed in slippery places because of His kindly hand. The difference between "faultless" and "blameless" should be known. A child's sketch is not faultless, but it may be blameless. As a work of art it lacks perfection through inexperience, but to the parent it reveals the love of a devoted heart. Presently we are like this — not without fault, yet blameless in God's sight through our heart's intention and aim towards Him. But one day we shall be "faultless," for Christ will present us so to God.

"He (Jesus) did not many mighty works there because of their unbelief" (Matt. 13:58). Christ was not able! Why? Unbelief is the only barrier preventing Him. Do we limit Him? Have we trust and confidence in Him to save, to succour, to satisfy, to keep us utterly? "Believe ye that I am *able* to do this?" "Yea, Lord." (Matt. 9:28). "Lord, I believe; help thou mine unbelief" (Mark 9:24).

7. Follow Me!

"Follow me ..."—Matthew 9:9

What does it mean to follow Jesus? The call is clear and the obvious meaning accepted. Just because this is familiar and commonplace, it is well to examine how the word was used by Jesus at the first lest we miss its true meaning. The word itself with its synonyms is found seventy-seven times in the Gospels. By sifting these in study, we find five basic ways of following Jesus.

I. *To Follow Immediately*. The compulsion of Jesus was overwhelming. There was an instant response. Obedience was not delayed. There was an urgency and decisiveness in the act. Here was something to live for and an inspiration to act in a great cause. Devotion to the Leader and Master was implied.

The fishermen "forsook their nets, and followed him" (Mark 1:18) . "Jesus ... saw a man ... Matthew ... and he saith unto him, Follow me. And he arose, and followed him" (Matt. 9:9) . These are examples of the truth that these men followed Jesus *at once*. The call of Jesus brooks no delay. We trifle at our peril. The summons is now and not tomorrow. Now is the accepted time; now is the day of salvation. When we follow Jesus it implies that we do so *without delay*.

II. *To Follow Closely*. Christ as the Example-Teacher expects His pupils or disciples to imitate Him. To follow Him suggests that we place our steps after His in the way. It has the idea of the copy-book for young children who learn by reproducing the top line, "precept upon precept, line upon line ... here a little, and there a little" (Isa. 28:10) .

"For even hereunto were ye called: because Christ also suffered for us, leaving us an example, that ye should follow his steps" (I Pet. 2:21) . Was Charles Sheldon wrong in the theme "What Would Jesus Do?" in his book *In His Steps*? Peter's fault in denial lay in lagging behind. He did not appreciate the set face going to Jerusalem. He objected to the cross then. His mind was worldly-wise. "Be it far from thee, Lord" was later changed to "ye should follow his steps." Thus it is to be right beside Him, step by step.

III. *To Follow Fully*. The word is used several times to point out the wisdom of committal with abandonment and no reservation. No halfhearted following will do for the kingdom of God. To attain fully in the teaching (I Tim. 4:6) , to follow on to know fully the teaching (II Tim. 3:10) , to investigate and understand thoroughly (Luke 1:3) speak of the same spirit of following.

To follow Jesus is to be *fully alongside* just as much as else-where one walks close behind. He calls us not to be servants but friends. A friend is fully trusted and fully shares. We keep in step in conformity and teaching. Matthew left all and was committed fully. His life did not narrow but widened. He brought his pen with him and his natural ability, and these were used in the service of the Lord.

IV. *To Follow in Company.* Following Jesus is never lonely: there are many companions on the way. When all forsook Him in the Garden and fled, we read that "a young man *followed with him*" (Mark 14:51). All honor to John Mark in his devotion and courage. Three "would-be" disciples did not follow Him aright (Luke 9:57-62).

Consider all the examples of the people who followed *together,* as the twelve, the women, the upper room group, the larger groups throughout the world, and then today with our world-wide fellowship of the universal church. We belong to a great company when we follow Jesus as our Saviour and Lord.

V. *To Follow Intently.* "The women which came with him (Jesus) from Galilee, followed *after* and also, beheld how the body was laid" (Luke 23:55). This following after was not one of location but of spirit. They had the zest of the explorer, the straining of the inventor on the eve of discovery, the intent and devotion of those who were caught up by a spirit not themselves. They searched eagerly; they were keyed up. Here was following without slackness.

The record has much more by way of example and word usage. It is sufficient to know that when we follow Jesus as Saviour and Lord we become like Him. The call is imperative to follow without delay, closely, fully, in fellowship, and devotedly. Garibaldi called the youth of Italy and Churchill called Great Britain in hours of crisis. Jesus calls to greater devotion and a richer sacrifice. "If any man will come after me, let him deny himself, and take up his cross daily, and *follow me*" (Luke 9:23).

8. What Is a Christian?

"The disciples were called Christians...."—Acts 11:26
"Almost thou persuadest me to be a Christian."—Acts 26:28
"Yet if any man suffer as a Christian...."—I Peter 4:16

To some the question is easily answered. The word "Christian" is current speech to such an extent that it becomes synonymous with anyone who professes to follow Jesus Christ. Unfortunately, it has been so used that many think it applies to any decent, law-abiding person. Coins from the mint are bright and clear when sent into circulation at first, but they can wear thin and lose their lustre by much handling. So it is with this word. The way to restore it is to find out how the New Testament used it long ago. The word used so universally is used only three times in the New Testament!

I. *The Name Initially.* "The disciples were called Christians first at Antioch" (Acts 11:26). Several terms were used at first to describe those who followed the Christ. "Disciples, brethren, saints, witnesses, friends, believers, the people of the way" were common. Now a new name was coined.

The change took place at Antioch, a cosmopolitan city. Greek commerce, Roman government, and Hebrew religion met. The world interlocked at that point. The new name was a judgment and a criticism. It indicated personal quality and relationship. It was a distinguishing name.

No reason is given, but, reading beneath the surface, there is a hint that Christ's followers had so penetrated the society of that day that the world recognized a new type of life. Perhaps as a nickname at first it was bandied about. Now it stuck. It was not selected by the people who bore it but was given by those outside the church of Christ. As "salt" and "light" (Matt. 5:13, 14), something new had challenged the conscience of that era. The name carries belief in Christ as Saviour-Messiah. A Christian, then, is one who reminds others of Jesus Christ.

II. *The Name Generally.* "Agrippa said unto Paul, Almost thou persuadest me to be a Christian" (Acts 26:28). An outsider is speaking with some contempt and in derision. The sneer is there. Imagine the ironical, contemptuous word as spoken by this man. So today there are those who would dismiss the claims of Christ. Here is no lover of the Christian faith. That is a valid view of *how* he spoke. On the other hand, supposing he spoke with some concern as if moved and almost persuaded. Paul the prisoner

27

pleaded with Agrippa and in his witness would have given his life to win him.

The dominating factor here is that the name Christian speaks of a spirit which seeks to love and win others outside of the church. The passion of this life is the passion of Christ. The expulsive power of this affection dominates the life of Paul. In that act and his spirit is the determining fact which reveals what a Christian is. In general a genuine Christian is one who does not live to himself but lives to persuade others. "To me to live is Christ..." (Phil. 1:21).

III. *The Name Particularly.* "But if a man suffer as a Christian, let him not be ashamed, but let him glorify God in this name" (I Pet. 4:16, R.V.). To be a Christian involved suffering. A wrong-doer may suffer deservedly by law; but, when a man follows Christ, he will find suffering because of his goodness and his life of doing good. That is part of the life of a Christian. The follower is like his Master, who suffered in the days of his flesh.

Physical suffering has been the lot of many Christians. Church history relates the tales of martyrdom and heroism on the part of Christians. Some parts of the world today find the same experience to be true. Not all suffering is physical. In business a Christian can suffer if he does not follow the crowd. In government circles a Christian may suffer if he stands for truth. In an age which worships human achievement, a Christian suffers if he stands for God's power. A pure life challenges impurity, and those who try to apply Christ's standards in social education and action may find opposition and suffering.

What is a Christian? A man true in his home, honest in business, thorough in work, clean in recreation, Christlike in life. He is Christ's man through faith and God's grace. He finds Christ's Spirit indwelling him. He is "a new creation, a new being." He reminds the world of the Lord and Master he serves. He bears this new name and new nature.

9. A World-wide Commission

"All power is given unto me in heaven and in earth. Go ye therefore, and teach all nations,... teaching them to observe all things whatsoever I have commanded you: and, lo, I am with you alway...."—Matthew 28:18-20

One simple way to remember this text is to note that there are four *"all's"* in it. Around these we gather the manifesto of missions, this world-wide commission.

I. *All Power. The Source of Authority.* Power, in this connection, is not that dynamic strength of doing something spectacular but the inherent right with the person to command. This speaks of "authority," something vested within Himself by native right as the Son of God above men. We are familiar today with ideas of authority. In industry we have the authority of the economist; in finance that of the banker; in education, the educator; in the state, the delegated rights of democratic government or the usurped might of despotic dictatorship, and in morals, God.

Moral authority derives its essence from the revelation of the majesty of God and the sufficiency of His justice. Conscience bows, not only to that starry heaven above, but to the moral law within. In Jesus Christ is the final unveiling of God, and He possesses all authority. It is His by right and sovereignty. God "horizoned" Him as Son of God by the resurrection (Rom. 1:4).

II. *All Nations. The Sphere of Activity.* The Great Commission begins with divine authority and sends disciples of Christ to all people. This corrects insularity and restricted outlook. What is our horizon today? Nothing less than the whole world and all people satisfy those who believe the Commission in its validity for all time.

Something is going on in other lands. Orient and Occident are closer than ever. Clash of color and strife of new movements is heard, and in the matrix of this generation millions await the one authentic word from God. Our sphere of activity is determined by the absence of man-made boundaries and obstacles. We see "the multitudes as sheep having no shepherd." "Mankind has struck its tents, and the great caravan of humanity is once more on the march" (Premier Jan Smuts, South Africa). Think of what is happening in other countries in their nationalism and the challenge of other faiths.

III. *All Things. The Scope of Audacity.* This universal manifesto tells of the gospel, "the good news of salvation," which is

29

distinct from all other messages. The sovereign Lord who commissions His servants sends them forth to evangelize. God is calling out His church from among the nations. The task is not easy, and the progress is slow (so it seems). But this must be measured in the light of what is taught. The gospel evangelizes, but it is a teaching evangelism. The convert is brought into a fellowship and educated in the Christian life. Growth and Christian nurture do not happen without the school of Christ in operation. Discuss some of the "all things" taught by the apostles and still taught by the church today.

It was a Jew who transmitted the truth to our European ancestors; it was a soldier who carried the message to France; an Irishman told it first to the Swiss, Italians, and Germans; a Scotsman freely gave it to the Irish before that; an Englishman carried it to the Dutch and the Danes; a Norwegian sent it to Iceland and Greenland; and so it has continued that men of other lands and races brought the glad tidings to Canada and the United States. You and I dare not hold back its teaching from others.

IV. *All the Days: Always. The Sweep of Ascendency.* The "go ye" is matched by a "lo, I." If we obey the command, we have the assurance of His promise to be with us alway. This has assured success in the missionary task and enterprise. That was David Livingstone's testimony — the personal assurance of the presence of the living Christ. He is with us all the days, alway. That is more than a promise: it is a fact! That presence is a reality as we carry out the world-wide commission.

"There's no sense in going further — it's the edge of cultivation,"
So they said, and I believed it — broke my land and sowed my crop —
Built my barns and strung my fences in the little border station
Tucked away below the foothills where the trail run out and stop.
Till a voice, as bad as Conscience, rang interminable changes
On one everlasting Whisper day and night repeated so:
"Something hidden. Go and find it. Go and look behind the Ranges.
Something lost behind the Ranges. Lost and waiting for you. Go!"
                                        Rudyard Kipling, "The Explorer"

10. Christ, the Church, the Crowd

"Jesus took the loaves ... he distributed to the disciples, and the disciples to them that were set down...."—John 6:11

We live in a hungry world. The hunger is deeper than the physical. It is the hunger of the soul. Around us is clamant need and inadequacy of mission. Christ is the index of divine resources to minister to the situation. The church stands between the crowd and the Christ. God may use other means, but generally He wills to use the church as the channel.

I. *The Crowd.* Always the multitude is difficult to number, but it is composed of individuals, each one of infinite worth.

The crowd is *great.* The apparent indifference should not deceive. At heart the multitude is not careless but concerned. The husks of a bankrupt life do not satisfy the heart hunger. Millions today are restless.

The crowd is *seeking.* Beneath the unrest and lawlessness of our generation is the desire and quest for ultimate satisfaction. Modern conditions accentuate the moral craving for certitude. "O that I knew where I might find him!"

The crowd is *needy.* A universal exhaustion characterizes the nations after war. Economic, social, political, intellectual unrest is an index of the heart through spiritual poverty of soul. The churchless millions "as sheep without a shepherd" make appeal to us in our plenty.

George Borrow in wild Wales met some gypsies who asked for help. He flung a few coins to them, but they shrieked at him in reply, "We have gold: give us God, give us God!" That is the clamor of the crowd underneath.

II. *The Church.* Over against the crowd stands the church as God's instrument. One problem is, not the "non-church goer" but the "non-going church." How does the church react to the world's need and cry?

There is *the wondering disciple.* Philip, the man of affairs and the business mind, was perplexed. Circumstances revealed his mathematical mind, calculating how much it would cost to feed the crowd. And then the thirty-five dollars would give but a ration, "a little," to each one. Such a spirit limits giving to missions.

There is *the watchful disciple.* Andrew was discerning, a man of few words but of rare deeds. His vision to meet the need is limited

as he sees the inadequate resources, but at least he was not
visionary and impractical.

There is *the willing boy*. His offering was small in the eyes of
others but mighty in God's hands. We should not despise the gifts
of anyone when dedicated and surrendered in sacrifice to the
Master of all circumstances. "There is a lad here," is the perennial
surprise of Christian service. The church must catch this spirit.

III. *The Christ*. The crowd was great, the hour late, the place
a desert, the circumstances unfavorable, and the task seemed impossible. It was the Lord who provided a table in the wilderness.
The method of our Saviour was threefold:

First, *obedience* was asked and received. In His compassion and
understanding He knew what to do. He ordered the crowd to the
place of blessing.

Second, *surrender* of means was expected. The loaves and fishes
are essential to the miracle of supply. The widow's cruse of oil,
David's sling and stones, Dorcas and her needle; each plays a part.

Third, the supply was *blessed, broken, distributed*. The arithmetic of Christ is different from the calculation of Philip. Philip
thought of giving "a little." Jesus gave "as much as they would."
Our Lord mutliplied by division and added by subtraction.

Today a hungry world looks wistfully to the church for the
ultimate satisfactions of life. The church is the divine channel to
dispense the Bread of Life. Christ is the miracle-worker in the
hour of extremity. The ministry and task of the church is to give
Bread, for "man does not live by bread alone." We need the
insight to feel the need of the crowd and the wisdom to know the
almighty power of Christ, for the measure of that need is also the
index of our resources in Him.

Jesus Christ is the Bread of life. "Corn for manna must be
bruised," so He was an offering on the cross. From that cross He
feeds the hungry.

> Thou bruised and broken Bread,
> My life-long wants supply;
> As living souls are fed,
> Oh, feed me, or I die.

11. The Uplift of God

*"When they cast thee down, thou shalt say,
There is lifting up."*—Job 22:29, R.V.

In this dramatic epic the friends of Job counsel him in his trouble and dilemma. Here aged Eliphaz uses pointed words concerning Job's moral and spiritual state. Not that his worldly-wise advice is to be accepted, but it is shot through with that grain of truth which is timeless. How true that if we are in touch with God it matters not when men cast us down or when we are discouraged: we remember there is a lifting up. The book of Job is concerned with this, as, indeed, it is a message from the whole Bible.

I. *God uplifts from the pit to the rock.* The Psalmist (Ps. 40:1-3) testifies to the grace of a mighty Creator-Saviour who brings the needy out of a dungeon, establishes life anew, and tunes the heart in harmony.

> In loving kindness Jesus came,
> My soul in mercy to reclaim,
> And from the depths of sin and shame,
> Through grace He lifted me.
> **Charlotte G. Homer**

This confession of experimental religion produces life on a higher plane of spiritual intelligence.

II. *God uplifts from depression to joy.* The world knows hours of depression in economic failure and lack. People are easily beset by worry and fear through these and other physical and mental states. Work, environment, company, and the threat of war produce fitful lives of doubt and gloom. Need of change is apparent for re-creation, to restore the lilt to the music.

Bunyan tells of the Slough of Despond where Christian was "bedaubed with dirt." Pliable asked, "Where are you now?" Christian said, "I do not know." Help comes and says, "Why did not you look for the steps?" Christian replied, "Fear followed me hard: I fled and fell in." In discouragement we have the "steps" to faith — the promises of God. "Be of good cheer; I have overcome the world" (John 16:33).

III. *God uplifts from defeat to conquest.* In Romans 6 and 7 Paul ends an inner struggle in victory. "Who shall deliver me?" "I thank God through Jesus Christ." Moral struggle is real, but here is the source of triumph. Later Paul counsels fearful sailors in a storm and shipwreck: "Be of good cheer: for I believe God"

(Acts 27:25). The Christian has radiant optimism in the presence of world storm. Men are afraid and despair about the future. Political, social, educational, and military solvents are tried and proved abortive.

A depressed fisherman is not the one to cast a line. Men in the mood of fear do not assist the struggling. Defeated men cannot help the tempted and tried in their moral battle.

IV. *God uplifts from death to immortality.* The end of life is not in the grave. There is lifting up even here. "Christ . . . hath brought life and immortality to light through the gospel" (II Tim. 2:10). Without Christian comfort the bereaved find darkness and hopelessness. But there is lifting up when the eternal Saviour appears alongside to beget hope and assurance in the hour of death. Thus comfort, not alone the idea of sympathy, but strength and courage, is imparted.

There is lifting up by God, and this is the guarantee of that Day to come when "the trumpet shall sound and the dead shall be raised incorruptible, and we shall be changed" (I Cor. 15:52).

V. *God uplifts from servitude to sanity.* A present and practical value of this truth of uplift is that the old slavery of sin is cancelled and liberty is granted. Without this uplift man's mind is clouded, intelligence is darkened, the will stultified, and the emotions perverted. But "God hath not given us the spirit of fear; but of power, and of love, and of a sound mind" — a disciplined mind (II Tim. 1:7).

Spiritual sanity of this kind brings poise and power to assist others to be lifted up. The uplift of God has been manifested in the divine drama of redemption. It comes through the Christ "who was lifted up out of the earth to be enthroned" according to John 3:14 and 12:32.

What was begun in Job has its counterpart in all of us. We live and work in a context of struggle. No one is exempt. In hours of weakness and discouragement we need to find the secret of the uplift of God through Christ.

> Say not, the struggle nought availeth,
> The labour and the wounds are vain,
> The enemy faints not, nor faileth,
> And as things have been they remain.
> **Arthur Hugh Clough**

In the weakest mood and the darkest hour there is the uplift.

12. Shadows

"Days ... are a shadow."—Job 8:9
"Shadow of death...."—Psalm 23:4
"Shadow of the Almighty."—Psalm 91:1
"Shadow of a great rock...."—Isaiah 32:2

Life is full of the unexpected and upsetting. Trials and difficulties confront every family. No one escapes the tests of character through that which is mysterious and unusual. Sickness, economic upset, family problems, and death itself await all. The Bible has this word to strengthen us: that which seems to be substance may be shadow. Some shadows bring their succour and blessing with them.

I. *What Life Seems to Be.* "Our days on earth are a shadow" (Job 8:9). Job anticipates James as he talks about the *brevity of life.* James speaks of life as vapor. Job's bodily affliction colored his speech as he sees a distorted perspective. What once was sweet to him is now bitter. Here is drudgery and not delight. As a hireling he longs for the evening shadows to end the long day, like a slave working long hours and desiring the shadow of evening with its wage and release. Life has become a dull procession of days and weeks, full of vanity and nights of weariness. Life is passing and unsubstantial. Whether the proud oak or the beautiful lily, age or youth, it is soon cut off.

> Thou thy world task hast done,
> Home art gone, and ta'en thy wages.

II. *What Death Seems to Be.* "The valley of the shadow of death. The psalmist's words are most familiar. Here is light even when he talks about the *bane of death.* Death stalks about us, waiting for us to fall, so man thinks. But in the immortal psalm there is another view. The shadow of death is "a darkness deep and dense, a great shade." As used for death, its true meaning has been missed. In the gorge of gloom with its overhanging cliff the psalmist-shepherd leads the sheep. In the heat of Palestine the shade is welcome and cooling. The sheep are led through and out into the pastureland beyond.

Death, then, is not a *cul de sac* or end. It is a way through into fuller life. Death's shadow is not substance. No fear need beset us. Its terror has gone. The valley is the "vale of soul-making" (John Keats) at its climax to fit us for the new life.

III. *What God Can Be.* "Abide under the shadow of the Almighty" (Ps. 9:11). These are words of Moses, the man of God, encouraging in the hour of trial. He talks about the *bounty of God.* When Israel marched through the wilderness, they were subject to fiery serpents, plagues, disease, heat, and enemies. As leader, Moses gave them the best of inspiration that God was *Shaddai,* who provided shade for them in protection and relief. God was all-sufficient.

The shadow of His wings and the shadow of His hand were realities to the believing Israelite. We must walk very close to our Companion if we are to have His shadow fall on us. It speaks of the constant presence of God. Dwelling in the secret place is the abiding condition of experience. To abide is to dwell or lodge and to share the host's hospitality. Thus God would offer us that. He knows our name and sets His love on us. This promise is also a request of prayer for us to take.

IV. *What We Can Be.* "The shadow of a great rock in a weary land" (Isa. 32:2). The picture of the prophet shows dreary waste in desert sand and dunes with blazing sun overhead. He talks of the *blessing of a Godly man.* The only place of rest and shade in the wilderness is a great rock. That rock stops the drift of sand as well as provides shade. Godly men are needed to do this in the world of drifting and shifting standards in morals. The drift away from God, the Bible, or divine standards calls for rock-like men to stand.

In the heat of the Eastern wilderness with its blazing sun and no shade, only a great rock provides that relief to the weary traveller. That is the ministry of the Christian man and the Christian church in time of trial and trouble for people. Refreshment, relief, renewal, restoration — these are ministries of grace by the godly man to those who are pilgrims across the wilderness of this world. Thirst is quenched, strength is revived, and a new beginning is possible.

When life seems but a shadow, when death brings fear, there is God the all-sufficient One, and there is the Christian man standing to give help.

13. Grant a Leader Bold!

"Now after the death of Moses the servant of the Lord it came to pass, that the Lord spake unto Joshua the son of Nun, Moses' minister, saying, Moses my servant is dead; now therefore arise...."—Joshua 1:1, 2

Leadership is always in demand. Men will follow a leader. "And grant a Leader bold and brave,/If not to conquer, born to save!" Thus sang Judas Maccabaeus in the struggle against despotic power in the intertestamental period. Handel immortalized these words in the oratorio. Recent years have seen conferences of world leaders. Casablanca, Quebec, Moscow, Cairo, Teheran, Berlin, Paris, San Francisco, and Geneva are names to remind us of the persons who met "at the summit." As in the state so in the church, leaders are sought for in men with qualifications of strength and ability.

I. *A National Emancipator.* Joshua was all of this. Before Abraham Lincoln was known as the emancipator of slaves, Joshua led a nation, once enslaved, into the Land of Promise. True leadership is given by those who have a sense of dedication to a task and a God-given destiny.

Horace Walpole said that during the American Revolution the citizens of Boston raised a special army of sixteen thousand men who were called "minute men" because they were ready for active service at a moment's notice. Joshua was a minute man and ready to serve God. The safety of our religious life depends upon our showing this attitude. We never know what emergencies or tests will confront us. Then our life depends upon readiness for action.

II. *Religious Devotion.* Another trait in this man's character is found in his spiritual convictions. "He departed not out of the house of God." We suffer by the breakdown in the observance of God's day and worship in His house. No one can be truly great or be a divinely appointed leader unless he has regard for these sanctities.

III. *Wisdom and Zeal.* Enthusiasm is a vital quality of creative activity. Inspiration, that indefinable power given to a man by which he is borne along by God's Spirit to act within the divine plan and purpose, is linked with spiritual understanding. Joshua had a knowledge of the sacred writings. "Only be thou strong and very courageous, that thou mayest observe to do according to all the law, which Moses my servant commanded thee.... This book of the law shall not depart out of thy mouth ... meditate therein ... observe to do ... all that is written ... then thou shalt make thy way prosperous, and then thou shalt have good success" (1:7, 8).

IV. *Education and Opportunity.* That he was God's choice to succeed Moses was forecast in the experience of the twelve spies who viewed the Land of Promise. Ten were afraid and cautioned delay in the invasion as they saw the giants and the walled cities. They saw God through their difficulties, and He appeared small and insufficient. But Caleb and Joshua saw the difficulties through faith in God which laughed at impossibilities. Joshua was a man of faith and courage and in training and experience well qualified for this post.

V. *Prepared for Work.* Faith is the one indispensable quality of life for achievement. The man of faith endures as seeing the invisible and is unafraid of the tests of life. Faith wins victories over the flesh and produces strong character for leadership. Thus Joshua "ran the errands of Moses" and served his apprenticeship.

Joshua means "Saviour." He delivered his people in hours of peril. "The walls of Jericho fell down" (Josh. 6:20; Heb. 11:30). Walled cities were captured, and giants were slain. Moses brought Israel out of Egypt, but Joshua took them into the Land of Promise. He gave them rest after warfare, and they possessed their possessions. During his leadership this was the record, "the people served the Lord all the days of Joshua" (Judg. 2:7).

Each age and nation looks for its leaders and emancipators. America knew Abraham Lincoln and George Washington. The church must have her leaders also in the outstanding persons given by God and richly endowed in wisdom, ability, and strength. The world needs a leader who will save. *He has come already.* The New Testament Joshua-*Jesus*-Saviour is God's gift to save ("I have given him for a leader and commander to the people," Isa. 55:4) — no political statesman, no national hero, no financial manipulator, no soldier, but the God-man, who delivers from sin and possesses His kingdom. He is Leader because He is the Lord.

14. As a Man Thinketh

"As he thinketh in his heart, so is he."—Proverbs 23:7

The text is taken out of the context to be an aphorism and principle of truth. Stated pithily as a maxim, it is accepted in common thought. Outward behavior is not always an index of the true man. What we think a man seems to be may not be what he really is.

A cab driver for thirty years in New York was shown to be an expert in the soloists and songs of opera. A jockey riding horses was revealed as an expert in art. A certain painter of Austria turned out to be a messianic leader and *fuhrer* of Germany, even Hitler. The inner thought, life, and mind determined the character and eventual action. We should not judge by the outward appearance. Find out what a man is in his thought-life.

1. *This is true psychologically.* When a man thinks in terms of hatred or frivolity or impurity, the mind sets the standards of what he is. Judas put a price on everything until his mind was like a mint. Thus he stooped to thirty pieces of silver as the betrayal price of Jesus. Richard III in Shakespeare is unveiled as the power behind the throne through his lust for power and greed of ambition. Not as the handicapped hunchback should he be judged or pitied, but as the unscrupulous, scheming, bloodthirsty man, warped in mind.

The mind fixes our attitudes to life. Secular education believes life is secular. Christian education believes it is sacred. The difference is shown when Christ is central in education. History becomes God's story. Geography is the study of God's world. Economics provides for God's stewardship. Mathematics is the science of God's order and design. Psychology looks at self in the measure of the stature of the fulness of Christ. Natural science teaches that the universe is created and controlled by God and not chance.

The mind is central in Christian philosophy. "Don't let the world around you squeeze you into its own mould, but let God re-mould your minds from within" (Rom. 12:2, Phillips translation). The power of thinking is important. Modern man seeks to find new techniques to power, but the New Testament teaches that the spirit of the mind can be renewed through Christ. This is moral rather than psychological in basis. Evil anesthetizes the mind, and it becomes insensitive to the difference between good and evil, right and wrong. When I sin, I need, not some new method of self-improvement, but to be forgiven. It is not belief in self but repentance and turning to God in Christ through the cross.

II. *This is effective spiritually*. Paul says, "Not I, but Christ in me." "To live is Christ." Christian faith brings experience of God's presence in the mind as, not it, but he; and not I, but Christ. To sit down for five minutes and really think should lead to conversion of mind. C. S. Lewis, in his story from atheism to Christ, sought for joy. God broke through to take hold of him unexpectedly. He was "surprised by joy." He was renewed in his mind.

This is true of the Holy Spirit's power. Whitsunday or Pentecost is the blind spot of the modern church. Some have never heard of the Spirit. The Spirit clothed Himself with Gideon. Bezaleel worked as a craftsman in the inspiration of the Spirit. Peter, the fearful man, became as rock and strength by the Holy Spirit.

This is true when the body is presented a living sacrifice (Rom. 12:1). This includes the mind, the avenue of spiritual power. The gift of the Spirit is power and fire. By this the mind is purified, empowered, and radiates new life. "He that abideth *with* you shall dwell *in* you." "The natural man receives not the things of the Spirit for they are foolishness to him: neither can he know them because they are spiritually discerned" (I Cor. 2:14). The things which are true, honest, just, pure, lovely, of good report, virtue, praise — of these we are to *keep on thinking* (Phil. 4:8). In that practice is the key to sound mental health and spiritual power.

Christian thinking is sincere against all that is spurious. It is spiritual over against the secular. The Holy Spirit is the secret to all our thinking. He energizes for strength. Service for Christ is rich and full when the mind is Christ-controlled. As a Christian *thinks,* so is he. In the inner life is found what a Christian is at the center of being. Do not judge a man by outward appearance, but find out what a man is thinking. In the thought-life is the key to his strength or weakness, his advance or failure.

What kind of people do they [the enemy] *think* we are? — Churchill
When I would pray and *think*. . . . — Shakespeare

15. The Secrets of the Lord

"I will build my church...."
"Jesus...suffer...and be killed...."
"The Son of man shall come...."—Matthew 16:18, 21, 27

The psalmist said that "the secret of the Lord is with them that fear him." That God shares His secrets with His own is well known. But not all have seen that Jesus had His secrets. They were truths hidden from the crowd and only hinted at to the apostles. At Caesarea Philippi, when Peter made his confession of faith, Jesus then disclosed His secrets. The word *"kingdom"* had been mentioned before, but now will come the secret of the *church*. The word *suffering* had been suggested, but now will come the secret of the *cross*. The word *consummation* or *end* had been hinted, but now will come the secret of His *coming*.

I. *The Secret of His Church.* "Upon this rock I will build my church; and the gates of hell shall not prevail against it" (vs. 18). Peter's confession was the height of spiritual illumination. Then it was that our Lord explained how this had come by divine revelation. In that context He speaks of the rock foundation of the church. This *rock* is obviously the heart of Peter's confession, that Jesus is "the Christ, the Son of the living God." Peter confirms this in his *Letter*.

What is the church? Here the New Testament idea is found in terms of a body of people called out from the nations, gathered together into a community and fellowship, and becoming a congregation or assembly to worship and serve God. Both Old Testament saints and New Testament saints are united in this oneness of faith and life.

In Matthew 18:17 there is a word about the corporate function of the church. This deals with differences between members. The fellowship is most important, and a man breaks it at his peril. The steps are outlined to deal with this offense. Christians of the church are not to be isolated units but members one of another.

As Jesus spoke of building His church, He set it alongside the "gates of hell." This indicates the place of authority in the unseen. Jesus had greater authority and power in time and in the unseen, hence this confident claim.

II. *The Secret of His Cross.* "From that time forth began Jesus to shew unto his disciples, how that he must go unto Jerusalem, and suffer many things..., and be killed, and be raised again the third day" (vs. 21). In our Christian experience the cross precedes the church, but here it was the reverse. The one is necessary to the other. Redeeming faith is linked to and within the orbit of the church.

He must go to Jerusalem. He set his face like a flint. Nothing intimidated and nothing hindered God's will in this act.

He must suffer many things. Trace in the record the *details* of this statement. His sufferings were many. Pray over them. See them. Consider the buffeting, spitting, plucking hair, exposure, agony, etc.

He must be killed. His death was like others in crucifixion, yet unlike others in its redemptive power. He laid down His life.

He must rise again. All references to His death in the record also include the resurrection (Rom. 1:4). How slow the apostles were to understand these secrets! (vss. 22, 24-26).

III. *The Secret of His Coming.* "The Son of man shall come in the glory of his Father with his angels; and then he shall reward every man according to his works" (vs. 27). The return or Second Advent of Christ is a prominent theme of the New Testament. Our creedal confessions embody it. Our hymns sing of that hope. The heart leaps in faith to this anticipation. In the above text Jesus revealed three secrets about His return:

The fact is declared. This is a plain statement without elaboration. We cannot explain it away, but must believe its truth.

The fashion is indicated: "in glory...." This speaks of a future event in history with manifestation of God's power. The First Advent was in humility: the Second Advent will be in majesty. The King of glory will be revealed in that hour.

The reward of works is promised. Some are blessed and others suffer loss. Judgment in crisis and division and government of God.

Following this disclosure, Jesus climbed the Mount of Transfiguration. There are presented pictures and signs of the secrets: the church through Moses, Elijah, apostles; the cross in talk about the decease (exodus); the coming in the glory displayed then (Luke 9:27). Do we share His secrets?

16. The Refusals of Christ

"Get thee hence, Satan...."—Matthew 4:10

A common conception of our Lord is His willingness and readiness to respond to the prayer and need of man. But such must never be interpreted as a nature that is pliable and easily led, as though He sought to please people. That would make Him to be weak and effeminate. There is this other aspect that He shocked and startled people by His refusals.

I. *He refused to yield to temptation* (Matt. 4:1-10). Jesus was not exempt from our common experiences in this matter. He refused *the easy way of life*. The false philosophy that a full stomach means satisfaction was rejected. The need of redemption is greater than social reform, and man lives by a Word of God, not of the earth. He refused the *spectacular way of life*. He did not run against God's promises or rush into danger at the risk of life. In the will of God he did not tempt or test out God. He refused *the political way of life*. The kingdoms of this world have been offered to others as well as to Jesus. Many would-be dictators have fallen. Our Lord refused to compromise by expediency or worship the Devil.

II. *He refused to answer prayer* (Matt. 6:5-7; Luke 13:25-27). There are some prayers He cannot grant. He may not grant some prayers because of *insincerity*. Unless prayer is real as the inmost desire of the heart and not a convention, that is the end of it. Or if *unbelief* or uncertainty (Jas. 1:6) are present, then heaven is closed. *Neglect of opportunity* may mean a belated prayer is in vain when the master of the house has shut the door. *In grace and wisdom* He may refuse; and, as in Paul's experience of the thorn unremoved, denial may work to the glory of God and enrichment of man.

III. *He refused to work miracles* (Luke 13:31-32; 23:8-12; Matt. 13:58). Truly He worked many miracles, but *at Herod's request* He declined. Our Lord called him "that fox," and when Herod hoped that some miracle would be performed, Jesus answered him nothing. Miracles are not wrought for show or for whims or caprice but always for a moral and spiritual end. "What sign shewest thou?" That was the cry of a generation which was evil. No sign was given by Jesus. And when some say today they will believe if they could see a miracle take place, there is no answer that is different. The one miracle of the Person of Christ and His resurrection to endless life is always present.

IV. *He refused to satisfy selfish ambition* (Matt. 20:17-28).
The mother of Zebedee's children expressed a selfish love for
James and John. She asked the impossible in a carnal and material
goal. In refusing her request, Jesus opened the way for fulfilment
by a spiritual baptism in blood which later gave them place beside
Him. We may easily ask amiss or be satisfied and have leanness
in our souls.

V. *He refused to use legitimate force* (Matt. 26:53-54). Here is
an amazing story of love's restraint in the presence of worldly
power. Legions were at His disposal, but He refuses the sword
that love might prevail. He was the incarnation of His teaching
to "turn the other cheek." The legitimate desires of life are sometimes to be surrendered by the Christian for a higher law and
principle. They may be lawful but not always expedient, as Paul
showed.

VI. *He refused to escape suffering* (Matt. 27:33, 34). When
offered the drugged wine to deaden pain and stupefy sensibility,
Jesus refused. He later accepted the moistening of His lips with
vingar to assuage His thirst, but He refused the opiate. He suffered
to the end. He was conscious and clear in mind as to what He
endured. His sufferings were real and no illusion. Pain is real,
and Jesus proves this.

VII. *He refused to come down from the cross* (Matt. 27:36-44).
There was no easy escape for Him out of suffering. When others
jeered, "save thyself . . . come down," our Lord did not, as *He
would save others*. With majestic bearing He died, not as a victim,
but as the Victor over sin and death. He who knew no sin *did not
refuse to become sin* that we might become the righteousness of
God in Him.

As Jesus refused in life and in death, so should we who follow
Him. Nehemiah said, "So *did not I,* because of the fear of God."
In that spirit we follow Christ.

17. Christ in the Midst

"In the midst . . . one like unto the Son of man."
—Revelation 1:13

Jesus Christ "in the midst" of life is the best news for a dis-illusioned world. Life fronts us with an untraversed pathway and unknown possibilities. We believe that He who promised to be with His own alway is adequate for every situation. The New Testament records for our encouragement that Jesus shares in all the common ways of life. Here are pictures of this truth.

I. *In the Midst of Earnest Inquiry.* "It came to pass, that after three days they found him in the temple, sitting *in the midst* of the doctors, both hearing them, and asking them questions (Luke 2:46) . His natural development led Him to this hour. Significantly, He is in the presence of the religious teachers. Truly, this is the symbol of all His life and work. He is the Center and Theme of Revelation, the Light of Knowledge, the Alpha and Omega, the Eternal Truth. The history of man is the history of asking ques-tions. It matters how we ask and where we ask. Bring your ques-tions about life, conduct, providence, and truth to Him who is in the midst of these with His divine wisdom.

II. *In the Midst of Disciplined Experience.* "I am *among you* as he that serveth" (Luke 22:27) . He who was *"in the things of my Father"* (Luke 2:49, Greek) , "subject unto" parents (Luke 2:51) , and tempted in the wilderness (Mark 1:13) shared human trials and limitations. He rebuked the spirit which sought carnal power and revealed greatness by service. The greatness of God is not in the throne but in stooping to man's need in humility. In all the discipline of our life Jesus shares and understands.

III. *In the Midst of Human Antagonisms* (Luke 4:16-30) . "He passing *through the midst* of them went his way" (Luke 4:30) . When beset by enemies, harassed by subtle wrath and enmity, endangered by violence, He proves to be Master. When the Chris-tian is misunderstood, assailed, ostracized, or lonely, we may find Him at hand to help and comfort. Many of our fellow-believers in other lands are in the throes of persecution. In trial and test, hates the spirit within the Christian who loves. In trial and test, Christ is near.

IV. *In the Midst of Spiritual Perplexity.* He "stood *in the midst* . . . and saith unto them, Peace be unto you" (Luke 24:36) . In the aftermath of tragedy, bewildered and beset by fear and anxiety, the disciples found Jesus at hand. His word became the solvent of doubt and the marks of His Passion the guarantee of peace to the troubled and distracted. They could not reconcile His promises of a kingdom with the providence which crucified their Lord and left them orphaned. His presence brings peace.

V. *In the Midst of the World's Sin.* "Where they crucified him, and two other with him, on either side one, and Jesus *in the midst*" (John 19:18). He who was the friend of sinners was also the Saviour of the world. His attitude and actions were not removed from sinning men but grappled with the problem of sin in every phase of human need. The cross is glorious today as salvation is found in the Crucified One. Sin is cancelled, and Jesus is still in the midst of the world's sin. He touches all men at this point of need.

VI. *In the Midst of Devout Worship.* "Where two or three are gathered together in my name, there am I *in the midst* of them" (Matt. 18:20). What was pledged here is also confirmed in the Seer of Patmos (Rev. 1:9-20). In that sublime vision He saw the Christ as Head of the church present among His people. The church is estimated, not by numbers, equipment, or sects, but where the presence of the living Christ is found among a gathered community of believers. The church meets to worship. Worship is the highest act and activity. Where Christ is, there is the whole church. In this view the church includes the redeemed of all ages and unites those within the eternal state and those militant upon the earth. The church worships the Lord of glory.

VII. *In the Midst of Divine Government.* "*In the midst* of the throne ... a great multitude.... The Lamb which is *in the midst* of the throne shall feed them and shall lead them unto living fountains of waters: and God shall wipe away all tears from their eyes" (Rev. 5:6; 7:9, 17). The final picture of Christ is of His victory over sin and death. The kingdoms of this world become His. When earthly thrones empty and governments fail, when empires pass away, then the throne of God is seen as unshaken. In this is our trust and confidence as we face the future. The optimism of the Christian is based on the realism of the divine government. Christ abides, and the future is bright in the light of His advent and triumph.

> For all wreaths of empire meet upon His brow,
> And our hearts confess Him King of glory now.
> **Caroline M. Noel**

In every situation Jesus is present to strengthen His people. He is in the midst of them always, all the days.

18. The Sifting of the Saint

"Simon, Simon, behold, Satan hath desired to have you, that he may sift you as wheat: but I have prayed for thee, that thy faith fail not...."—Luke 22:31, 32

Socrates said, "An unexamined life is not worth living." It is also true that the life worth living is sure to be tested. Peter was a marked man. We see here one natural person and two supernatural beings. The saint is set between Satan and the Saviour. He is the object of Hell and of Heaven. Both contend for the supremacy and the mastery of a man's life.

I. *The Power of Satan.* "Satan hath desired to have you." Peter's downfall was in mind and also his conversion. Who was this who came to tempt and try the apostle?

A Personality. We speak of evil and its influence, but behind is the sinister spirit of evil. Recognize the existence of an evil spirit just as we believe in the good, the Holy Spirit. Names given include, "Satan — Adversary; Devil — Accuser; Beelzebub — Corrupter."

A Powerful Spirit. "...Asked to have" — demanded (as a lesser to a greater). "Obtained permission — claimed the right — obtained you by asking." Compare several versions and the original for meaning.

Evil Intent. Already he held Judas, the son of perdition (John 17:12), but he wanted the whole group. The "you" is *plural.* He was not content with one: he bid for Peter, to take *all.*

Right to Tempt? God permits testing in order to try us. See Job 1:9-12 and 2:1-10 as evidence of this unseen warfare behind the scenes of a man's life.

Marks Certain Individuals. Satan doesn't bother some people. It is a tribute to our worth if we are tempted and tried.

Persons Used to Help. Peter was rebuked for wrong words used — "thou art an offense unto me." Does our speech offend, and is it used against God's people? Note how Satan used Job's friends.

Warnings Given by the Lord. "Simon, Simon" — the old name used and repeated — significant.

II. *The Probing of the Saint.* "...that he may sift you...." We may compare the Eastern custom of winnowing grain. There the stick or flail is used. A tribulation experience in this. No one way is used to sift the Christian. Winnowing was done by hand and often at night when there was more wind.

The occasion and need for this testing is found in verses 24 to 30. At the table the apostles disputed who should be the greatest. Peter then was full of dross and needed sifting and purging. In John 1:42 Jesus had predicted that Simon would become Peter. The shiftless would become as rock. Nature takes a long time to produce rock: slowly, by heat, pressure, upheaval, and denudation.

Sifting here is by divine permission. The evil is used under the ultimate authority of God. Puritan John Trapp said: "Jesus uses the fan and sifts to get rid of chaff; but the devil uses a fan and sifts to get rid of the wheat."

III. *The Prayer of the Saviour.* "But I have prayed for thee. . . ." This is the heart of the message, its outcome being the saving of Peter, who, when turned, becomes strength to others.

Intercession of the High Priest. The Lord prayed for all the apostles and Peter in particular. His prayer is mightier than the force of the Devil. His advocacy is over against the testing and sifting. No grain is lost by Christ.

Invincibility of Faith. Here is prayer which avails, which overcomes the world, and faith does not suffer eclipse. If there is any setback, it is temporary and not final. Satan is no match for the supplicating Saviour at the throne of God.

Issue of Sifting Process and Prayer. "When thou art converted, strengthen. . . ." This is to establish, confirm, make fast. In verses 31 and 32 when Peter "turns" they are all turned. Satan asks, and Jesus asks.

We learn that there is a spiritual conflict over the souls of men. Possible failure is there, but overcoming is also present. Heaven and Hell, God and the world, Spirit and flesh, Christ and the Devil are in tension and conflict.

Fowls of the air may snatch away the seed (Matt. 13), but the Sower is busy also. "In the hour of trial, Jesus plead for me." The devil plays upon fear and emotion, appealing to the lowest in us, seeking to destroy. Jesus comes to save us as He prays when we are tempted and sifted in the sieve.

> O loving wisdom of our God!
> When all was sin and shame,
> A second Adam to the fight,
> And to the rescue came.

19. A Clear Conscience

"I exercise myself, to have always a conscience void of offence toward God, and toward men."—Acts 24:16

The philosopher Kant said that "two things fill me with ever increasing wonder and awe, the more I ponder them; the starry heavens above me, and the moral law within me." Because wonder is the origin of true worship, it is worth while thinking about this moral law or conscience. Paul's claim has been made by many others. Is this possible and how?

I. By way of *definition,* we note that the word is not used in the Old Testament, but everywhere there is the evidence of the operation of conscience. Some thirty times it is found in the New Testament, chiefly by Paul. Conscience is a *knowing of oneself.* Man's distinguishing feature, whereby he perceives what is good and bad and which prompts him to do good and shun the bad, is this goad within us. Bishop Butler has it, "a principle of reflection in man, by which he distinguishes between, approves or disapproves his own actions, a judgment, not merely of fact, but upon fact."
Conscience is an imperative, "I ought," and troubles us to make us triumphant in moral action. Offering a crown of thorns, its coronation is the noblest splendor that can come to man. Thomas Carlyle wrote: "There is an Infinite in man which, with all his cunning, he cannot quite bury under the finite." And John Wesley said: "This is a faculty or power implanted by God in the soul by which every man perceives what is right or wrong in his own heart or life, in his tempers, thoughts, words or actions."
Present-day psychology has other ways of speaking of this moral imperative, and these might well be studied. The biblical basis and point of view is that God has placed within our moral nature this voice which cannot be stilled.

II. Any *description* must take note of what men speak of as "the voice of God." Thus we speak of conscience in this way of accommodation. Contrast that a Hindu mother obeys that urge and treats her child cruelly, whereas a Christian mother obeys by sending her child to Sunday school. Saul (Paul) said: "I verily thought within myself that *I ought to do* many things contrary to the name of Jesus Christ" (Acts 26:9). Here is conscience in action against God! Certainly not "the voice of God." Why these seeming contradictions? Why differences in conduct? The answer is that the human eye records what it looks at, and the eye of the soul registers what it has in focus.

49

The New Testament indicates a good, pure, clear, perfect, witnessing conscience, and also a weak, defiled, seared, evil conscience. Conscience is not infallible and, like the sundial, acts correctly according to the light shining upon it. Let that light be Christ and conduct is readjusted, for He is greater than nature, law, or conscience. Fuller knowledge by some Christians means more sensitive reacting to the will of God. Some irregular behavior is due to that which is lacking in range. Some are responsible to public obligation but dull to private indebtedness. Some are awake to needs at home but lack any imperative about lands afar. Men can be exact in observing membership in club, fraternity, or other association by their presence and payments but lax about their so-called church covenant and fellowship.

III. Some *deductions* can be made and the demands of conscience met. That supreme biographer of the soul, John Bunyan, confessed at one stage in his agitations that "he envied the beasts of the field which have no conscience of God." However, this is not a separate faculty but the entire personality in its active knowing, loving, and choosing.

Conscience needs to be *cleansed* (Heb. 9:14; 10:2, 22). The vilest can be made clean, the good ennobled, the sinful holy, the hardened mellowed. The blood of Christ's cross is God's wholesome way of cleansing the conscience from dead works. The great literature of the ages recognizes this struggle of sin with the majesty of that moral law. In *Les Miserables* by Victor Hugo, the novels of George Eliot, *The Scarlet Letter* by Nathaniel Hawthorne, and in *Macbeth* (as well as others) by William Shakespeare we trace this theme under soul struggle. If conscience is spurned and disobeyed, there is the nemesis of sin.

Conscience can be *clean*. Paul found the secret: it is by choosing between our rights and the higher law of love in the interests of a weaker brother, discriminating between the legitimate and the expedient, and by being exercised concerning the good, the better, and the best as well as between right and wrong. The apostle John wrote: "If we walk in the light, as he is in the light, we have fellowship one with another, and the blood of Jesus Christ his Son cleanseth us from all sin" (I John 1:7). Is that the way of a clear conscience?

20. Jesus Knows What Is in Man

"Many believed in his name, when they saw the miracles which he did. But Jesus did not commit himself unto them, because he knew all men, and needed not that any should testify of man: for he knew what was in man."—John 2:23-25

Our Lord did not accept everyone at face value! The faith which was based on signs did not receive His approval as that which believed without signs. Thus He divided men even as He sought to win them. Some people know others in terms of official-dom. There is the view of the expert and the cynic. Our Lord knew men in their motive and intention. This claim of His gives:

I. *Authority to His Teaching.* We never find Him saying, "I suppose, surmise, guess; it may be; perhaps; it seems to me," or, "I apologize." No reference is made to any authorities: He is the authority. No advance in science or knowledge nor any progress in civilization has invalidated His sayings. His teaching was marked by authority and by such supernal wisdom that men marvelled. "Whence hath this man letters, having never learned?" "Never man spake like this man."

His themes are the essential subjects of human thought and life. They refer to *God*: His being, wisdom, and power; to *man*: his nature, achievement of personality, and struggle; to *sin*: its bane and remedy; to *salvation*: its provision and nature. Because He knew man, He needed no help from others. He had divine insight.

II. *Potency to His Sympathy.* The enigma and problem of *suffering* was ever before Him. What was dark He illumined by His own experience as Son of Man. Faber sings: "There is no place where earth's sorrows are more felt than up in heaven." *Sorrow* or lack was known to Christ. His knowledge of that is seen in the gospel story as He stands alongside the needy. The *sins* of life found poignancy in Gethsemane and in His Passion. He is able to succour the tempted.

The sympathy of Jesus is deeper than human feeilng. It is an empathy, wherein He reveals intimate knowledge of man.

III. *Sovereignty to His Claims.* He knows man as a *sinner,* although He knew no sin. Only the truly righteous one can give righteousness to the unrighteous. He knows man needs *mastery,* that choice between God and Mammon is necessary. The all-powerful Christ proved His claims over demon-possessed, over disease, over the powers of darkness, and over death.

Calling men to Himself to follow Him, He knew their potentialities — Matthew to write a Gospel, a widow to give her mite, a Nathanael without guile, the fiery nature of John, the setting of the child in the midst, and "that fox, Herod." Because He knew human nature, He knew the transformations possible.

IV. *Finality to His Work*. Our work is necessarily incomplete. He alone could say, "It is finished." He was never flurried, never late, never made mistakes to correct. Each day's work was done completely. He moved majestically to the consummation of His supreme task at the cross. Much of what we attempt is abortive. Some of it needs to be wiped out and forgotten. A little is blessed when we seek the highest and the best. His life was wholly mature and poised. The work He came to do was completed. The cross became His throne. "Are there not twelve hours in the day?" "Mine hour is not yet come." "I must work the works of him that sent me." "Which of you convinces me of sin?" We speak of "the finished work of Christ," referring to the redemption of the cross and resurrection. This is the work He came to accomplish. It was completed and offered up to God. God endorsed and was well pleased with His Son in all His work.

V. *Adequacy to His Salvation*. No additions are possible and none are needed to His sacrifice for sin. "There is none other name," "none beside thee." "There is none other name under heaven given among men, whereby we must be saved." Knowing what was in man, Jesus knew what to do to redeem the sinner. No case was hopeless to Him and no life outside the orbit of His power to cure. He is well named "The Great Physician" as we sing. Every diagnosis is correct. Every prescription of individual need is the way of life and moral and spiritual health.

He commits Himself to the poor and needy but not to the self-sufficient. "What a work is man!" said Shakespeare. "What a Saviour is Jesus!" cries the Christian. He knows what is in us.

21. Take Heed How Ye Hear!

"He [Jesus] spake ... in parables, saying, Behold, a sower went forth to sow; and when he sowed, some seeds fell...."

—Matthew 13:3, 4

The familiar Parable of the Sower is better interpreted as the Parable of the Soils. We have no doubt about the sower and the seed. Here the emphasis is to unveil the various types of soil and measure the response given to the sowing.

I. *Some seed fell by the wayside.* The *Indifferent Hearer.* The birds came and devoured the seed. It was trodden under foot. Anyone hearing the Word and understanding it not, the Evil One comes and steals it away. This is the gospel summary.

Learn there are hindrances to truth. One is that *attention is lacking.* A life hardened by sin or familiarity is not pliable or responsive. Because of insensibility, the seed lies without. It is *never in* and no germination follows. Life is a thoroughfare, as Pharaoh, Judas, and Esau. We *contend with evil powers* which steal the seed, for example, gossip, criticism, frivolity, and sensuality. To be dull of heart, ear, and mind is a state wherein a message of God leaves no lasting impression. There is *hearing without thinking.* Conscience is not aroused as Obstinate in *The Pilgrim's Progress.* The seed gets no hold. The only remedy is to *hear with understanding.* We need to break up the fallow ground. It is not the seed in the heart which is responsible but the man who lets the Devil snatch it away. Here *the seed is stolen.*

II. *Some seed fell upon stony places.* The *Superficial Hearer.* There is not much earth. The seed springs up at once but without depth; when the sun arises, the seed is scorched, and, having no root, it withers away. Moisture is lacking also.

Learn there is mushroom growth, quick to sprout, quick to stumble. The trouble here is that *reflection is lacking.* A shallow soil over a substratum of rock is not good. Man hears and assents, but conviction does not grip life. Revival time or evangelistic thrust brings profession of faith and conversion, but some do not last. A surface crop has enthusiasm and impulse but lacks stability. There is no depth. The seed is *in* but *not down. Testing comes* by temptation, tribulation, persecution, ridicule, fear of man, or taking stand on moral issues. The seed withers, having no root, as Pliable in *The Pilgrim's Progress* or as Mr. Temporary, easily offended and soured. There is *hearing without deliberation and conviction.* Ananias or John Mark were like this, although Mark

53

made good later. When the flinty heart is broken, the seed takes root. *The Seed is starved.*

III. *Some seed fell among thorns.* The *Preoccupied Hearer.* The thorns sprang up and choked the seed. They grew with the seed. The Word is heard, but the cares of the world and the deceitfulness of riches choke the Word and the life becomes unfruitful.

The soil in this instance is good but has become impure by thorns. *Devotion is lacking.* Weeds prefer good soil, and thorns have vitality. The double-minded heart finds good seed is crowded out. Divided attention is fatal to truth. God and Mammon compete as in Demas, who loved this present world. He lost apostleship for an apostate. The heart is limited and has no room for thorns as extra. *Temptations of the world* are real. Cares of life, pursuit of wealth, anxiety, fear, methods and maxims of the age, the gambling fever, the demon of getting on, and pleasure: these cut the nerve of spirituality. Vision is blighted, and growth is stultified. The God-given capacity for fun, laughter, pleasure, and recreation is easily perverted in wrong ways. Selection must be on highest good and end. Hearing without *separation* or discrimination brings disaster. Think of the lust of "other things" as Mr. Worldly Wiseman in *The Pilgrim's Progress.* Thorns can be uprooted and life become single-minded. *The Seed is strangled.*

IV. *Some seed fell into good ground.* The *True Hearer.* This seed brought forth fruit, some thirty, some sixty, some an hundred fold. The good soil is the heart which *hears and understands,* keeps the seed fast, and patiently brings forth fruit. This soil is free from hindrances of the other soils: it is *not hard but soft; not shallow but deep; not dirty but clean.* The Devil cannot steal the seed; the flesh cannot starve it; the world cannot strangle it. The seed gets hold and grows. Think of Nathanael, without guile; Barnabas, a good man; Lydia, whose heart was opened to attend to the Word of God; and Timothy, knowing the Scriptures from a child: these gave the seed a chance. Faithful in *The Pilgrim's Progress* is an example also, "turned and converted."

The *end* of the parable is in verses 36 to 43 and 52. Its application is clear. "Lest we should see and hear and understand with our heart and be *converted.*" That accounts for the trinity of evil through stealing, starving, and strangling the seed. What kind of soil are we? The soil determines the outcome of the sowing. Believe that the various soils can be changed to become good, soft, deep, and clean, and *fruitful.*

22. Learning by Experience

"I have learned by experience that the Lord hath blessed me for thy sake."—Genesis 30:27

Such is the story of Laban in relation to Jacob. Some years before (26:24), Isaac was blessed for the sake of Abraham. A few years later (39:5), Potiphar's house was blessed for the sake of Joseph. We can understand these two examples, but how is Laban blessed through Jacob when Jacob deceived and defrauded? There is much that is mysterious in life, and what is dark is illumined by providence in the discipline of God's overruling. The wise man of Ecclesiastes said his heart had great experience (1:16). Our Lord learned obedience by the things He suffered.

We also learn by experience. In all walks of life this is true. In business the boy must be taught and trained. The scientist learns by experiment. The doctor and nurse profit by the work of the operating theater and sick room. The mother is enriched by the child and the home. In preaching, the servant of God learns, not only from textbooks, but through his inadequate efforts and many embarrassments. If wise, he will go on learning all his life. Dr. J. H. Jowett said at the close of his gracious ministry that, if he could begin over again, he would have a ministry of comfort. Experience had taught him that congregations wait for that note more than any other. And the Bible owes its chief appeal to the fact that it was written, under God, in and through the experience of men known of God. It has become a mirror of our life, and it testifies to experience. Learn then how this truth is true of the Christian life. We learn by experience some vital things:

I. *The Deceitfulness of Sin.* No need for us to look askance at Jacob the deceiver and condemn him. Look into our own hearts for evidence of this twisted, crooked nature. Have we been caught in the mesh of unholy desire? Have we awakened to the guilt of base passion? Have we been made aware of pride, jealousy, and greed? What happens in "the chambers of imagery"?

Does sin appal us? Set in the light of God's holy love, we see that the Christian is more sensitive to sin than the calloused and ungodly life. Alexander Whyte, Edinburgh, was a preacher who made much of sin. His people thought he overdid it, but he had smarted under it and knew its terrible depths.

II. *The Vanity of the World.* Learn that man's heart cannot find rest except in God. Recall the well-known words of Augustine that "man is restless until he rests in Thee." Qualify this in the light of modern man's frustration-complex life in a world of uncertainties. Pleasures pall, money-making ceases, quests fail, and ambitions mock when men are satiated with the temporal things. "Vanity of vanities, all is vanity." Was the preacher right? By experience we learn that earthly props fail and nothing lasts.

III. *The Goodness of God.* The Bible is full of this. "Goodness and mercy . . . follow me . . . ," said the psalmist. Christians testify to this rich experience even when circumstances are not always pleasant or affluent. "When thou passest through the waters, I will be with thee . . . ," said the prophet. Is that still a reality? Do we find a presence and a power to sustain in times of need?

IV. *The Gain of Godliness.* We discover that moral and spiritual prosperity is greater than material gain. Christians suffer persecution and loss, but character is built up. Tribulation works experience. "I have learned, in whatsoever state I am, therewith to be content." "Godliness . . . is great gain" (Paul).

Compare Psalm 1 for a picture of the godly man in contrast to the ungodly.

V. *The Grace of God in Suffering.* Faith sings her song in the darkest night. Choice spirits in the crucible of pain learn what grace can achieve. In fiery discipline Christians radiate the nobility of saints. At the last "our people die well" as John Wesley has said. In sorrow we find the peace of God. In disappointment we learn of God's providence. Out of suffering come the riches of creative love and beauty.

VI. *Christ a Mighty Savior.* Personal experience is worth much. The hallmark of evidence and conviction is when we can say, "I know." It is not sufficient to admire the Saviour: we must know Him in forgiveness and power. An actor may recite the Twenty-third Psalm from a study of the lines; but, when a Christian believer recites it from heart-knowledge, it is evident that the divine Shepherd is known in a personal way.

Laban was blessed through Jacob, but we have a richer confession of faith: we have learned by experience that the Lord has blessed us *for Christ's sake.*

23. What Think ye of Christ?

"What think ye of Christ?"—Matthew 22:42

This is the one question which haunts the minds of men in every age. It is crucial for life and destiny. On Christ's pathway to the cross this question was asked, and Peter answered with a sublime confession of faith (Matt. 16:15, 16). Our Lord, in the context of the text above, was in conflict and argument with the people who disputed His claims of Messiahship. He pointedly put this question to them as He stripped away all the externals of argument.

To answer this question each one must express it in his own way as in the words of Peter or The Apostles' Creed. Some may wish to rewrite their confession of faith in some simple, nontheological manner. Men may be suspicious of dogma, but they are hungry for faith. Our Christian faith is expressed in this dogma or final word concerning the Person of Christ.

I. *Christ — Saviour, Divider.* Whenever our Lord met people, He separated them as well as saved some. The question is, Is He *Lord* or only a Leader? Is He a pilgrim on the way, or is He *the way?* Is He a landmark on the journey or the *end* and *goal?* Is He a sign, pointing to truth, or is He *the truth?* Is He one of many teachers, or is He the *revealer of God?* Is Christ unique, final, and absolute?

Christ is the most controversial figure of history. Millions of books have been written about Him. Thousands of sermons and addresses are delivered each week concerning Him. More people acclaim Him as Saviour and Lord than ever before. We affirm, then, that He is the one solitary figure which haunts the minds of men. He is the glory of the past, the life of the present, and the hope of the future.

II. *The Unique Character of Christ.* Personality is the greatest thing in life. Christ is the supreme personality. Consider the qualities of character at their finest. He has patience surpassing Job, strength surpassing Samson, meekness surpassing Moses, faith surpassing Abraham, and love surpassing John. While outstanding men express national characteristics and traits, Jesus is the Son of Man having universal appeal.

Renan said, "Jesus will not be surpassed. All the ages will proclaim that among the sons of men there is none born who is greater than Jesus."

III. *The Interpretation.* How shall we account for Him? He fought no battles, organized no armies, had few friends, wrote no books, and died a felon's death. We may test his life by heredity, environment, race, family, education, and opportunity; and He remains the enigma of all time — unless He is the God-man. He is the unaccountable One by human standards and canons of criticism. Who is He?

IV. *The Question and the Answer.* This is not an academic question. This is not strictly Jewish as some think. A Jewish proverb says, "The secret of man is the secret of the Messiah." We believe Christ is the Messiah and the Saviour of the world. In Him all the purposes of God are fulfilled. History coheres in Him, philosophy centers in Him, literature is inspired by Him, life is enriched by Him. He is the center and theme of revelation, the controller and end of history, the Redeemer of men.

The alternative is that, if this claim is not true and cannot be substantiated, then He would be a blasphemer, a deceiver, a liar, and an impostor. Then our faith would be in vain and empty. We believe that He indeed is what He claimed to be in the beauty of His character, in the sublimity of His teaching, in the dynamic of His ethic and influence.

Christ has moral authority, forgiving sin and recreating life. All men feel guilty and separate from God, but Jesus alone was perfect in oneness with God. Both enemies and friends found no fault in Him, and the centuries confirm that He is the miracle of the ages.

V. *The Claims of Christ.* The fact of Christ becomes a factor in our lives. His claims included: "I will build my church . . ."; "I will give . . . the keys of the kingdom . . ."; "Destroy this temple [His body] and in three days I will raise it up . . ."; "I will send . . . the Spirit . . ."; "I will come again. . . ." His word is unbroken. The church is world-wide, the kingdom expands, His sacrifice redeems, His Spirit is with us, and we await the advent of His flaming feet with hope.

What think ye of Christ? What is your response?

24. The Saviour of the Unfit

"Every one that was in distress, and every one that was in debt, and every one that was discontented, gathered themselves unto him; and he became a captain over them."—I Samuel 22:2

The stories of David make fascinating reading. They touch life at all points. He, himself, was a remarkable character in the appeal he made to his fellow-men. The victor over Goliath had no calm passage to the kingship of the nation. He lived in turbulent times, and the difficulties were many. His greatness is seen in commanding the respect and loyalty of needy men. Four hundred once marched under his banner, and they were not first-class men. At the Cave of Adullam they rallied under David that he might train them to become mighty men of valor. The sorry crowd, the unfit, the rejects, were remade by him.

The period reflects the chaotic conditions which prevailed: distress because of false method of government under Saul; debt because of the oppressive taxation then in vogue; discontent because of the righteous indignation over wrongs.

The Cave of Adullam marks the turning point in David's life. His kingliness is now seen in his power over the unfit. He who had known rejection now gathers together the rejects of the nation for enlistment under his banner. All this suggests a parable of action in the light of "great David's greater Son." The unfit of the world gather unto Him for hope and salvation.

I. *Those in Distress* — "Straits or Stress." When the government of life is misused and wrong sits on the throne, men see evil in control by false designs. Man is made for God but is now in chains through sin. That distress is:

Mental in the perplexity of life which is baffled by the enigma of the universe, the riddle unread. Providences of life cannot be reconciled with the suffering and tragedy in fear and anxiety.

Physical in the suffering and pain of broken and bruised bodies and maimed lives. This is a suffering world, and many do not see why.

Moral in the temptations to the spirit as well as the flesh. Think of those who start life handicapped through heredity and environment. The innocent suffer because of the guilt of others. Distress is everywhere in our moral order. Man protests and rebels.

II. *Those in Debt* — "One with a Creditor." Sin leaves men bankrupt. In David's day the government took its toll, and men groaned under taxation. Later, after Solomon's death, it would be worse (II Chron. 10:10, 11) under Rehoboam. Then there was no David to help.

The picture of life under sin's taskmaster is that of debt. Sin pays wages, the wages of death. Man cannot raise sufficient to pay the debt. He is bankrupt and a beggar. He must cast himself upon the mercy of the creditor. (Cf. Paul's argument in Romans.)

III. *Those in Discontent* — "Bitter of Soul." Worse than physical ill is often the bitterness of soul. When the iron enters and there is hardness and calloused condition, how terrible that state can be. Life here is seen as worthless, as not worth living. Disharmony in the universe is now seen as the disorders of family, group, and society. Men become lawless and defy authority. They fret and chafe under law. The rise of Marx with his *Das Capital* and Hitler with his *Mein Kampf* reflects this mood in the modern day. The world has been plunged into blood and anarchy because they were discontented. So it is with the sinful man who struggles in tension and frustration in an age of anxiety. He is ready to defy God.

As in David, so in Christ, we find the remedy:

The distressed seek for security. This is found in the Shepherd whose sheep hear His voice and follow Him. They find rest and succour as well as deliverance from evil and the Evil One.

The indebted seek for settlement. This is found in the King whose rule is wise and beneficent. They find in Christ the answer to their quest. He pays the debt and grants pardon and peace.

The discontented seek for satisfaction. This is found in the Father whose love wipes away all tears and whose hand stills the unrest of soul. This is love's way to bring abundant life and fulness.

> David conquered the giant and drew four hundred unfit.
> Christ conquered sin and draws all men unto Himself.

The unlikely, the unfit, the unattractive, are called by Christ. It is not our fitness but our *need* which counts. The Cave of Adullam was not like Saul's Palace. The cross is not attractive or beautiful to some, but it is the only shelter for salvation. Christ is the Saviour of the unfit, and "He will in no wise cast out."

25. According to My Gospel

"...according to my gospel."—Romans 2:16

Over two hundred years ago an English merchant visited Scotland and, on his return, related that he had heard three preachers in the course of his travels. "The first," said he, "Robert Blair, showed me the majesty of God; the second, Samuel Rutherford, showed me the loveliness of Christ; and the third, Andrew Dickson, showed me all my heart!" In setting forth the gospel, these are three notes to be stressed. Let us express our own basic beliefs in the divine revelation.

I. *The Majesty of God* (Isa. 6). Without God life is tragic. Confusion and distress abound. We live in a distracted world of insecurity. Evil passions and selfish ambition blind many. Multitudes have lost God by their blindness of unbelief. Man has made himself central and crowded God to the circumference of life. A revival of God's sovereignty is needed to restore life to its proper balance and perspective. God is not imprisoned within His universe, and He is not at the mercy of man's capricious whims. His majesty is all around us. Nature sings His glory and power:

> Every flower is a hint of His beauty,
> Every grain of wheat a token of His beneficence,
> Every blade of grass a revelation of His power.

Jonathan Edwards experienced that majesty while walking alone in his father's pasture and when he looked up at the skies and clouds: "There came into my mind so sweet a sense of the glorious majesty and grace of God, that I know not how to express. I seemed to see them both in a sweet conjunction, majesty and meekness joined together; it was a sweet and gentle and holy majesty and also a majestic meekness; and awful sweetness; a high and great and holy gentleness."

In history and providence God is found, as Moses at the burning bush, Job in suffering, and Isaiah in the Temple. In that awesome vision is a song: "Holy, holy, holy, is the Lord of hosts." To lose this sense of God's majesty is to be bankrupt: to know it is to be enriched spiritually. The lofty view brings dignity to life and duty.

II. *The Loveliness of Christ* (I Cor. 13). When Paul sings about love, he has Jesus Christ in mind.

Love found incarnation in His Person. Love is seen in its realistic setting of human life. Keats sang that "a thing of beauty is a joy for ever." How true when related to Jesus. The petals of love's flowers do not wither, and the fragrance never ceases. To be brought face to face with Him is to behold the unutterable beauty and to see the undying sin of our own lives.

When we compare our lives with the lives of others, it is easy to pride ourselves that we are not as other men; but the standard is not high and not flattering. But bring life into the light of Christ's loveliness and we see and know Peter's cry: "Depart from me; for I am a sinful man, O Lord." Our secret sins are seen in the light of that glory.

Knowledge of this leads to meditation on His glory. In love we see truth and grace balanced, speech that is kindly, spirit that is forgiving, actions which are beneficent. Tertullian said: "Jesus turns all our sunsets into sunrises." Life becomes, then, many-splendored, and we sing Faber's song with new meaning:

> How beautiful, how beautiful,
> The sight of Thee must be;
> Thine endless wisdom, boundless power
> And awful purity!

III. *All My Heart* (Rom. 7). This is the inevitable sequence of glory and beauty. We see ourselves as we are. A man never knows his heart of sin until he has come under the holy light of God's majesty and Christ's beauty. Paul cried: "O wretched man that I am; who shall deliver me from the body of this death? I thank God *through Jesus Christ.*"

Sin is not mere ignorance; it is not a casual infirmity: it is a deep-seated malady of human nature. The unveiling of the heart is the precursor of grace abounding to the sinner. We cannot establish our own righteousness. Sin is the leveler of society in the pride of man and his rebellion against God. No education or science or human ability can remove it or cancel its disability. Only the grace of God operating through the gospel overpowers it.

This bankruptcy of life is found in all spiritual confession from Augustine: "O foolish man that I am . . . all things look ghastly . . . O madness!" from John Bunyan: "Poor wretch as I was, I was all this while ignorant of Jesus Christ and going about to establish my own righteousness." In Christ the sovereign God has reached us, and at the cross majesty and mercy meet.

26. The Stigmata of Jesus

"The mark ... of the beast. ..."—Revelation 13:17
"The marks of the Lord Jesus."—Galatians 6:17

Everyone is a marked person. Some habit in speech, walk, or gesture gives us away. We are eccentric in this. We speak of men as marked men in other ways: the criminal in prison with his special dress; a sailor with tattooing on his arm; cattle branded for the ranges; and a promising youth marked by ability for advancement. The New Testament speaks of two brandings. These contrast to heighten the greater character.

I. *The Mark of the Beast* (Rev. 13:17). The Greek word used here means a stamp or engraving. The Book of the Revelation deals with the final victory of the Christ. His enemies are defeated. In conflict there is the opposing figure of the beast, a symbol of evil, antagonizing and opposing the Saviour. In prophecy and apocalypse the end is seen in climax. What are the evidences of this mark?

In war there is rapine, cruelty, destruction.

In history there are Nebuchadnezzar, marked as brutish; Hitler with his gas chambers to destroy the Jews; and Stalin with purges of blood and concentration camp brain-washing.

In morals there are the lusts, indulgences, drunkenness, greed, jealousy, and the demoralization of men through evil.

Sorokin, Sociologist of Harvard, speaks of the arts in sensate culture as marked today by "demoralization, dehumanization, and brutalization," so that the human form is distorted and is no longer seen in the light of the divine.

The beast of the Revelation represents sorcery and superstition trying to enforce emperor worship as a cult. Deissmann, New Testament scholar of Berlin, found in Egypt documents stamped with the name of the emperor of Rome. In Berlin Museum is a plate stamped with the seal of Augustus. That is the usage of the word to stamp or to *mark.*

At the end of history there may be a final meaning to this as we see it recurring throughout the centuries. What final mark of the beast will be enjoined upon the multitudes? When God is dethroned and man is defied, then the mark is soon in evidence.

II. *The Marks of the Lord Jesus* (Gal. 6:17). The original word used here means a tattooed mark or one burnt in, a brand, akin to "prick" (cf. the mark of the beast, Rev. 13:16).

Religiously from the Middle Ages some assumed this meant that

marks resembling the wounds of Jesus were impressed on the body
of saints with supernatural power. St. Francis of Assisi, meditating
in a cell, fell into a trance and had a vision of Jesus. He claimed
that after awaking he was branded by the wounds of the crucified.
This is not proved, and science is slow to accept such, although
sensitive people may induce mental states producing bodily changes.

Practically, Paul knew the practice of his day in branding slaves.
A devotee of the heathen temple would also be branded in dedication to the god. Paul testifies here that he was a slave of Jesus
Christ, the Lord. He speaks of his love and loyalty and much
more. He tells particularly of *his wounds and scars* earned in the
service of God. In toil, prison, trial, and persecution he was
branded with the marks.

Read II Corinthians 11:23-28 slowly and carefully, and compare
what he went through, and then think of our easygoing lives.

Compare various translations to light up this text:

WEYMOUTH — I bear on my body the brand-marks of Jesus.

A. S. WAY — I bear the brands which proclaim me Jesus' bond-
man.

R. KNOX — I bear the scars of the Lord Jesus printed on my body.

GOODSPEED -- I bear in my body the scars that mark me as a
slave of Jesus.

MOFFATT — I bear branded on my body the owner's stamp of
the Lord Jesus.

PHILLIPS — I carry on my scarred body the marks of my Owner,
the Lord Jesus.

R.S.V. — I bear on my body the marks of Jesus.

Compare Acts 16:23 — the marks of the lash reminded Paul that
he was infamous in the eyes of men, but *in honor* as a servant of
Christ. See also II Corinthians 4:10-11, where Paul cites the truth
of bearing in the body the *dying* of Christ in order to manifest *life.*

Conclusion: Two marks are contrasted in order to heighten the
Christian's. What do we suffer for Christ's sake? What marks and
scars will we carry to be witness that we have fought His battles
for Him who will be our rewarder? Will the "trumpets sound for
us on the other side" (as for Bunyan's Mr. Valiant-for-Truth) ?

The stigmata of Jesus bind all Christians in fighting the spiritual
warfare.

27. The School of the Cross

"I have been crucified with Christ...."—Galatians 2:20, R.V.

According to John Bunyan, that wise interpreter of the inner life, "the school of the cross is the school of light." The Christian life begins at the cross of Christ. It is there, according to Bunyan, where the sinner stands with his burden of sin, and then that burden rolls off his back and enters the sepulchre to be seen no more. Christian experience and life develop by association with the cross. Advance in discipleship is inspired by the cross. Galatians treats this by its several interpretations of the cross.

I. *Christ Crucified for Us.* "Christ hath redeemed us from the curse of the law, being made a curse for us" (Gal. 3:13). The truth of *substitution* is revealed. The natural man does not relish this doctrine. The New Testament draws attention to the fact that the sinner is undone and under judgment. Here Christ takes the place of the sinner in the experience of the cross. God was in Christ in this death. By the sacrifice in which righteousness and grace, holiness and justice, meet, Christ brings the sinner out of bondage to be free from the curse. The law's demands have been met; and, because of the Substitute, the prisoner is free.

> Upon a Life I did not live,
> Upon a Death I did not die,
> Another's Life — Another's Death —
> I stake my whole eternity.

The beginning of discipleship is at the cross.

II. *Christ Crucified among Us.* "O foolish Galatians, who hath bewitched you, that ye should not obey the truth, before whose eyes Jesus Christ hath been evidently set forth, crucified among you?" (Gal. 3:1). The doctrine of *proclamation* is revealed. Nothing should rob us of the glory of that cross. An evil eye may fascinate and bewitch some. There are those who would charm us away from the simplicity that is in Christ. Beginning in the Spirit, we are not perfected in the flesh. We grow through the cross experience, never without it. We see the Crucified One as "placarded" among us. As a highway sign is clear in its message, so the cross is clear in its message for all to read. The cross is central. It is the heart of the gospel and the core of the Christian message.

III. *The Christian Crucified with Christ.* "I am crucified with Christ: nevertheless I live; yet not I, but Christ liveth in me: and the life which I now live in the flesh I live by the faith of the Son of God, who loved me, and gave himself for me" (Gal. 2:20).

The message of *identification* is stressed. This mystical saying expresses oneness with Christ in His death. When He died, I died with Him. Union brings communion. After the new life is begun, we return to the cross experience to find we are associated with Him. There is an exchanged life, and now Christ lives in us.

Taking up the cross is not wearing one on a chain but bearing it in the knowledge that we are risen to new life through identification.

IV. *The Flesh Crucified in Us.* "They that are Christ's have crucified the flesh with the affections and lusts" (Gal. 5:24). The dogma of *sanctification* is presented. This is not a popular truth but necessary in the whole counsel of God. Holiness of life implies growth and progress. It speaks of maturity and dedication to God. By "flesh" is meant the self-life. Here the Christly life must hold sway over the self. Negatively, the "works of the self" cease to master one; positively, the "fruit of the Spirit" is seen in the Christ-control of the new life.

This does not mean the old nature will not make demands, but the self-life is now a vehicle of the new life divine. The Christian reveals he is different in motive and standards, acts and conduct. Dead to the old, he is alive to the new. The profession of conversion is matched by the converted life.

V. *The Christian Crucified to the World and the World to the Christian.* "But God forbid that I should glory, save in the cross of our Lord Jesus Christ, by whom the world is crucified unto me, and I unto the world" (Gal. 6:14). The doctrine of *separation* is manifested. God would not cancel out the beauties and benefits of the natural world in which we live (cf. Paul, I Cor. 3:22, "all things are yours . . . the world"). But the natural world looks for a social order with a spirit not in line with God's will. It is this world which antagonizes the Christian and brings persecution and crucifixion. The disciple challenges that world system and order in civic, economic, and religious relations. It was that world which crucified Jesus.

Paul reckoned himself dead to the opinions, maxims, standards of the world and teaches us to live in that light. Therefore, he glories in the cross of his Lord. We, too, advance in the light as we learn in the school of the cross.

28. Beneath the Cross of Jesus

"Bearing his cross...."—John 19:17

Nowhere are details more important than at the cross of Jesus. Reverent imagination and historical accuracy blend to portray the greatest drama ever staged. Painting and poetry have sought to interpret the travail of the soul of Jesus. Words are suggestive. Many hymns have enshrined much of the truth revealed. The cross is central here.

I. *Bearing the Cross* (vss. 17-18). Jesus was compelled to carry the tree of torture as customary. He was no criminal yet bore this shame. Simon the Cyrenian is reported in the Gospels as a conscript who was made to share the cross with Jesus. With lacerated back and sleepless hours Jesus was weak and faint.

John does not tell everything in detail. Nothing is said about the agonies of this cruel method of death, and nothing is told about the reaction of the two criminals who died with Jesus. He bore the cross — that is everything, and He bore it as our Redeemer and Saviour.

II. *On the Cross* (vss. 19-22). The title was required by Roman law so that all might read the charge of the crime. This placard hung around the victim's neck as he walked to the cross and then fastened above. Pilate's intention had in it revenge in ridicule of the Jews. It was a subtle honor paid to Jesus. Unknown to Pilate, it was the truth, for He was and is the King of kings. What he wrote, Pilate did not erase. His witness stands. How solemn that all we write abides in its finality. Thus the Lord was "lifted up" (John 12:32) and began to draw men without distinction. He reigns from the tree.

III. *Beneath the Cross* (vss. 23-24). The soldiers took Jesus' clothes as prerequisites. The seamless coat, a one-piece garment, indicated the simplicity of His attire, and they gambled for this (cf. Ps. 22:18). What were the soldiers doing? Compare the Gospel accounts and see how they not only gambled, but they "watched." Check this word to see that they "guarded" their prisoner.

Think of the mockery of those hours when evil men tossed the dice for greed of gain when the Son of God laid down His life.

IV. *By the Cross* (vss. 25-27). In contrast to wicked men, although at the post of duty, the loved ones of Jesus expressed their devotion by standing by. The women make an interesting study as we trace them one by one. Their faith and love stand out in contrast to others who have followed afar off.

To Mary, His mother, Jesus gave special attention in that hour. She was granted comfort and protection. Jesus always cared for His mother, although He did not place her first in His life. She will enter heaven redeemed by His sacrifice. She will see Him as the Redeemer and join the worshipping throng. She does not share the throne or the adoration. No Mariolatry here or there.

V. *Above the Cross* (vss. 28-30). Another cry from Jesus indicates that the end is drawing near. The sorrows of the Crucified will soon be ended in His timeless victory and triumph. His sufferings were real, and in the cries of desolation and thirst we are aware of both physical and spiritual anguish. Jesus was the sin offering for the race. His soul was made an offering for sin. In weakness He refused the drugged wine to deaden pain, and in clearness of mind He accepts the vinegar to moisten his lips ere He cries out in triumph. Jesus tasted the sharpness of death and opened the kingdom of heaven to all who would believe.

The victory of Jesus over sin was announced in the cry, "finished" or accomplished. The finished work of Calvary is here. He who died on the cross is above the cross in His triumph.

VI. *Down from the Cross* (vss. 31-42). The body of Jesus is taken down, and reverent hands give it burial. Those who attended the spectacle made choice of the Crucified in their acceptance or rejection of Him. Sinful men rejected, while men of faith accepted. Actions speak louder than words. Joseph and Nicodemus with the women and a few disciples are given honor because of their devotion.

VII. *Beyond the Cross* (chaps. 20-21). Jesus came down, not when the crowd cried out for Him to do so, but after He had won His victory. Now He is the Christ beyond the cross in resurrection and Easter life. That is why the crucifix cannot be the symbol of Christianity. We see not a dead Christ with impaled body on a cross, but we worship a living Lord.

29. The Face of Jesus

"His visage was so marred more than any man."—Isaiah 52:14

In the art galleries of the world there are many pictures of Jesus. Reverent imagination, meditation in the Gospels, and fragments of tradition have combined to produce these masterpieces. Yet no one knows how Jesus looked. The words of the Gospels are pictographic, and by these we may trace out something of the likeness to the young Prince of glory.

I. *An Attractive Face.* The foregleam of Isaiah has given many the impression that Jesus had no beauty, whereas others have insisted that He was fairer than the children of men. A mental picture of "the man of sorrows" would not necessarily cancel the thought of "the king in his beauty."

At the wedding of Cana He was the center of laughter and joy. His face would light up with a smile. In the Temple there was the purity of an open face asking questions. Children came to Him, and a young man ran to Him as though constrained.

II. *A Strong Face.* Some faces are weak and effeminate; some are dissipated and scarred. Sin distorts, but holiness is strength. Jesus combined masculine and feminine graces but never in weakness. Napoleon's "pale Galilean" is questioned. Jesus was bronzed and tanned from open air and honest toil. His countenance evidenced strength in the indignation against evil that He manifested in cleansing the Temple. Men fled from Him in the blazing zeal which flashed from eye and expression of face.

III. *A Sorrowing Face.* Although only thirty-three years of age at His death, there were those who said that He was "not yet fifty" as if to indicate Jesus looked much older than His years. Truly He was the "man of sorrows and acquainted with grief."

Jesus wept over Jerusalem and at the grave of Lazarus. He was cruelly buffeted in His betrayal and trial and endured the contradiction of sinners against Himself in the crucifixion. His visage was marred more than the face of any man. The sorrowing heart was expressed in the sorrowing face, eloquent with the love and compassion of God seeking the lost. His face was wracked with pain through the sufferings of the cross.

IV. *A Transfigured Face.* On the mount of glory "his face did shine as the sun." Sometimes men are radiant when devoted to a great cause, and the commonplace shines because of deep emotion. The dedicated life is reflected in the outshining of a choice spirit.

In the Transfiguration there is manifested the glory of God, the majesty of the mountain experience. The light on His face was not something from without (as in floodlighting) but the outshining of the inner spirit, deep in communion with God. Here deity was ablaze in light ineffable and glorious.

V. *A Resolute Face.* On the way to the cross and approaching the Passion, Jesus "steadfastly set his face to go to Jerusalem." In the Garden of Gethsemane He fell on His face and prayed. On the cross a thief saw the wondrous look of that face, not in defeat or despair, but in victory.

Our Lord made His choice early in His life out of messianic consciousness to lay down His life as a ransom for the sins of the world. Before He called His disciples to take up their cross and follow Him, He resolutely bore His own cross of sacrifice. It is thus that we enter into the fellowship of His sufferings and the power of His resurrection.

The face of youth is prophecy; the face of old age is history. In Jesus is the face which appeals to all ages and to all peoples. No one knows how He looked, for the records are brief and only suggestions are given. How does He appeal to us? He was all that we have found and much more.

We see *the light of the knowledge of the glory of God* in the face of Jesus Christ. That face was like the sun shining in its strength. His servants shall see His face, and they shall serve Him. The unrepentant hide from the face of Him that sitteth on the throne. We shall be like Him, for we shall see Him as He is.

Before Thomas Carlyle wrote about his *Heroes,* he placed a picture of the hero before him to absorb influence and inspiration. The Christian contemplates the face of the One who lives and reigns for ever. That face haunts and fascinates all men. It is awesome because it is the face of God, yet it blesses with the benediction of eternal life.

30. The Precious Blood of Christ

"Redeemed ... with the precious blood of Christ."
—I Peter 1:18, 19

The New Testament speaks of many precious things, for example, precious faith, precious promises, precious stone, and the preciousness of Christ to them that believe. The highest place is given to the blood of the Lamb who was slain. If we ask why this insistence upon blood, we discover it to be central and the heart of the gospel.

I. *Interpretation finds help in the Old Testament background.* The human race was taught that the way to God was by sacrifice, and worship is by Another. Therein was revealed the heinousness of sin, its guilt and stain, so that without shedding of blood there was no remission of sin. The blood stood for guilt and death, life and salvation, as Abel's blood crying for vengeance, or the prohibition of food with blood to the eater, or as in the Passover feast: "When I see the blood, I will pass over" — a token of deliverance.

The life is in the blood. Science has known but a short time (only since Harvey's discovery of the circulation of blood) of the power of blood in its organism and resistance. Harvey said: "Blood is the fountain of life, the first to live, the last to die, and the primary seat of the animal soul." A commentary!

II. *Affirmation finds a basis in New Testament pictures.* A selection of texts will serve to illustrate this:
"This cup is the new testament in my *blood*" (Luke 22:20)
"Except ye ... drink his *blood,* ye have no life in you" (John 6:53). "The church purchased with his own *blood*" (Acts 20:28). "Propitiation through faith in his *blood*" (Rom. 3:25). "Justified by his *blood*" (Rom. 5:9). "Redemption through his *blood* (Eph. 1:7). "Made nigh by the *blood*" (Eph. 2:13). "Peace through the *blood*" (Col. 1:20). "Without shedding of *blood* is no remission" (Heb. 9:22). "Sanctify ... with his own *blood*" (Heb. 13:12). "The *blood* of Jesus Christ ... cleanseth us from all sin" (I John 1:7). "Washed us from our sins in his own *blood*" (Rev. 1:5). "Washed their robes, and made them white in the *blood* of the Lamb" (Rev. 7:14). "They overcame ... by the *blood* of the Lamb" (Rev. 12:11).

The New Testament speaks for itself in this regard. Whatever man may think about this truth matters little. The New Testament is saturated with the witness to the blood of Christ.. The blood is the life. He "offered *himself* without spot to God" (Heb. 9:14). He "gave *himself* for me" (Gal. 2:20).

III. *Objections find answer in faith's insight.* We are told that "the blood is out of date, crude, vulgar, too literal, and savors of the shambles rather than the sacred place. The reply is that any grossness is *not* in the blood, but in man's sin. Blood is sacred, holy, precious. In war time no one spoke disparagingly of a soldier who gave his blood to die for his country. A soldier's life-giving is not sacrificial for sin. Here we speak of the very life and blood of the Son of God! The criticism that belief in atonement by blood is too crude and too literal comes from those who distort the testimony of the Scriptures concerning the sacrifice of Christ. Some would change the language and cancel the essential truth. But that would lighten sin and therefore lighten the cost of redemption. The objector to "the *blood* of God" *is* the literalist, the crude thinker, the materially-minded and blind. The penitent and believer sees the truth with the insight of faith and love.

IV. *Conviction abides because of the power of the blood.* The blood is *precious,* held in *honor* and *reverence because:*

It belongs to Jesus Christ. There is none like Him. Although man's blood is of value, *His* is beyond compare. His is a life of beauty and grace, without sin or fault, without taint or imperfection.

It is the blood of God. A daring word and startling, yet this is the claim which is substantiated. God was in Christ reconciling the world unto Himself. Do not materialize or mar the picture of eternal love sacrificing itself for us.

It is the blood of the everlasting covenant (Heb. 13:20) This is God's pledge and security of eternal life expressed in the cross throughout all ages. The cross is the expression in time of the eternal, redeeming reality. The cross was always in the heart of God. The Lamb was slain from before the foundation of the ages.

It cancels sin. Guilt, fear, dominion, and pollution of sin are affected. To be thus "redeemed" is to escape from the dead hand of man's tradition and from an aimless life of emptiness. William Cowper wrote: "There is a fountain filled with blood . . ." because he had found freedom.

It cleanses life. All sin is dealt with. The blood *shed* has been *offered:* it now must be *sprinkled* by faith. As natural blood affects the health and purity of the body, so Christ's *blood* washes the stain of the heart. "Believing — drinking — washing — cleansing": no material concept should rob us of spiritual power.

31. Casual, Causal, Crucial

"One Jesus, which was dead, . . . affirmed to be alive."
—Acts 25:19

Easter brings joy and gladness to a disillusioned world. The church renews her faith and finds creative power again in her mission and worship. Christians celebrate the heart of their faith.

This chapter of the Acts tells the story of an attack on Christianity. The fact of the resurrection is the crux of it. One word stands out in the discussion and argument which deals with the subject. Sometimes one word gives a man away. When Festus reported to Agrippa about Paul the prisoner, he stated the central thing in the accusation against him. Festus spoke as an outsider, yet his blatant remark touched the heart of the matter when he used the words of the text. Notice the relationship of these vital truths.

I. *Casual.* "One Jesus. . . ." Some refer to Easter and its message in a casual way. In conversation a remark is passed, and that is all. So Festus sought to dismiss Christianity by a reference to a man of Nazareth, a certain Jesus, who bore a common name of that day and who might be forgotten thereafter. Who was He anyway, was the sneer and the imputation? Some try to dismiss Christianity with a quip, a jest, a sneer, or a shrug of the shoulders. That is brought out forcibly in the novel of Anatole France, *Mother of Pearl,* in which Pilate, in retirement, is asked if he remembered Jesus. Pilate contracts his brows, touches his forehead with his hand as he pretends to think, and then, after a silence, says, "Jesus? Jesus of Nazareth? I cannot call him to mind."

That is the novelist's daring insight and imagination, but could Pilate forget Jesus? His wife's dream and letter, the silence of Jesus before the accusers, his own "Behold the man!" After the trial that day, was there no mention of Jesus in the dispatches to Rome? How many today try to forget Jesus or attempt to dismiss Him from the contemporary scene. If that is all that can be said about Jesus — "one Jesus" — then He is lost to us.

II. *Causal.* "One Jesus, which was dead. . . ." The casual becomes causal when you speak of this death. The fact of Good Friday cannot be overlooked. That strange death, the death of the cross, was shameful in the eyes of men. So Jesus died the lowest death possible, but not for himself. Generally when one person dies, the life of the general public goes on the same, unchanged; but the death of Jesus affects all men without exception. What seemed to

73

be disaster and defeat for Jesus became the mighty means of man's release from sin and shame and death.

What about the sequence of cause and effect? John Buchan, in one of his Rede Lectures, tells of this. History is an art which is always trying to become more of a science. As a science it is concerned with causation. The past, if it is to satisfy our minds, must be presented as a sequence of effects and causes. So in the life and death of Jesus we should expect this causation to be demonstrated. He who died has strangely moved the heart of the world. "I, if I be lifted up . . . will draw all men unto me." That death was no ordinary death: it was a sacrifice for sin, a redeeming death for us. That death is causal in history.

III. *Crucial.* "One Jesus, which was dead . . . affirmed to be alive." The causal becomes crucial when we affirm the resurrection from the dead. Christianity stands or falls by this fact. This is the crucial fact of life and time. Without this nothing else is certain in history. We believe that this is the only fact in history: all else is relative. The fact becomes a factor in our lives. We are now talking about Jesus alive from the dead. If we talked only about Jesus, that would not be sufficient, or even Jesus crucified, however important. The Christian faith finds its focus in the risen, living Christ. If no resurrection, then Christ is not risen. That would mean a dead Christ, a tomb in Palestine, a mecca for pilgrims. If no resurrection, then preaching is vain and foolish. We have no gospel of glad tidings now and no salvation to offer. If no resurrection, then faith is empty. Nothing would be stable. Then there is no certainty in personal faith in Christ. If no resurrection, then Christianity is false. It would become one of the many comparative religions. If no resurrection, then we are yet in our sins. We would have no hope of the future life, no New Testament, no Lord's Day, no church being built. We affirm Christ is *alive!* The casual is displaced by the causal: the causal issues in the crucial!

32. The Easter Victory

"Christ . . . hath abolished death, and hath brought life and immortality to light through the gospel."—II Timothy 1:10

The story is told of Sir William Burne-Jones, the artist, relative of Premier Stanley Baldwin, that he was moved to say something about the funeral service of Robert Browning in Westminster Abbey. He said: "It was too somber; impressive? — yes, but the funeral lacked the note of victory. It just needed, in addition to the singing and order, a chorister to sing out or *a trumpet blast of victory!"*

In the Christian faith we find this trumpet blast of victory at Easter and on every occasion when we triumph in Christ. The heart of the Easter message is in this text for three reasons:

I. *Christ abolished death.* This means He has "taken away its power, put an end to it, put it down." But "he has not," cries a disillusioned world! The facts of life seem against this view. The cynic scornfully derides it as false as he points to war and bloodshed. The pessimist cries out against such a view as he broods over the darkness and despair of life. The stoic refutes this even as he urges men to endure and have courage in the midst of trial. And the worldling laughs at the futility of such a possibility as he walks amid the ruins of humanity.

The trumpet blast of victory does not deny the presence of death. It recognizes it as "the last enemy," "the king of terrors," and "the wages of sin." "It is appointed unto men once to die, but after this the judgment." But there is a difference now, for Christ delivers us from the fear of death. Instead of its bondage, we are free. The "sting" and "horror" are gone for us, and "death is swallowed up in victory." Death is now an incidence but not the end of life.

II. *Christ brought life and immortality to light.* Death, to many, means darkness, but Jesus has turned the light upon it. He has photographed or illumined it by the disclosures he made. What was dark and mysterious is now glorious. Read Wordsworth's "Intimations of Immortality," with its yearning of something beyond death, and then think upon the assurance Christ gives. The Old Testament also anticipated "intimations," but it needed the New Testament with its glorious words of hope to bring finality of conviction. In this light we trace the meaning of life now. Others have viewed life's tangled skein, but our Lord brings the perfect pattern for the other side of death. God is not the God of the dead but of the living. The mortal is exchanged for the immortal and the natural for the spiritual. Here work and service are necessarily incomplete: beyond is completeness and fulness. Immortality crowns our life with the likeness of Christ. In Him we are made perfect and made like unto Him (I John 3:2). By the resurrection we are given assurance that God will complete the work thus begun. The Christ of history and of experience is now the Christ of eternity and glory.

III. *Christ brings this through the gospel.* A trumpet blast of victory is not a mere note but harmony. It is not a one-fingered tune of monotony but melody and harmony as in a symphony. The gospel is the "good news" of God's love coming to all men. By means of it character is changed and life is transformed. When Paul declared the gospel (I Cor. 15:1-11), he was not giving any fairy tale but the eternal word of God with power from on high.

This victory means that *all false religions are rejected.* There are many cults and religions, but Christianity is the one, final, redeeming faith. All others are partial in their light and distorted in their life. In Christ is salvation. The laden altars, the repeated ritual, and the enslaved lives are evidence of the futility of religion without redemption.

> Not all the blood of beasts
>   On Jewish altars slain,
> Could give the guilty conscience peace,
>   Or wash away the stain:
> But Christ, the heavenly Lamb
>   Takes all our sins away,
> A sacrifice of nobler name
>   And richer blood than they.

This victory means that *all imperfect cultures are inadequate.* The loveliness of nature and the wisdom of the mind do not bring redemption. Salvation is not by gnostic or secret rites of man. Not by hedonistic pleasure does it come. Human nature, with its abysmal depths of darkness, needs rebirth and resurrection power.

This victory means that *all material and moral might of man is abortive to achieve eternal destiny.* Mammon worship, good works, pride of life, and achievement cannot save. Only Christ's victory over sin and death guarantees man's redemption and life eternal. This gospel sounds forth as a trumpet blast. He is the Victor on the field of conflict with sin. We can enter into His victory.

33. Intending After Easter

"Herod ... intending after Easter ...."—Acts 12:4

After Easter is a crucial time for everyone. It is then we demonstrate whether we believe in Easter or only give lip-service to its influence. Many churches have crowds of people on Easter Sunday and then suffer a slump thereafter. We should be concerned with what happens *after* Easter.

The word "Easter" occurs in this text, the only time in the New Testament. Herod had killed James, an apostle, and had imprisoned Peter. The intention of Herod was clear — to keep Peter in prison over the Easter season and then kill him. God's answer to that was a church praying and then deliverance. This raises the question of intention, the inner motive and desire of life. How is it with us after Easter? Are we still of the same mind? Every Sunday is an Easter Day, a day of resurrection.

I. *Intending to Seek the Things Above.* When people are stirred during Easter with its thrilling music and its matchless message, then ask if they intended to seek the things above. "Seek those things which are above ... set your affection on things above, not on things on the earth" (Col. 3:1, 2). The vision of a higher life spurred someone to dream of a new life after Easter. Eternal values impressed so that material things were to be handled lightly thereafter. But were they?

John Bunyan, in *The Pilgrim's Progress,* tells of the "man with the muckrake." The poor fellow grubbed away among the rubbish because he never lifted up his eyes to see the crown above his head. Man today is like that in his feverish quest for earthly success. Business, pleasure, and material pursuits keep man looking down and not up. What if Easter brought the call to seek the higher things of the spiritual world? That intention should be implemented and carried out now.

II. *Intending to Seek First God's Kingdom.* First things first. Some things matter more than others. There are priorities in life. "Seek ye first the kingdom of God, ... and all these things shall be added unto you" (Matt. 6:33). Thus our Lord spoke of the supreme intention of life. In this is the will of God translated in decisions and commitment of life.

What is this kingdom of God? There is the earthly and the heavenly, the temporal and the spiritual. When a life submits to Jesus Christ as Saviour and Lord, then it is born into that kingdom. We are linked under the sovereignty of God. The future and climactic expression of that kingdom will cover the world, but meantime we see it built slowly and surely in men's hearts and lives. Within that kingdom we are given a place of service. Not as an armchair critic, but as one who takes up the cross, do we serve. Many intend to seek that kingdom first in their lives, but after Easter we ask, How is it now? Are you realistic in carrying out the mandate and the implications of discipleship? Is your life thus disciplined?

III. *Intending to Live a Full-orbed Life.* Is not this the core of your intention after Easter? This is why Christ came living, dying, and rising again. "Seek, and ye shall find..." (Luke 11:9, 10). Jesus said that He came to give us "life, and ... more abundantly." The charge against professing Christians is that they are content to be only *partially* Christian. Just to observe Easter once a year is not sufficient. The total life of the Christian is the totally committed life. A full-orbed life is one that is without reservation.

Leonardo da Vinci said, "Man and the intention of his soul are a good painter's paramount objects." And Alexander Pope said, "The proper study of mankind is man." That study has not been neglected. But our stress is on man's *intention.* We do not know a man by any other means except in this realm of motive. Peter, who said he would not forsake his Master, denied Him. Yet Peter loved Jesus. Later he is converted and became strength to others. Final judgment of a man should be deferred until we know his intention and motive.

Are we partial Christians only? What is the reality of Easter unless it be the fulness of life in Christ, who is alive? What took place on Easter Day? Did you *intend* to commit yourself in fulness and devotion? Has the vision waned? Have the prayers and inspiration of Easter been forgotten? There is no fulness of life except we *carry out our intentions* so formulated.

34. Triumph in Christ

"Now thanks be unto God, which always causeth us to triumph in Christ."—II Corinthians 2:14

In play, work, or war, we like to be on the winning side. No one wishes to admit defeat. This is the spirit of Paul's letters when he reflects upon his relationship to Christ. To be a Christian means to be in the train of Christ's triumph. He thought of himself in God's triumphal march of the ages.

The metaphor is taken from the triumphal procession of a victorious general. In the Roman Empire the captives were sometimes kept at Rome for a few years in order to grace the conqueror's procession when it took place. To Paul, God celebrates His triumph over His enemies. Paul sees himself, once an enemy, as part of that procession. Connected with this is the idea of the incense-bearer, scattering incense, which was done as the procession moved on. Some of the captives might be put to death when the procession ended at the capitol: to them the smell of incense was an odor unto death. Others, who would be spared to serve their new master, would find the incense an odor unto life.

"Thanks be to God who leads me on from place to place in the train of his triumph, to celebrate his victory over the enemies of Christ; and by me sends forth the knowledge of him, a steam of fragrant incense. . . . For Christ's is the fragrance which I offer up to God" (Conybeare's translation).

I. *God gains His greatest victories out of apparent defeats and disasters.* If the kingdom of God not only got over the murder of Christ but made it its great lever, there is nothing that it cannot get over and nothing that it cannot turn to eternal blessing and to the glory of the holy Name. In the cross we have the supreme demonstration of this principle. Think of the three youths in the fiery furnace (Dan. 3:19-26) : what seemed defeat turned out to be God's way of triumph – a fourth was found in the fire. Joseph (Gen. 39:7-23), tempted to impurity, seemed to be in jeopardy, but under God he was able to overcome. Evil scheming and prison did not defeat his stand of purity and character.

The trials of life need not be disasters. They are opportunities for God to reveal His power on our behalf. Sins abound, but grace is mightier. God will not be defeated or thwarted in His love. What are our inner resources of faith? What are we living by? True character is shown in the hour of trial.

II. *God wins His best servants out of those who have become*

79

His bond-slaves. Paul, once an enemy, is now a servant of Christ. His former religion was not Christian; and, although zealous, he sinned against God. His conversion on the Damascus Road was the turning point in his life. He was made captive by Christ:

> Make me a captive, Lord,
> And then I shall be free.
> Help me to render up my sword,
> And I shall conqueror be.

George Matheson sang that out of his blindness and lost love to find eternal love could make him a servant of God.

In selfish freedom Paul was a slave to sin. Now in slavery to Christ he finds true freedom of spirit. In the procession of triumph he is one of the prisoners of love. The rebel heart is stilled, and devotion is born. Defiance becomes devotion, and despair becomes joy: hatred becomes love. Thus Paul, in the procession, is made captive to Christ's will and plan.

III. *God uses the Christian servant to scatter the fragrance of the gospel.* In the Roman world the victor who led the procession was acclaimed because of the number and quality of his captives. Incense burned on many altars, and the acolytes scattered it all along the route. Paul saw in this a corresponding procession of those who had become Christ's. Wherever he and they passed, the fragrance of the saving gospel was diffused. To the disobedient it prefaced death; to the saved it meant life. Accepted, this gospel brings salvation; rejected, it brings doom and judgment.

Is not this the true picture of how the Christian faith has been spread abroad? By the lives of those who are the captives of Christ, by their witness in life and word, by the testimony of the truth to all men, the gospel was thus taken to Rome, the citadel of the empire; to Corinth, the city of commerce; to Athens, the city of culture; and it has been carried to all the lands.

The train of His triumph is before us. What a spectacle as we see the march of victory over the centuries! Are we marching in that victorious procession of Christ's captives? Do we diffuse the fragrance of the gospel?

35. The God Who Remembers

"They that feared the Lord spake often one to another: and the Lord hearkened, and heard it, and a book of remembrance was written before him for them that feared the Lord and that thought upon his name."—Malachi 3:16

This is part of a prophecy in which a nation is called upon to repent. Israel had been guilty of profanity, sacrilege, greed, weariness in service, treason, robbery, and blasphemy. The people expostulated and excused themselves at the charge of God, but the indictment was confirmed. In the presence of this disappointment concerning His chosen people, God remembers a remnant who keep alive the flame of spiritual devotion. When others live disobediently, they live devotedly.

I. *The Activity of the Remnant.* The doctrine of the remnant is vital to the Old Testament.

These *fear* the Lord and reverence His name. There is awe and holy regard for God's majesty and holiness. Their lives are lived in the light of that holy light wherein is no darkness and before which no sin is allowed.

They *think* upon His name. Isaiah (53:3) spoke of those who esteemed not the Messiah. This word is also used by Malachi. Here are people who do esteem the name of Jehovah. When others are blasphemous and guilty of treason against that holy name, they prize and set value upon His name as the chief name among all nations. Here is their faith expressed in a day of apostasy and backsliding.

Naturally, they *speak* one to another concerning their God. The reality of a rich fellowship is disclosed. This is not a service of worship or a prayer meeting, although worship and prayer may be present, but a fellowship gathering. In an age of spiritual declension small groups met to maintain the spiritual life. As in Israel, so in the early church, with Christ in the midst, the disciples continued steadfastly in the fellowship (Acts 2:46). Godly conversation and Christ-centered devotion found an outlet in the groups rich in faith.

God's approval came — *"They shall be mine"* — a purchased, redeemed people, God's spiritual treasure, His *jewels.* When others forgot Him, He rejoiced in this remnant. There were Noah, Nehemiah, Elijah, and Malachi in Old Testament days. We recall Christians in the catacombs of Rome, Covenanters in Scotland, Huguenots in France, Puritans in England, and other groups "of whom the world was not worthy" (Heb. 11:38).

II. *The Attitude of the Lord.* God's response to the remnant is set forth in striking words.

God hearkened — He "pricked up the ear." Just as a horse shows pleasure and familiarity at the sound of a well-known voice, so God shows his sensitivity towards His own. As a receiving set, delicately poised, picks up messages, so God reacts to the faintest whisper of His own people who are looking to Him.

God *heard* — not that He should be thought of as hearing on the special occasion, but not missing a syllable of the conversation and the thought of His own. How patient God is as He listens to us. The remnant is not always aware.

God *remembered* — this is the supreme fact of divine grace. Man neglects, but God cares. Man forgets, but God remembers. We have erected our war memorials and monuments to those who have served their day and generation, but many forget those who have gone before us. How significant that God remembers His own in a day of forgetfulness. The prophet speaks of the "book of remembrance" with its indelible record of the faithful remnant. Compare the current practice of displaying books of remembrance in new church buildings and some of the outstanding memorials erected.

The last book of the Old Testament ends with this "book of remembrance." The last book of the New Testament ends with another "book of life," the Lamb's book, wherein are the names of those who are the redeemed of the ages. As we think of this truth, we know that: God remembers our sins and forgives them by His grace; God remembers our failures and gives us strength to overcome; God remembers our endowments and offers opportunities of service. Are our names on God's scroll of honor? He remembers the faithfulness of those who stand in a day of declension.

Compare in Esther 6:1 the custom of a monarch to list names of benefactors in a book: so God does this in His heart concerning His remnant, faithful people. As reward, God promises to the faithful "the Sun of righteousness" (Mal. 4:2) to bless. Life and energy will come in the rays of that sunshine of love from God.

36. John Wesley—The Methodist

"There was a man sent from God, whose name was John."
—John 1:6

One of the fascinating and profitable means of preaching is to use church history through its outstanding personalities. Biography is a useful method of setting forth spiritual truth. The Bible is rich in biography and can be so used. Here we use men outside of the Bible in whom we see *the life of God in the soul of man.* Consider William Carey, Charles H. Spurgeon, Dwight L. Moody, Jonathan Edwards, and, in this case, John Wesley. Others will come to mind in John Knox, John Calvin, John Wyclif, and Martin Luther. In the standard biographies of Wesley, in the history of the Evangelical Revival, and most of all in his own *Journal* the data is found.

I. *A Man of Great Virtue. His Religious Experience.* Born in 1703, his life was crowned with eternity in 1791.

Influence of Home. Brought up in a manse, father a minister of the Episcopal Church in England, a remarkable mother (Susannah) : "make religion the business of your life, the one thing necessary" her counsel; as a child, saved from burning of the Epworth manse.

Oxford College Days. Joined the Holy Club, a methodical way of spiritual life; economy of time; religious discipline; habitual reverence; rule for life a little pharisaical; student, tutor. Christian?

Georgia as Missionary. "To save his own soul and convert Indians." Meets Spangenberg (Moravian), who asked, "Have you the witness yourself? Do you know that Christ has saved you?" "I hope so." Failure in America: returns discredited, and feels keenly.

London and Aldersgate Street. Meeting, May 24, 1738: one read Preface of *Luther's Commentary* to *Romans:* "About quarter to nine, describing the change God works in heart through faith in Christ, *I felt my heart strangely warmed.* I felt I did trust in Christ alone for salvation, and an assurance was given me that He had taken away my sins" (cf. influence of Moravians and Reformation).

II. *A Man of Great Views. His Christian Doctrines.* He had received much in early training, but now it came to life.

New Birth. He preached *justification by faith.* His life was written across the sky for all to see. He had nothing to conceal. Preached according to his experience. Conversion and rebirth strong in his message (see sermons).

Sanctification. The doctrine of holiness of life was prominent in Wesley. He was raised up to testify to this more than anything else. "This doctrine is the grand depositum of Methodists... for this we are raised up." The sinner is saved; the saint is sanctified. The work of the Holy Spirit is manifested: "The work of God does not prosper where perfect love is not preached." The Class meeting fostered this warm religion.

Portrait of a Methodist. "A Methodist is one who has the love of God shed abroad in his heart by the Holy Spirit given unto him. He rejoices... prays... gives thanks. His heart is full of love to all... is purified. His desire is to do God's will. He keeps God's commandments.... He follows not the customs of the world. He fares not sumptuously every day.... He cannot lay up treasures.... He cannot speak evil.... He cannot join in diversions to evil.... He does good to all.... These are the principles... marks... by these alone do Methodists desire to be distinguished from all other men."

III. *A Man of Great Vision. His Righteous Crusades.* Southey called attention to the great energy of Wesley.

The Age. The eighteenth century, known for its drunkenness, immorality, crime, and vice: gin shops — drunk for a penny, etc. Wit was filth, amusement degraded. Religiously at low ebb: empty churches, bad clergy, coarse people. Night darkest before dawn, when the fire of God fell upon Wesley and England. "People of discernment thought Christianity fictitious" (Butler). Reason eclipsed faith.

His Aim. He attacked sin in every form — slavery, the liquor traffic, degrading sports, and all vested interests in church and state. "The Evangelical Revival saved England from French revolution and godless civilization" (Lecky). Cf. Helevey, French historian. He affirmed Christianity, not as social reform first, but in personal salvation. Education inspired, and encouraged. Prison reform.

His Achievements. His writings — 50 volumes; preached 40,000 sermons, travelled 250,000 miles; open air evangelist. New moral enthusiasm swept the land: society cleansed; Methodist Church founded. Evangelical Revival the watershed of modern advance. "The world my parish" true. All this from "a warmed heart." Wesley never at leisure in this crusade. The rebirth of a soul becomes the way of rebirth in a nation's life. Missionary societies and social agencies resulted from this movement through Wesley.

37. Mary the Mother of Jesus

"Blessed art thou among women."—Luke 1:28

The words of Gabriel addressed to Mary told of the awful and tremendous secret of the coming birth of Jesus. She was addressed with respect and honor. She was given a place of greatness and "endured with grace" as befitted the mother of Jesus. Mother's Day or Christmas are times to re-examine her position and the influence she has exerted.

The Christian church has fallen into two attitudes toward her, one of which is wrong and the other mistaken. The Roman church has placed her between humanity and the Son of God. This is idolatry and has brought disastrous effects. The Protestant church, in a warranted rebound from Mariolatry, has forgotten to hold the mother of Jesus in the esteem due to her.

Mary was a member of the race, a sinner like others, and needed and shared in the redemption which was provided by her Son. However, the honor conferred upon her was of the highest, and our thought of her and our language concerning her should at least not lack the dignity and respect manifested in the angelic messenger. Hers was the crown and glory of motherhood, and we should ever think and speak of her with understanding.

I. *The Events in Mary's Life.* The record is brief in comparison to that of our Lord, yet what we have is suggestive. The references are grouped thus:

At the Birth of Jesus. Here she is the virgin-mother, the maiden in the glory of dawning womanhood. Lineage of King David, she hoped for the Messiah's coming like others. Humbly she accepts the honor and task before her. After the birth of Jesus nothing is told about her for twelve years, except —

At the Dedication of Jesus. After forty days at Bethlehem, she and Joseph took Jesus to present Him in the Temple and offer two turtle doves (cf. Lev. 11:2, 6, 8). Simeon rejoiced in the Child at this time and foretold Mary's future sorrow.

At the Passover. Mary was living now at Nazareth and trained her child. Did she understand Jesus' word of Luke 2:49, "My Father's business"? "She kept all these sayings in her heart" (Luke 2:51).

At Nazareth and in the Home. In the Nazareth home there were other children born to her through Joseph (Mark 6:3). She attended a wedding (John 2:1-10). She learned that her Son had a special mission (Matt. 12:50). For eighteen years Jesus was "subject" to Mary and Joseph, living and working. What did she tell Him about that wondrous birth? What conversation did they share together about the work of God?

At the Crucifixion and the Upper Room. She is with other women. She followed Jesus to the end (John 7:5). She is given a new home and guardian (John 19:25). She is one of the group at Pentecost (Acts 1:14). She is a devoted woman of grace and love.

II. *The Elements of Mary's Character.* What kind of person was she? A sword pierced her heart, but she was strong in faith and rich in devotion to Christ.

Faith. She had this to accept God's command; she believed God "that nothing was impossible" (Luke 1:37); cf. her faith in the song of thanksgiving (Luke 1:46-55) and her trust in the Lord.

Obedience. The will of God came first, and she placed her life in God's hands: "Be it unto me according to thy word" (Luke 1:38). At Cana she said, "Whatsoever he saith unto you, do it" (John 2:5).

Humility and Modesty. Read the Magnificat (Luke 1:48, 52, 53) and trace the references to this: "her low estate... low degree... filled hungry...": we find nothing of self-exaltation, but self-forgetfulness and humility.

Purity. The song of thanksgiving reveals a purity of spirit and disposition. The pure in heart see God. Herod sought the life of Jesus, but Mary sheltered the Child. In a time of sensuality and evil, Mary shines out in the white light of her strength.

Thoughtfulness. Mary kept much in heart (Luke 2:19). She was cultured and expressed herself poetically. She sang in her soul as she rejoiced in God's wisdom (Luke 1:46-47).

III. *The Example of Mary's Faith.* Women especially and all Christians can learn from her.

Her Influence as a Mother. That has been profound and far-reaching. Gentle, strong, obedient, unselfish — these qualities prevail. She was not sinless, but she was the highest of women.

Her Crown of Womanhood. As the mother of Jesus she brought forth the Saviour. He has lifted womanhood and sanctified motherhood. No one else can have Mary's distinction, but other women by faith can share her ideals and follow her example.

38. Love Is Loyalty

"Many waters cannot quench love...."—Song of Solomon 8:7

The loyalties of life are among the master qualities. We are what our loyalties make us. Either noble or base, they control our actions and indicate our influence in character. The Old Testament illustrates this truth that loyalty is the test of love. In three short books there are these well-known stories of three women, obviously young women, in the choice and testing of love's loyalty. Each embodies a primary loyalty of life: (1) to plighted troth; (2) to kinsfolk and family; (3) to people and country.

I. *Song of Solomon:* The Shulamite Bride, *Loyal to Lover.* The interpretation of this book is not easy. The simplest among many views is that of a story of human love between a king and this maiden. (This is interpreted by the church as a revelation of the nature of true love which leads us to understand the divine love to man, Christ to His church, and the highest spiritual and mystical experience of the soul.) The king finds and woos this maiden in the vineyards of Lebanon. She refuses him. Later there is another wooing by her true shepherd lover. He wins her. Then follows the betrothal and marriage. Here is idyllic recollection of that experience. The soul expresses love in these terms: the bridegroom — "As the lily among thorns, so is my love among the daughters" (2:2); and the bride — "His banner over me was love" (2:4).

Loyalty is seen in the devotion to the object of love. "Many waters cannot quench love, neither can the floods drown it: if a man would give all the substance of his house for love, it would utterly be contemned" (8:7). Compare the modern laxity about the marriage bond and the sanctities of life with reference to sex and family. This unnamed heroine is loyal to her lover. There is need today for this high and holy devotion in modern human relations. A nation stands or falls by its family life.

II. *Ruth: Loyal to Her Mother-in-Law, Kinsfolk, Family.* This story is from the days of the judges, when "every man did that which was right in his own eyes, "a time of chaos in the nation. Religious apostasy, political irresponsibility, moral decline, social bankruptcy — these brought trouble and sorrow.

Ruth's life stands out unsullied in a time of lowered standards. Recall her background in the load of Moab and the tragic circumstances which led her to Palestine. Her choice to follow Naomi is a moving story: "Intreat me not to leave thee, or to return from following after thee: for whither thou goest, I will go; and where thou lodgest, I will lodge: thy people shall be my people, and thy God my God" (1:16). In a pastoral setting, harvest, home, and family, this young woman commits herself to the high end of devotion within the family and the community. The issues were not seen then, but later came the link in the Messianic line of promise through Boaz and David to Christ.

Ruth's experience was one of loyalty to the best she knew and the devotion of a life to the highest in spite of sorrow and suffering love. Great ends depend upon a choice of this kind. Relate a modern example to this principle for today. Think of those who risk their lives to stay with their fellows in time of peril and danger. Love is loyalty.

III. *Esther: Loyal to Her Nation and People.* When the plot against Israel became known to her uncle, this young woman was God's agent to save a nation. Wicked Haman schemes to get rid of Mordecai and the Jews, but God overrules through Esther's faith and obedience. This is a thrilling story of plot and counter-plot, intrigue and faith. The opposing forces are deployed skill-fully, and the heroine is set forth in her modesty and courage. That courage came from her love in which she showed her essential loyalty to principle and so to her people.

Her resolve in "come to the kingdom for such a time as this" (4:14) and "so will I go in unto the king, which is not according to the law: and if I perish, I perish" (4:16) suggests how one in a difficult position socially and politically can yet stand for the right under God and be honored by God.

What about our loyalties? Where is our devotion given? Can God depend upon us in choice of friends, use of time, giving our money, the worship of God, and our responsibilities within the family and the church and the nation? Think of Christ's love and loyalty to His own. "He loved them unto the end [utterly]" (John 13:1). Can we match Him? If love spells loyalty, what influence do we exert for the kingdom of God? What does the cross mean?

39. Faith

"Faith is the substance of things hoped for, the evidence of things not seen."—Hebrews 11:1

If love is the greatest thing in the world, faith is primary. It cannot be defined, but it may be described. If hope is love waiting, then faith is love trusting. Faith begins with an experiment and ends in an experience. We cannot live without faith. We live by what we believe. Every day people live and trust themselves to others. Why not faith in God?

I. *Faith is a means of knowledge.* The objects of faith are the unseen and the invisible. The office of faith is to give present substance to future things and vital reality to the unseen. Faith is not credulity and not superstition. The difference between "secular" and "religious" belief is not in the exercise of faith but in the object.

Concerning *God* it is written, "Without faith it is impossible to please him: for he that cometh to God must believe that he is, and that he is a rewarder of them that diligently seek him" (Heb. 11:6). The existence of God is assumed in the revelation of the Bible: "In the beginning God." Our knowledge of God rests upon faith. It is not by reason or searching.

Concerning *truth* and *doctrine,* Jesus said: "If any man will do his will he shall know of the doctrine, whether it be of God" (John 7:17). Obedience is the divine organ of spiritual revelation. It is not knowing in order to believe but believing to know.

II. *Faith is a means of power.* Concerning *salvation* and the *Christian life,* we read, "For by grace are ye saved through faith" (Eph. 2:8). Personal commitment and trust in the Saviour is power. Coming to Christ for pardon and forgiveness leads to power over sin in newness of life. The new creation begins by the power of faith and issues in reasoned living. Faith is not unreasonable. We may know little and yet become Christian. A Christian's knowledge is power.

Concerning *prayer* and the *needs of life,* we may "ask in faith, nothing wavering . . ." (Jas. 1:6). Here reason is allied to faith, but faith will supersede reason. Reason is the handmaid of faith. Where reason cannot aspire, faith will wing its upward way. The records of individuals, churches, hospitals, orphanages, missionary societies, and the like are eloquent testimony to the dynamic energy of faith in God and the unseen.

89

III. *Faith is a means of action.* Concerning the *unknown* and *our future,* we must live by this confident trust in God. Our ground of confidence, the title deed to our spiritual inheritance, is that upon which we act. Call it conviction, a feeling of certitude, a bias or prejudice, yet it is a reality. Faith takes the long view of life and sees it whole and steady. The alarmist and pessimist is not a man of faith. To have faith is to be calm and steady, poised and understanding in time of uncertainty.

> Peace, perfect peace, Our future all unknown?
> Jesus we know, And He is on the throne.

Concerning *the world,* we are told that "this is the victory that overcometh the world, even our faith" (I John 5:4). Paul writes, "taking the shield of faith" (Eph. 6:16). Facing life with its insistent demands and its unexpected events, we know that faith is not for comfort but for character. Overcoming life's handicaps of mind and body is the energy released through faith. Deliverance is promised from the assaults of pessimism, cynicism, fear, and evil powers which molest the soul. Faith overcomes.

IV. *Faith is a means of living.* Concerning our *daily life,* there is no substitute for faith. No one wishes fate or fanaticism. "We walk by faith, not by sight" (II Cor. 5:7). This is the working principle of each day for the Christian. No rational person is creedless. Belief in God, in Christ, in the Holy Spirit, in the Bible, and in the church counts! It matters vitally in a personal way *where* we repose our trust and confidence.

Concerning our *moral life and conduct,* "faith without works is dead" (Jas. 2:20). The men and women of faith are not idlers but workers. What we believe determines how we act and live. Conduct issues from creed, behavior from belief. "A man's action is the only picture-book of his creed" (Emerson). Read again Hebrews 11, and see what faith has done in the lives of humble and ordinary people.

40. Song in Strange Surroundings

"How shall we sing the Lord's song in a strange land?"
—Psalm 137:4
"At midnight Paul and Silas . . . sang praises unto God."
—Acts 16:25

Two texts indicate two different views of and attitudes to life. On the one hand is the futility of song in time of trouble. On the other hand is the music of contentment in trying surroundings. These are not necessarily the contrasting views of the Old Testament and the New Testament but simply come out of these two experiences.

I. *In exile it is difficult to sing.* During the exile the Hebrew people were treated as prisoners who might provide sport for their captors. They were not only treated cruelly and punished, but in this instance they were placed in the position of mockery and abuse. For them not to attempt any singing would be interpreted as disobedience to their captors. For them to attempt to sing meant for the moment a hardship of poignant memory and wistful longing which would well-nigh crush the soul in tears and sorrow.

Imagine, then, their problem as Israelites. As prisoners in a foreign land and away from home, without their Temple of worship, they found it almost a desecration. To sing before those whose religion denied the true and living God was a degradation of their sacred ideals of worship. Away from home they had little heart or spirit for such a task. Solitude tended to silence, and to sing would be forced mirth.

They thought themselves to be victims, overwhelmed by trouble. A medical specialist in London estimated that suffering hardens fifty per cent of the people. Complaints, groaning, rebellion — these elements led the Israelites at first to think that their harps should hang on the willows. The absence of joy led to the loss of testimony that they were God's people. How true this can be in time of trouble. God's people may find it difficult to sing then. But perhaps this is the time to sing, so that others might know the spirit of overcoming trouble. Man's reason would say that it is impossible to sing in this experience. The Israelites found it so.

II. *In prison it is not impossible to sing.* In contrast to the Israelites, here is another exile experience. Christ's men are in prison because of their witness to the faith. Here are no open spaces, no river of Babylon, no plain or trees, and no harp! The dungeon at Philippi, the Roman garrison town, is dark, and the stocks are secure and scourging is cruel. Midnight is hardly the time for bright spirits.

Yet this was the place and the time of singing. The words suggest that Paul and Silas *worshipped* God in their prayers and praises. The prison became a sanctuary. What was it they sang? Was it one of the familiar psalms of Israel or some new Christian hymn? Did Paul carry the tune or air and Silas take a part? In this hour two men of faith overcame their circumstances. Trouble did not crush them. They learned and expressed the secret of Christian contentment.

Anyone can sing outside a prison in the sunshine; it requires faith to sing in prison and at midnight! Our Lord on the eve of His betrayal and trial shared in the song of the *Hallel* in the upper room in the Passover and Lord's Supper. Madam Guyon, in a French prison for ten years, sang:

> A little bird am I.
> My cage confines me round,
> Abroad I cannot fly,
> But though my wings are tightly bound,
> My heart's at liberty.
> My prison walls cannot control
> The Flight, the Freedom, of my soul.

The nightingale never sings so sweetly as when its breast is pierced by a thorn.

"The prisoners heard. . . ." There was an unseen and unknown congregation for Christ's men. It is always so. We cannot count the unseen audience at any time, whether at home or church or radio. We are surrounded by a great host of worshippers anyway, according to Hebrews 12:22-24. Jesus Christ is present with His own people no matter where they are found. If in prison, then He shares the scourging, the stocks, the terrors of the condemned, the darkness of the midnight hour. We little know who is watching or listening to us in our time of trial. If we *sing* then, we are witnessing to others.

Midnights can become as midday; darkness as light; wounds as messages of love; and strange surroundings the sanctuary of praise to God.

41. The Work of the Holy Spirit

"He shall give you another Comforter...."—John 14:16

It was expedient for Jesus to leave His disciples. He told them that by going He would send to them the Holy Spirit to abide with them. As the Spirit of Christ He would be in them and with them. In that capacity Christ could be everywhere and with all His people at any time. This work of the Spirit of God is most important for the Christian to understand. Among the many ministries of the ascended Lord are those which relate to the function of the Holy Spirit. As the Comforter He comes as the Paraclete, the one alongside to help, to stand by in need, and to speak for the disciple. Other works are indicated in this study:

I. *Regeneration:* "Ye must be born again...born of the Spirit" (John 3:7, 8). This relates to the change which Christ works in the heart. It is not reformation alone, not a process of change by man's effort. It is the communication of a new nature which is divine and holy. "Born over again" (Goodspeed). "Born again is to be born from above." Charles Wesley sings in the Christmas hymn "Hark the Herald Angels Sing,...Born to raise the sons of earth, born to give them *second birth.*"

II. *Baptism:* "baptized in the Holy Spirit" (Acts 1:5, R.V.). This secures the position of the believer in the family of God or the body of Christ. We are put into Christ as our inheritance. Baptism makes possible all other graces of the Christian life. At the time of regeneration we are baptized into this experience. This is initial and complete. The Holy Spirit is the agent of Christ for the "One Lord,...one baptism" (Eph. 4:5); "For by one Spirit are we all baptized into one body" (I Cor. 12:13). The baptism is also linked to the filling of the Spirit (Acts 2:4).

III. *Sealing:* "the Holy Spirit of God, in whom ye were sealed" (Eph. 4:30, R.V.). The seal speaks of the stamp of ownership. The Roman emperor used a seal to mark those who belonged to him by conquest and enslavement. God in Christ owns those who are thus stamped by the Holy Spirit. II Timothy 2:19-21 suggests what the seal implies in the Christian life. The hallmark of the true life is here by the foundation and witness of the Spirit within our lives.

IV. *Indwelling:* "ye are the temple of God, and...the Spirit of

93

God dwelleth in you" (I Cor. 3:16). We should not doubt this even if we lack emotional feeling about it. Faith rests upon fact and not feeling. Union with Christ, forgiveness of sin, and inner peace are here. Our lives, our bodies included, are shrines of God's indwelling presence. God takes up His abode in us. We are now temples of worship. We must reverence and honor the temple of God in purity.

V. *Gift:* "ye shall receive the gift of the Holy Spirit" (Acts 2:38, R.V.). Peter linked this with man's repentance from sin and confession of faith in Christ (Acts 2:38; 11:14-17). In Acts 1:5 and 11:16 it is referred to as a *baptism*; in 2:4 as being *filled*; in 2:17 and 10:45 as being *poured out*; in 2:33 as being *shed forth*. In 8:20 Peter rejected a man who thought the *gift* could be bought.

VI. *Earnest:* ". . . ye were sealed with the Holy Spirit of promise, . . . an earnest of our inheritance" (Eph. 1:13-14, R.V.). As in the idea of being sealed, there is the same concept of a foretaste of what is to come, an earnest. Money is deposited for a purchase, and that percentage is an earnest. When two young people become engaged to marry, a ring is usually given as an earnest or pledge of what is to follow. The Holy Spirit is "the engagement ring" for the Christian from Christ.

VII. *Anointing:* ". . . he . . . anointed us, . . . also sealed us . . ." (II Cor. 1:21). The thought here is linked with the Old Testament practice of anointing a king or priest for holy service. I John 2:20, 27 speaks of this anointing as teaching us. The Spirit was given to lead us into all truth. As oil is rubbed in, so the Spirit is the invisible presence to give us quickened minds.

VIII. *Filling:* ". . . be filled *with* the Spirit" (Eph. 5:18). The preposition is in the case which means "by." Thus the Spirit fills us with Christ, not Himself. Living in the Spirit, we are led to further affusions of His presence and power, which is Christ in us. Verses 14 to 21 speak of the results of this. The ministry of the Holy Spirit is varied and manifold in power.

42. The Work of the Church

"Ye shall be witnesses unto me...."—Acts 1:8

What does the church exist to do? What is its primary task in the world? The answer seems easy, but the church has done many things in the course of history.

I. *What the Church Has Done.* In the field of *education* she has produced scholars and thinkers. What would have happened without them in the Middle Ages? Christianity made possible the benefits of the Renaissance. Now the State has taken over education more and more. Yet education is not the primary task of the church. In *social reform* the church has been active. In other centuries the church broke the power of slavery, brought prison reform, cancelled child labor, gave relief to the suffering, built hospitals and institutions to alleviate the needs of men. Yet social reform is not the primary task of the church. In *political affairs* the church has had a voice. She has spoken to the conscience of nations and governments. Statesmen have looked to the church for guidance. In time of crisis and in city and community work the church has led in the advance of all that is best for the welfare of people. Yet politics is not the primary task of the church.

II. *What the Church Exists to Do:* simply "to be a *witness* to Christ." But what is witnessing? The modern view of a witness is that of one who bears testimony to what he knows or has seen. The original meaning of the word "witness" is "martyr." A martyr today is thought of as one who dies for his faith or principles. But by the original meaning of the word a man was not a martyr because he died for his faith: he died for his faith because he was a martyr (a witness).

This word for witness (martyr) occurs about thirty times in the Book of the Acts, an indication of the primary task of the church. Jesus selected men to serve Him, and they were set apart to be witnesses. He promised them power to do this. That work does not rest upon political influence or social prestige or intellectual authority. It is something given by God as an enduement of power and authority. It comes by the presence and power of the Holy Spirit, Christ's vice-regent in the assembly of God and in the hearts of His people.

The *Sufficiency* of Witnessing: "Ye shall be witnesses." The personal element is important. God did not carry through His plan by organization as such, but by the choice of selected men. In Acts 8:1 we read, "they were *all* scattered abroad, *except the apostles,"* and in Acts 8:4, "they that were scattered abroad went everywhere preaching the word." Every Christian a witness and missionary was the ideal.

Why was the early church given this task in this way? To perpetuate the work of Christ. His ministry of three and a half years in teaching was not enough; now the ministry was extended through them.

How? by practicing the message they proclaimed. Christianity was not a faith only but a life to be lived. The personal touch is necessary.

When? in proclaiming the gospel of Christ. They seized upon the most tragic incident in the life of Jesus for their best news.

The *Secret* of Witnessing: "unto me." This was not testimony to the church as such, but to the Person of Jesus, the living Lord, not witness to the resources of the church or their own achievements, certainly not to their wealth (which was negligible) or prestige (they were nobodies then). They gave witness to Christ Himself in His saving and redeeming power for life. Luke 24:47 suggests part of that message as given at Jerusalem and beyond. Love dominated their spirit as they witnessed to Christ. "By this shall all men know..." (John 13:35).

The *Sphere* of Witnessing: "Jerusalem...." From the holy city, out through Judaea, Samaria, and then to the uttermost parts of the Roman world they went with this message and gospel. The Book of the Acts illustrates the expanding sphere of witness: chapters 1 to 7, Jewish, with Jerusalem as center; chapters 8 to 12, transitional, with Antioch as center; chapters 13 to 28, world-wide, with Rome as center.

The missionary outreach gave them their life-task in the light of the Great Commission (Matt. 28:19, 20; Acts 1:8).

III. *What the Church Rests upon:* the promise of Christ, "ye shall receive power." This power is that of the Holy Spirit given at Pentecost. It *united* the disciples in one bond of love. It *gave* them a sense of *mission and destiny.* That power *is spiritual and moral* in its dynamic quality for life and deed. God inbreathed upon them His grace and strength. They went out to "turn the world upside down."

43. A Young Crusader

"While he [Josiah] was yet young, he began to seek God."
—II Chronicles 34:3

The tragedy of two world wars has served to emphasize the necessity for youth to enter upon leadership. Forces of evil bid for the perversion of youth. It is time that forces of good should offer to youth the challenge of sacrifice and a godly life. The future may well be in the hands of youth who are even now making supreme decisions with and for their lives. This story points to *a prince who led a great crusade.*

I. *Before His Conversion.* The inner life of the young prince was uncorrupted and undefiled. His youthful heart was open towards God.

The *influences* surrounding Josiah were fourfold. Two lives were evil and two were good. His grandfather, Manasseh, was a bad man, and his father, Amon, not much better. The first eight years of a child's life are most impressionable. Offsetting two bad examples, we find his mother, Jedidah, who brought grace and purity to him. Who can estimate the influence of a godly mother? Samuel had Hannah; Augustine had Monica; the Wesleys had Susannah Wesley. Josiah's ancestor David was a man after God's own heart. Josiah's heritage was not to be despised.

The *inheritance* he entered upon was not encouraging for a youth. The nation was given over to idolatry and sin with formal hypocrisy. The court was corrupt and the Temple in ruins. But the prophets Jeremiah and Huldah were his spiritual advisers, and this was good.

II. *At His Conversion.* "He did that which was right in the sight of the Lord, and walked in the ways of David his father, and declined neither to the right hand, nor to the left. For in the eighth year of his reign, while he was yet young, he began to seek after the God of David his father." Thus the change of life for Josiah was decisive.

He decided for the *right person* — "God." God is the source of all moral and spiritual life and grace.

He decided at the *right time* — "while ... yet young." This is the best time and when most decisions of life are registered.

He decided in the *right manner* — "to seek after ... God." Here is earnestness — doing the right and honoring God; intelligence — he knew which way of life was best; determination — steadfastness in conviction and resoluteness of purpose marked the life and habit

97

of the young prince. Any time is the right time to turn away from sin and self to God, but the best time is in youth.

III. *After His Conversion.* Conversion leads to a converted life. Personal and social effects are the result. Christianity offers abundant evidence in history of its power to influence and alter environment through dedicated lives in a great crusade.

Reformation came through Josiah. At home the idols were thrown down and the worship of Jehovah resumed. At Jerusalem and throughout the land false teachers and the treacherous leaders were removed. City and state had a time of house-cleaning. The shams and the injustices, the hypocrisies, the abuses and vested interests with their devilries were not only challenged, but overthrown. Josiah is the forerunner of Nehemiah, Luther, Calvin, Knox, Wyclif, Hus, and many another.

Reconstruction meant destruction of evil things and the construction of good things. The House of God, the Temple, was repaired and the worship of God enthroned again at the heart of the nation's life. Josiah enlisted repairers and subscribers, workers for many tasks. The period of reconstruction is one of peril from vested interests, but Josiah seems to have handled it aright.

Revival crowned the witness and zeal of young Josiah. The *discovery of the old Bible* led the way. Lost to the nation for around sixty years, the dark days of ignorance were banished when this scroll was found. When read again it touched the conscience of the people. Then came the *dedication of the people.* A cleansing stream swept through the land.

Whenever people make a covenant with God in such an experience as Josiah's, there is the renewal of ancient loyalties and a dedication to new and holier fidelities. God honored them under Josiah. Compare New England in the eighteenth century and its revival, the influence of the Wesleys, and the social, moral, and political changes which resulted. As in Josiah's day, what about ours? and our lives?

44. First Things First!

"Seek ye first the kingdom of God...."—Matthew 6:33

The familiar phrase comes out of the well-known text. The Bible reveals a sacred regard for order, Heaven's first law. There is first that which is natural, then that which is spiritual. There are times and seasons, and God has given us priorities. In the light of that "seek ye first...," note:

I. *First, the Gospel.* "I delivered unto you first of all that which I also received, how that Christ died for our sins according to the scriptures; and that he was buried, and that he rose again..." (I Cor. 15:3, 4).

The experience of the gospel was that which was declared by Paul and received by the converts who now stood in this faith. Their faith centered in the redeeming acts of God. The Scriptures had foretold, and now testified to, these acts of death and resurrection.

The faith has priority over ethics, education, and eugenics and points to an evangelical experience as the key to eternal life.

II. *First, the Church.* "God at the first did visit the Gentiles, to take out of them a people for his name" (Acts 15:14). "The disciples were called Christians first in Antioch" (Acts 11:26).

The priority of God in this age of grace is to call out a people for Himself. Out of all nations He adds to the elect. The nature of the church is determined by this activity of God (see Acts 2:44). The universal or catholic body of Christ is world-wide and is not restricted to any one people or place.

Do not disparage the church. Within it are those who have become Christians, the people of "the way." The church is God's instrument.

III. *First, Worship.* Worth-ship is the root of worship. It must be spiritual — in spirit and in truth — not formal or superficial, but heartfelt and genuine, nothing to be allowed to mar the fellowship.

"First *be reconciled to thy brother,* and then come and offer thy gift" (Matt. 5:24).

"First *cast out the beam out of thine own eye"* (Matt. 7:5). Beware of censorious judgment. Carping criticism is condemned, but not constructive appraisal; but first, the self-scrutiny of your own life.

"He began to say unto his disciples first of all, *"Beware ye of*

99

the leaven of the Pharisees, which is *hypocrisy*" (Luke 12:1) — this for worship.

IV. *First, Giving.* "Now concerning the collection . . . as I have given order . . . so do ye. Upon the first day of the week let every one of you lay by him in store . . ." (I Cor. 16:1, 2). "They (the Macedonian Christians) . . . first gave their own selves to the Lord . . ." (II Cor. 8:5). In the spirit of Romans 12:1 they "presented their bodies . . ." and this meant the giving of time, strength, ability, and here *money*. But giving was first to God. The way to raise money is to give it weekly, regularly, consistently, proportionately, and systematically. John Wesley: "Get all you can: save all you can: give all you can." Giving is the acid test of consecration.

V. *First, Prayer.* "I exhort . . . first of all, supplications, prayers, intercessions, and giving of thanks, be made for all . . ." (I Tim. 2:1). This requirement has priority in the Christian community. Prayer is not only in private but in public. Groups and churches must pray for all men. Notice the description given — "for kings, and for all that are in authority." We pray for our nation and our leaders. The end of such prayer is "that ["they"? no, not "they," but "we"] may lead a quiet and peaceable life in all godliness and honesty." The result of prayer is that *we* receive peace in our nation with the attendant blessings in the state and land.

VI. *First, Judgment.* "For the time is come that judgment must begin at the house of God: and if it first begin at us, what shall the end be of them that obey not the gospel of God?" (I Pet. 4:17). In days of crisis with fiery trials and persecutions the church realizes anew her state of being judged. Before God judges the world, He begins within the church. God is a consuming fire. Where do we stand in the church?

VII. *First, Prophecy.* "Knowing this first, that no prophecy of the scripture is of any private interpretation" (II Pet. 1:20). This refers to the prophet's grasp, not the reader's. A genuine man of God is inspired by the Holy Spirit. First, be certain that the message is not of man but from God.

"First of all" is also "last of all." Christ is Alpha and Omega. Study the divine priorities. God is a God of order. To "seek first" implies that we are not like the men of Luke 9:57-62.

45. A Temperance Message

A 3 5 2 8

"By this craft we have our wealth."—Acts 19:25

Increasingly the Christian church must pay attention to the evils and abuses of intoxicating liquors. To combat them we need to know the facts and to face them squarely. Temperance in the New Testament means "self-control." This does not imply prohibition, but it can mean self-denial. In our mechanical age with its hazards of speed and strain, we find we are facing social implications.

What can be said for those who refuse to commit themselves? What does the nation get out of the liquor trade? Any credit? Yes: money for the exchequer, minimum of work for a limited number of people, good dividends to those whose money is invested; but it can be "blood-money." What about the debit side? The moral and physical results are disastrous. Spiritually, souls are blighted. Alcoholics Anonymous can tell its story of heartache and sorrow.

Paul here at Ephesus upset the city and its social structure because he dared to oppose the evils of vested interest. One Demetrius, a silversmith, represented his trade of idol-making and fought the battle. There was a "stir about that *way*" (vs. 23) ; the Christian "way" of life disturbed Demetrius and his followers. In the text we have the crux of the matter as applied to our problem:

I. By this craft we have our *wealth*. "Vested interests" are spoken of concerning those whose chief interest in the traffic is money and profits. Examination of the returns of private ownership, State-controlled outlets, and other avenues of distribution as well as manufacture indicate one thing — the enormous profits from this drink industry. The national amount spent by the people on liquor is also staggering as it reaches about four billion dollars, according to the Bureau of Business Economics, of the United States Bureau of Census. Such a sum far exceeds the amounts we spend on education and other worth while projects.

Legitimate business is entitled to fair and just profits. But is this traffic in liquor legitimate? It is listed as a dangerous business. It requires government sanction, is buttressed by strict laws and enactments to protect the public, and is taxed abnormally, all this because even governments of men know that money gain is the chief interest of the business. This is a strong indictment against such traffic.

II. By this craft we have our *worship*. This is true of the Ephesian silversmiths and true of any liquor traffic. Verses 26 and 27 of this chapter picture the concern of these Ephesian craftsmen: "almost throughout all Asia, this Paul hath persuaded and turned away much people, saying that they be no gods, which are made with hands; so that not only this our craft is in danger to be set at nought; but also that the temple of the great goddess Diana should be despised, and her magnificence should be destroyed, whom all Asia . . . worshippeth."

The craftsmen were devotees of the goddess. What touched their trade affected their hearts. Religion and money were tied together. The most sensitive part of civilized man is his pocket. Haven't we heard the slogan, "Our trade, our politics"? What about "Our trade, our party, our religion"? Whatever influence the liquor interests promote bears upon people, party, church, or government: that means government of the people by whoever will regard their first concern to be the interest of the liquor traffic. This is the end and object of devotion by those in the business — selves and profits — thereby creating an idol and binding multitudes in religious devotion to it.

III. By this craft we have our *wickedness*. Wealth is great; worship is greater; but this is greatest. It is an evil in the sight of God, and Christ came to destroy the works of the Devil. His servants must take their stand concerning the evils of the liquor traffic.

A Physical Evil. The action of alcohol in the human organism is given in medical and scientific testimony. Hospitals learn to do without it. Life insurance companies know that the abstainer is a better risk. Our cities have many derelicts who are so because of the liquor traffic.

A Mental and Moral Evil. Inmates of institutions are weakened through indulgence. Moral judgment is warped and self-control is lost when liquor takes over.

A Social and Economic Evil. Its blight is found in family life, community welfare, economic breakdown. Waste of money and time, hazards in auto-driving, crime, and spiritual loss are seen.

What shall we do? Take our stand. Remember Jesus allowed swine to be destroyed to save souls (Luke 8:33-37). Paul fought the silversmith at Ephesus. We love people: we hate evil.

46. Afterward!

"For ye know how that afterward...."—Hebrews 12:17
"Nevertheless afterward...."—Hebrews 12:11
"Then would he not afterward...."—Hebrews 4:8

This is an arresting and provocative word. It requires no context. The future may not trouble some in their concern for the present. But effects have causes, and the tomorrows of life are certain. What harvests await us should cause us to think a little about the afterward. Three uses of the word are found in the *Letter to the Hebrews*.

I. The Afterward of *Regret and Remorse....* "Esau, who for one morsel of meat sold his birthright. For ye know how that *afterward,* when he would have inherited the blessing, he was rejected: for he found no place of repentance, though he sought it carefully with tears" (Heb. 12:17). This needs little elaboration in the well-known story of the deceit of Jacob and the profanity of Esau. Esau bartered his spiritual birthright for selfish indulgence. He wasted the future for the passion of the moment. Esau's meal was quickly over, but the payment for it endured throughout his life. There was, indeed, plenty of cause to regret that act!

Others have been like Esau: the rich young ruler, Peter, and Judas are examples of men who bartered spiritual riches for a moment's selfishness. Sorrow, shame, and suicide were the results afterward. Often there is remorse and repentance leading to restitution. Some are too late, and life is strewn with regrets and wasted opportunities. The abuse of privilege, the friendship despised, the love neglected, the birthright sold — these speak of the sacrifice of eternal values for temporal and carnal gain.

Every act, word, habit, and error of life brings an afterward. If we thought of this we would be careful to cultivate kindness and consideration in relation to others.

II. The Afterward of *Recompense or Reward.* "Now no chastening for the present seemeth to be joyous, but grievous: nevertheless *afterward* it yieldeth the peaceable fruit of righteousness unto them which are exercised thereby" (Heb. 12:11). There is a gospel of restitution at the heart of life. The compensations for conflict abound. Chastening or discipline is part of God's training of the soul. Man sees it as pain and displeasure, often punishment, but discipline is necessary and reasonable. A father must discipline his child if he is to bring out the best in the young life. Fruit trees need to be pruned, and the tests of a storm reveal the depths of rootage.

Do we consider God's treatment of us severe or unfair? Character is built slowly and under discipline. "Jesus ... for the joy that was set before him endured the cross." In sorrow we can trace the difference in reaction among people. Some rebel, and others accept. Some see an enemy: others see discipline and enrichment. Duty also is seen as drudgery to some: to others it is a means to skill and achievement. In Job's life there was pain and loss, even tragedy; but he found, beyond, the recompense. In this a man must be exercised; that is, he must relate himself aright to God by faith. Only then is there an afterward of reward.

III. The Afterward of *Rest or Renewal.* "For if Joshua had given them rest, then he would not have spoken of another day" (Heb. 4:8, R.V.). This refers to Israel under Joshua, who led them into the Promised Land, successor to Moses, who had delivered them from Egypt. Hope sustained them in the wilderness, but the rest came in the land. Moses brought them out; Joshua brought them in. But Joshua was not able to give them rest. There were walled cities to be captured and giants to be fought. Only in a limited way did the Israelites possess their possessions and enjoy rest in the land.

"There remaineth ... a rest to the people of God." This led to "Let us labour therefore to enter into that rest." What happened to Israel became a type of spiritual life for the church. We have been brought out of Egypt's bondage but not yet into the full rest of the Promised Land. *But we can* enter into that full rest, says this writer to the Hebrews. What Joshua failed to do, our Joshua-*Jesus* can.

All restlessness, fear, anxiety, and distrust are overcome in the *rest* of the rest-giver, even Jesus. It is the rest of faith, not rest from, but rest in, labor. This is the afterward for us, incomplete until in eternity in heaven, but increasingly in this life of pilgrimage now. Rest and renewal are given by God.

The afterwards of life are momentous.

47. The God We Adore

"Now the God of...."—Romans 15:5, 13, 33

Sometimes a chapter of the Bible will light up with new meaning as we see its sweep and scope. Instead of the text or even the paragraph, the whole chapter is illumined by a recurring phrase or word. As Paul reaches the climax of the Letter to Rome and stresses the practical ethical note for life, he presents aspects of God's character in the light of needs to be met. *Each description answers to special need.*

I. He is the God of *patience* (vs. 5). How remarkable this is *in the light of our impatience.* God is never in a hurry and never acts impulsively or impartially. Man is quick to find fault and ready to condemn. We become out of sorts and petulant. We lose our temper under strain and are easily upset. These are the marks of imperfection.

In contrast, God is longsuffering, bearing with us, feeling with us, and patiently carries our burdens. As a mother in the home with children or a teacher in the classroom with students, so God bears and forbears with the dull, the stupid, the slow of heart to believe. Where man is in a hurry, God takes His time. Think of the divine patience in the light of our sins and wrongdoing. As we worship and adore our God, we learn by His grace to overcome our impatience.

II. He is the God of *consolation* (vs. 5). Human discouragement is a root problem of life. This is seen over against God's consolation or comfort. When Jesus said good-bye to His own, He promised them the gift of the Holy Spirit, who was named the Paraclete or Comforter (John 14:16, 16:17). In this was the thought of "one called alongside" to help the needy. As an advocate in court stands beside someone on trial, so the Holy Spirit stands beside us in our need. Consolation is not alone sympathy but strength given.

Think of God's consolation as He binds up the wounds of sin, heals the brokenhearted, strengthens the weak, and abides with the lonely. The gods of the heathen are idols and cruel in their disregard of human needs, capricious in their forgetfulness. The Christian view of God is that of one who shares and contributes. Even Job finds strength in faith.

III. He is the God of *hope* (vs. 13). When Paul wrote, *the world was in a state of despair* and moral breakdown. We see the revelation of God in that light. Tracing the history of man can be a discouraging experience in one aspect. Man's sin and failure are everywhere portrayed. Pessimism could be an easy way out for some. Multitudes live without hope now and have none for the hereafter. A heathen symbol of death was a broken column or a torch upside down. In contrast, the Christian symbol is based on the resurrection of Christ, and hope brightens our sky.

In the conflict of the centuries, right against wrong, righteousness against sin, it is our Christian hope which gives us the ground of assurance that God must win finally. We believe in "The Hound of Heaven" (F. Thompson) and "O Love that wilt not let me go" (G. Matheson). They express for us the conviction that our God keeps alive the flame of hope because He is the hopeful God.

IV. He is the God of *peace* (vs. 33). In a world of unrest, tension, strife, trouble, war, and a future uncertain through man's selfishness and sin there is no anchorage of the soul for many. Religious unrest, moral breakdowns, lives adrift, and the feverishness of the pace of our modern ways — all these cry out that peace is not possible. Our lawless age does not warrant an optimism for peaceful coexistence.

Here the Christian message offers peace to the troubled and distracted. Peace is love resting in the knowledge of God. In that confidence or faith our trust is caught up in the divine awareness of a peace which passes understanding. It is not human but God-given. It is not earned but received as a gift from God. This peace garrisons the heart of the one who trusts, and the soul has peace with God and is at peace with others in this world.

The God we worship and adore is One who is patient, encouraging, hopeful, and peaceful. All this is true as we take time to worship Him. As we worship He imparts to us of His nature so that we begin to have similar qualities of character. In this way we face the world's demands with serenity and good hope. Peace entwines hope and courage and patience.

48. The Divine Love

"God so loved the world. . . ."—John 3:16
"Christ also loved the church. . . ."—Ephesians 5:25
"He loved me. . . ."—Galatians 2:20

There are three circles of divine love. The greatest thing in the world is the love of God. No one can exhaust the theme, and no one is able to fathom the depths of its meaning. Human love at its best is a wonderful experience, but who can measure the quality of the love of God? That "God is love" means that God is *holy* love, and therefore it is the love of creation, passion, and grace. It is the love that cannot accept sin, and consequently it is a sacrificing and suffering love in order to make reconciliation.

Love pervades every virtue. Joy is love smiling. Peace is love resting. Patience is love waiting. Faith is love trusting. Meekness is love yielding. Hope is love expecting. Righteousness is love judging. In contrast, sin is the violation of love. God's love is seen in its depth and scope. There is the impulse to *give* and the impulse to *have*. The objects of God's love are three:

I. The Outer Circle — "God so loved the *world*" (John 3:16). How can we conceive of this? How vast and stupendous a concept — to take in the whole world! Human love is restricted to the individual or family or a group, but here all men are included. Men draw a circle and shut others out, but God's circle is all-inclusive. There are no limits or boundaries. Those who may be against God and enemies are nevertheless included in this. Man reasons that we should love only those who are lovely or who respond to us, but God's love seeks in order to save the lost. His love is not dependent upon a similar return. It is good for evil. It gives, not to get, but to bless.

The *breadth* of that love: "God so loved the world"; the *length* of that love: "he gave his only begotten Son"; the *depth* of that love: "that whosoever believeth in him should not perish"; the *height* of that love: "But have everlasting life": these four dimensions exceed human calculation. The cruelties of life, war, lust, passion — these do not cancel divine love. They serve to accentuate it. It beckons sinning man to the heart of God. When it seems difficult to believe in the love of God, look to the cross, which expresses His suffering love for all.

II. The Inner Circle — Christ also loved the *church*" (Eph. 5:25). God loved the world, but not all the world responded. The group responding is the church. The world is made up of groups —

national, racial, linguistic, religious, cultural, economic, and social.
The mightiest group today is the church. Greater than guilds,
clubs, societies, associations, and orders is this group of Christians.
It is that part of the world which has come home to God by love.

When men talk unthinkingly about the fatherhood of God, we
need to know that God is the Father of all by creation. He is, however, the Father by redemption only to those who have responded
to His love in Christ. The larger family of the race (Acts 17:26) is
now without: the inner family is that of the redeemed, the family
of God by spiritual faith and nature. This is through new birth
or second birth by the Holy Spirit.

The brotherhood of man is racial in its solidarity of blood and
sin. The church is another brotherhood of those who have come
home like the prodigal (Luke 15:20). God the Father has welcomed back His lost and sinning children. The church is the body
and bride of Christ, who "loved the church, and gave himself for
it." This is the inner circle of the elect people.

III. The Select Circle — "He loved *me* . . ." (Gal. 2:20). No
father loves his children in general without loving each one in
particular. It is this wonder which startles Paul. To say God loved
the world is to imagine the individual lost in the crowd. To say
Christ loved the church is to say that a group is favored. But to
say "He loved me" is to invite an experience which transcends all
others. Love is personal in its outgoing.

The parable of the lost things (Luke 15) has that in view. Jesus
showed the worth of the individual. Truth is powerful when it is
personal. "God cares for each of us, as if He cared for us alone;
and so for all of us as if all were but one" (Augustine). This love
affirms that all souls are of value. No one is lost or is too small.
A librarian with thousands of books knows them one by one. So is
this love of Christ. It flows from the heart of the eternal God to
the whole world of man; it finds acceptance within the church;
but it is that which pulsates in the heart of each one who trusts in
Christ. The cross of Calvary is the gauge and measure of that love
to us.

> "Love so amazing, so divine,
> Shall have my soul, my life, my all."

49. The God of Bethel

"He called the name of that place Bethel...."—Genesis 28:19
"I am the God of Bethel...."—Genesis 31:13

This theme is linked with enduring memories. Christians think of the heritage that is given from one generation to another. Like Jacob, the church celebrates its anniversaries with this in mind. People and place are one in spirit. Not that God cannot be found or worshipped everywhere, but there are places hallowed by association in worship.

> "O God of Bethel, by whose hand
> Thy people still are fed;
> Who through this weary pilgrimage
> Hast all our fathers led."

To Jacob, and to us, this means:

I. *Bethel opened a new world.* In verse 10 of the context, "Jacob went out from Beersheba and went toward Haran." The reasons behind this act included flight from the anger of Esau his brother, losing friends and leaving home, seeking a wife and a new life in a new place. Jacob was lonely, destitute, and fearful.

Some leave home voluntarily; some are forced to go; most go of necessity for work and family reasons. Jacob left a limited sphere for a wider outlook. He gave up a narrow world for space. Space is not always emptiness, but it is the openness to see the stars and planets, climb mountains, cross seas, walk the fields. A new world brings new horizons and often God Himself. Think of the Pilgrim Fathers and the new world of this America. Follow the immigrants of the old world who came to the prairies and the plains of the new.

Bethel is the place of beginning again. It speaks of crisis, choice, and commitment in the soul. It marks the dividing line between the old and the new, the well known and the untried. Here may be vision and venture.

II. *Bethel offered a new way.* In verse 11 we read, "a certain place . . . night . . . stones . . . pillow . . . sleep"; in verse 12, "dreamed . . ladder . . . earth . . . heaven . . . angels"; in verse 13, "and, behold, the Lord. . . ." All this spoke of an experience unknown before. A new outlook was born through this. This was a spiritual crisis in the soul. Crafty, crooked, deceiving Jacob was converted. This was the hour of decision and committal. The old nature gave place to the new man. Jacob is about to become Israel. The crooked is made straight.

In this the earth-bound soul is freed and soars to heights unknown. The eyes of the soul are opened, and he sees eternal things.

A vision of God is granted to him. The *angels* "ascending" — they had been there then in his life, already bringing him to this hour, and he did not know it. "Descending" tells of the possibility, the actuality, of communication with heaven and of answered prayer. The *ladder* is a symbol of that dream experience. The slabs of rock toward the mountain slope brought reality nearer. A dream fades, symbols pass, but the fact abides as truth in life for ever.

A new life opened for Jacob. Under God he would live a different life. His moral standards and actions would exemplify a newly cleansed conscience. What is the ladder? God coming into life to touch ours. Compare John 1:51, where Jesus talks with Nathanael and tells of the ladder and presents Himself as that ladder. Through Him God comes to us and we go to God. The gulf between is removed or overcome. The shining stairway is Christ Himself. "Nearer, my God, to Thee, Nearer to Thee! E'en though it be a cross, That raiseth me. . . ." is the interpretation of the symbol.

III. *Bethel ordained a new will.* No longer did Jacob have his selfish way. The highest relationship of life was begun in worship and obedience to the will of God. Verses 14 to 22 speak of this experience. The new Jacob is Israel, "a prince." In this converted life there is a changed spirit. He tithes his possessions in devotion and vows a vow of allegiance.

In verse 17 "how dreadful is this place" speaks of the reverence and awe which filled the soul as Jacob learned to offer spiritual worship. "This is none other than the house of God, and this is the gate of heaven": how these words sum up Jacob's transforming hour at Bethel! We, too, learn that this is not alone for the Sabbath or a sanctuary but on a Saturday and in the shop. The highway is linked with the holy place; the shrine with the forge; and home with the church.

Francis Thompson wrote about "Jacob's ladder pitched betwixt Heaven and Charing Cross . . . Christ walking on the water, not on Genesareth, but on Thames."

When we come to our "Bethel," the "house of God," we are joined with the past and its heritage. The God of Jacob is the God of Bethel, and we are "at home" with Him.

50. Two Church Members

"Aaron and Hur stayed up his hands. . . ."—Exodus 17:12

Some years ago a newspaper reported the year's work of a certain church and said that as long as Aaron and Hur were on the church roll the church would prosper! No doubt a few who read that would be puzzled as to the identity of the above-mentioned members. Their names are not familiar and commonplace on any church roll in our day. But the reference is easy to understand. We might rewrite this ancient report in modern terms and say: "As long as Mr. and Mrs. . . . are on the church roll, the church will prosper." Would it prosper? It would depend upon the persons identified and how they related themselves to prayer.

I. In the struggle with Rephidim in the wilderness, Israel won the battle through the leadership of Joshua in fight and by the *intercession* of Moses supported by Aaron and Hur. The nation was inexperienced as fighters, yet after years of slavery behind them they were victorious by the power and presence of God. Oliver Cromwell said, "Trust in God and keep your powder dry." Moses at eighty years of age was unsuited for the bustle of battle but able to intercede on the mountain top. Each man is suited for a particular post in the service of God. The prayer of Moses was an essential to success as the fighting of the army. Real prayer is difficult, exhausting work. Prayer in view of the battle is not detached but fed by knowledge and accompanied by watching.

II. The *influence* of prayer cannot be overrated. It decides battles and sways the tides of history. It opens shut windows and releases spiritual blessing. James tells of Elijah that "he prayed earnestly" (Jas. 5:17, 18). Prayer routs our spiritual foes. As the church is today, we have garlanded the altar of sacrifice with flowers and damped down the fires of prayer and holy passion. No longer does the church advance as an army on the offensive but is like a beleaguered garrison hiding behind the bastions of past orthodoxies and cold indifference to the world. In the valleys of human need the enemy of souls routs the small forces unsupported in the hour of trial. Amalek, the enemy of Israel, suggests that self-life which overrules the life of the Spirit. Amalek is overcome when the weapon of *all-prayer* is used. When the arms of the church are uplifted in prayer, the fighters prevail; when they are let down, the soldiers are defeated. Amalek cannot connect these things, but the church discerns their relationship.

111

III. When the equipment of the church seems greater than ever in money and manpower, there is the lack of *inspiration*. We live in an activist society. The world despises the mystic, and the church writes off the man of prayer as too passive. We may mock the suppliant or criticize the seer, but remember that the decisions of spiritual battle are the result of the work of Aaron and Hur who uphold Moses' hands. Mary, Queen of Scots, said she feared the prayers of John Knox more than the armies of England. It was Knox who prayed, "Lord, give me Scotland or I die." Epaphras, when far from his people, *labored in prayer* for the Colossian Church. Paul said, "Without ceasing I make mention of you always in my prayers" (Rom. 1:9).

IV. Prayer is needed for the nations, the world, for the vast regions of earth untouched with the gospel. Do we know anything about *identification* in this need? Prayer is required for the missionary forces of the church and for a revival of vital Christianity in the congregations of the church. Organization, wealth, social prestige, and numbers may count with the standards of success in the world, but God has no power to bestow upon a church which is without prayer and impotent. We advance on our knees.

The true work of the church depends upon Aaron and Hur. Aaron we know. But who is Hur? He is the unknown, often out of sight, exercising this ministry of prayer which counts. The only difference between men in a church is the difference between men who pray and men who do not pray. Would it make any difference in your church whether you came together with others to pray or whether you refrained? Could two church members like Aaron and Hur make all the difference to the onward progress of the church?

51. The Christian Extra

"What do ye more?"—Matthew 5:47

In this word is summed up the secret of the Christian life in its moral and ethical outreach. To the disciples has been given more than to non-Christians, therefore more is expected from them. The Sermon on the Mount, from which this text is taken, is the manifesto of the King of kings. It reveals the laws of His kingdom. By it is stressed the dynamic of the blessed life to be lived by those who follow Christ. We are not called to moral mediocrity nor to average morality, but to the higher levels of holy living by the power of the spirit of God. Christianity is not a code of ethics, but it is intensely ethical and moral in its demands, hence this question. This surpassing goodness — this extra — is reflected in these ways:

I. In Its *Infinite Range* — Its *Comprehensiveness*. This is claimed by our Lord in His teaching in the Sermon on the Mount. His goodness is greater than the morality of the world. The vast sweep of revelation is awe-inspiring when we study the wholeness of that teaching. Nowhere in all literature is there to be found such a sweep and horizon of thought and power. Jesus surpasses all others in this regard.

It is like the difference between ancient and modern astronomy. The ancients had a narrow sky and few stars. The moderns think in terms of the mysterious universe with its myriads of worlds upon worlds. The vastness of the universe staggers the mind of a Jeans or Eddington or Einstein.

It is the comparison between going one mile and going two. The Roman legions could demand of their captive-subjects that they assist the soldiers by carrying their packs at least one mile. That was compulsory. Jesus taught that a Christian should surpass others in volunteering to carry baggage for double the distance. We are to exceed the claims of duty with cheerfulness and go the second mile.

It is the comparison between the Old Testament and the New Testament revelation of man's work. While the Bible is a unity, God saw fit to reveal Himself gradually and in stages. The Old Testament stresses the law, whereas the New Testament speaks of the gospel. The Old Testament made demands of "doing to live," and the New Testament speaks of "believing to do." Beyond the words of prophets, psalmists, and others is the crown of Chist's teaching, climaxing in His cross and resurrection. In the subject of forgiveness, think of the range of His teaching. Man does not

easily forgive. Jesus spoke of "seventy times seven" as the spirit
and range of forgiveness.

II. In Its *Inward Challenge* — Its *Thoroughness*. There is pene
tration and depth. The Christian not only matches the non-Chris
tian in doing good but surpasses him in the spirit and motive
The disciple does the unexpected. He turns the other cheek, loves
his enemies, and finds a distinction between the legitimate, the
lawful, and the expedient. He does not measure his work by its
reward but by the overflow of love.

The weather vane has four quarters, N, S, E, W, and is a guide
when the wind blows. But the mariner's compass has thirty-two
points marked and is a finer instrument. The world has its general
notions of right and wrong, but the Christian has a more sensitive
reaction in conscience and in love. The rule of thumb measure
(35 inches) may suffice for the careless, but the Christian must
abide by the standard yard. The light of the sun is preferred to
that of the candle. Sin, to the worldling, is a mistake made; but
to the Christian, sin is sin against God as well as against others
We distinguish the things that differ and have a sense of what i
vital. Through Christ we see the best over the better and the
better over the good.

III. In Its *Imperative Demand* — Its *Loftiness*. The sweep of
Christ's demand is far reaching. To bring Moore's Almanac with
its predictions alongside of the teaching of Christ is to see how
high is the latter above men. Christian living is not regulated by
the spirit of the age but by the teaching of Jesus Christ. Honesty
is not being as honest as you can but being as honest as you ought
Compare the words of Jesus as he said "Except..." on *righteous
ness* (Matt. 5:20), *conversion* (Matt. 18:3), *new birth* (John
3:3, 5); and take the Sermon on the Mount in summary for appli
cation of this Christian extra. Even love is not enough: it must be
love "even as I loved you" (John 13:34, R.V.).

By the mount of the cross we ascend the mount of moral obliga
tion as disciples. God's imperative is that we be perfect, even as
He is perfect (Matt. 5:48).

52. The Life I Now Live

"The life which I now live...."—Galatians 2:20

This is of supreme importance. Most of us can say, "life with its way before us lies." But what is its "goal and prize"? No two lives are exactly the same. What is the one aim or the chief goal of life? It is this which concerns us.

To some, life is complicated. Few seem to find their way to the desired end and accomplishment. If only we could find that one dominant principle and passion! Remember there is the man seen by others, the man understood by his loved ones, the man known to himself, and the man as judged by God. But the four are really one. How does that one live?

I. *Pursuit of Things.* This is the common lot of the crowd. Selfishness appears to be the mainspring of life. To "get" and to "save their lives" are the aims. Ambition and energy are directed to that end. Desire for satisfaction is bound up with material pursuits. Business, sport, politics, education, art, religion — these all indicate areas wherein you can trace this spirit.

The fatalist speaks of blind chance or fate or luck. He feels helpless in a cycle of hate and frustration. The pessimist thinks of life as an enemy and a misfortune. Pleasures pall, money-making ceases, and every physical and emotional enjoyment passes. In this, life can miss the highest and the best. Man was made for something higher than material things. What is the chief end of man?

II. *Solvent of Theories.* To others, life is a quest, ever seeking a goal which eludes them. Theories of life beckon. Philosophies offer a road of enchantment. What is the latest theory? Like the Athenians in Paul's visit, they lived for "some new thing," ever dreaming, always seeking, but never finding.

Think of the many cults and isms, the new religions which arise. They offer means of "escape" from reality; and they promise "peace" when there is no peace. Their veneer of Christian labels is deceptive. Basically they provide a religion without Christ as Lord, a faith without revelation, and a life without redemption. They bolster pride in man's self-sufficiency and self-effort.

III. *Dedication to Ideals.* For some there is the goal of idealism. It has an appeal to the altruistic and unselfish. Serving others, giving time and strength to good causes, philanthropy and charity, the talk about the Golden Rule — these are methods of life for well-intentioned people. But some ideals can mock you in their height of unattainment. High ideals without Christ at the heart

115

are not Christian. We may have a godless goodness. Many today are living on the dividends from Christian investment of life and character. They enjoy the benefits from other Christian lives. Think of the many service organizations which become substitutes for Christian faith and life. Courage, independence, adventure, freedom, and service are watchwords. Ideals are not sufficient for life.

IV. *Secret of Power.* In Christ alone is found the way to fulness of life. He came to bring "life and that ... more abundantly." Paul gives the secret in the text. "The life which I now live ... *I live by the faith of the Son of God, who loved me, and gave himself for me.*" All other aims and goals of life, however good in themselves, do not measure up to this complete commitment of life. A master-passion is a necessity if life is to reach the highest end. Not through self-love or lust or greed or ambition, but through faith comes fulfilment.

What is your master-passion? What are you living for? If it is less than this, you are dead even as you appear to live. You are blind even as you seem to seek. Your best service for man is still far short of the glory of God. "The fashion of this world passes away, and it is with what is abiding that I would fain concern myself" (Goethe).

This is the true life, the full life, the abiding life.

> Without the Way, there is no going,
> Without the Truth, there is no knowing,
> Without the Life, there is no living,

"The life I now live, I live by" — what? Fill it in. Let it be Christ. "Such is my faith, and such my reasons for it, and I find them strong enough. And you? You want to argue? Well, I can't. It is a choice. I choose the Christ!"

53. The Man Who Betrayed His Master

"Judas, one of the twelve . . . that betrayed him."
—Matthew 26:47, 48

The study of character is most important for all. In it we trace the strength and weakness of human nature. Truth finds its entrance often by the picture of a life held up for all to see. What mystery there is in this character and what a subject for the biographer!

I. *The Apostle.* As we gather the evidence from the record, we find very little mentioned about Judas. He was *"one of the twelve"* and so had the distinction of being selected by Jesus for good work. He shared the privileges and responsibilities of that honored position. He sat under Jesus' ministry and teaching like the others.

He was *"chosen after a night of prayer"* so that we do not see Jesus making a casual choice of this man. Jesus wished him for the service he could render and knew the capacity of the man's mind.

Judas *"carried the bag,"* evidence that he was a trusted man at first. As treasurer of the group his position was honorable, and he sat on the left hand of Jesus at the feast of the Passover in the upper room. Perhaps he was the man with greatest potential?

II. *The Traitor.* What depths are found in personality! Was Judas politically minded more than spiritually motivated that he gave way?" It is noted, *"who became a traitor."* Outwardly he was the same as the others, but there was a gradual change in spirit and attitude. His motives altered, and he lost sympathy for Jesus' end and goal, becoming the Devil's tool and medium of attack against Jesus.

A man's questions reveal his interests and keen insights. *"Why this waste?"* That was when Mary brought her love offering to Jesus in the precious ointment. Judas calculated quickly its value on the market and the dead loss of 300 pence then. To say it might have been sold and given to the poor was bluff, for he did not care for the poor. Already he was a *thief* in intent and motive.

Had temptation overtaken him already by pilfering from the treasury bag? Was his heart set on riches so that he had a passion for prices? Did he set a price on everything now? Later, when he deals with the authorities, his word is, *"What will you give me?"* When he cannot get the full price for the ointment, he will settle for the lesser amount for the price of a slave! Thus greed and

avarice devour a man in covetousness. From disregard of the poor
he stoops later to selling his Master!

We read that Judas *"sought opportunity."* The foul spirit in
him hugged the devil of chance, and it was not long until evil
had its way. The house of his heart was swept and garnered, but
the demons returned sevenfold to indwell. The last state is worse
than the first. Let avarice and ambition wed and soon he abandons
the Lord of his life.

Before the Passover Judas and the priests are plotting: *at* the
Passover Judas and Jesus are dining. At the *dipping of the sop* in
the dish of friendship, Jesus made the gesture of love and forgiveness. Then Judas *"went immediately out: and it was night."* After
the Passover Judas is not with the twelve, and then in the Garden
we see *"Judas standing with the soldiers."* His stand is clear then.
"He kissed him much" (lit.) was the undoing of a parade of
affection which was artificial. Although Jesus spoke of him as
"friend," He also said, "it had been *good for that man* if he had
not been born." Was this spoken of Judas "as a sinner and not
as a man"?

III. *The Suicide.* In this tragic story no heavenly coercion compelled Judas to his destiny. He is not on record as a suppliant for
mercy. He never came to Jesus seeking forgiveness. There is no
word of *repentance.* What was spoken of as "repent" is the word
for *remorse,* but not godly sorrow and change of heart. He made
no restitution as evidence of conversion. He confessed that he had
"sinned" and threw back the blood-money to his connivers in evil,
but then he went and hanged himself. Was this *retribution?*

Consider the terror of the lost, afraid of the issues of sin but not
of sin itself. He went *"to his own place."* He made it. Why did
Jesus choose Judas? A mystery? Another question: Why has He
chosen me?

The mystery of Judas is not resolved easily. Sovereignty and
free will interplay, and we trace a man's choices bringing final
disaster and doom. Are we selling Christ? For what? Beware that
our temptation is not as Judas': we fall easily.

54. The Man Who Made Good

"Take Mark . . . for he is profitable to me for the ministry."
—II Timothy 4:11

Behind the New Testament stories is the romance of personal failure and achievement. Character is revealed as it is tested and tried by the demands of the unexpected. John Mark is the young man who was full of promise, failed in a critical hour, and then "made good" in the final act of the drama.

I. *Setting Out.* Every life begins in hope and faith. Background is important. Mark's *home* is seen when Peter went there out of prison (Acts 12:11-12). His mother's house was the meeting place of the infant church. Sister to Barnabas, she has position and means. Was this the same house where the Last Supper was observed by Jesus and His apostles? Did Mark know the upper room intimately? Peter calls Mark "Marcus my son" (I Pet. 5:13), a hint that Peter was his spiritual father, having led him into the Christian faith. In the garden of Gethsemane there was a certain young man (Mark 14:51) who witnessed the scene, heard the prayer of Jesus, and tells the story later. When they left the house that night, Mark probably had listened and followed, not yet fully dressed.

Mark's *zeal* was obvious in his venture with Saul and uncle Barnabas in the missionary journey. The opportunity revealed character. Fine impulses, generous nature, youthful enthusiasm, and a willing spirit led Mark into that experience of service.

II. *Falling Back.* Missionary service had its realism as well as romanticism. Mark's *trial* came in the tests of the journey with its rigor. The visit to Cyprus, then Asia Minor, the Taurus Range, brigands, perils and dangers of travel, persecutions — these faced Mark. Was he soon hot, then soon cold? Discouraged and homesick, he would turn back. The Romans marked a deserter by cutting off a little finger. Hippolytus calls Mark "the man with the finger wanting." Bunyan spoke of Mr. Temporary. Was this Mark, the man who went but halfway? Did he lack stedfast courage?

Mark's *tragedy* is written in the record (Acts 13:13), for his return was not in glory but in disappointment and shame. Inexperience brought disaster in the face of testing. Returning to his home at Jerusalem alone was in contrast to his going out with Saul and Barnabas (Acts 12:25). Persecution brings to light the hidden weaknesses as in the parable of the soils (Matt. 13:18-23). In Acts 15:36-40 a second journey is attempted by the missionaries.

This time Saul would not take Mark with him. He and Barnabas differ in their judgment as to his fitness. II Cor. 2:11-12 suggests that Satan was too strong for someone if Saul's judgment was right. Barnabas would stand by his nephew, but Saul would not have him. Because Mark fell away, he was the occasion of disruption between two friends.

III. *Making Good*. It was the sympathy and understanding of Barnabas which saved Mark. He may have been unfitted for the task of a pioneer missionary, but there was another sphere of service for him. Mark was not an apostate nor a castaway. Later Paul will acknowledge that he is "profitable for the ministry."

In Col. 4:10-11 Paul commends Mark, indicating that the breach he had with Barnabas is now healed. Mark is rated a "fellow worker" and as a "comfort unto me." Paul has also given a directive about Mark which suggests that he has been reinstated in the highest esteem and confidence of the apostle. The church at Colossae is to receive and welcome Mark. Was Mark now in Rome when Paul thus wrote? Was he now sharing Paul's hardships? Many a ragged colt makes a noble horse, and the unruly Mark becomes a strong man of God. Although a man fails and makes mistakes, he can change and return to the old standards and find himself again restored.

In verse 24 of his letter to Philemon Paul speaks of Mark as one of his "fellow labourers." II Timothy 4:11 testifies to him as "profitable." The ministry has turned out the opportunity to make good for Mark. The qualifications of II Tim. 2:21, "a vessel unto honour ... meet for the Master's use ..." now applied to Mark, who now had "fled youthful lusts." The Gospel According to Mark is the crowning evidence of the faithful servant who made good. Jesus as the busy Servant of God is a reflection of Mark's own life relived through his style of composition. The weak youth is now the strong man. The fearful disciple is now the brave Christian. The once defeated runaway is now the courageous victor in the long campaign.

The man who makes good could be our story. Who has not failed at some point of temptation and trial? Who has not come back to win another day through Christ?

55. The Man Who was a Secret Disciple

"Joseph . . . being a disciple of Jesus, but secretly. . . ."
—John 19:38

One of the tragedies of life is to express love too late. Joseph of Arimathaea with Nicodemus elicits our sympathy as they are typical of many who manifest faith in Christ at the eleventh hour. Some question whether a man can be a disciple in secret.

I. *His Record.* We must take the gospel account for what it is — brief and fragmentary. Not all is told but enough to suggest what is vital.

The Past. This was blameless. Joseph "wore the white flower of a blameless life." Four Gospels refer to him: a member of the highest tribunal of Judaism, the Sanhedrin; one of the seventy members of the council which had the high priest as presiding officer, seventy-one in all — a counsellor and law maker — wealthy, affluent, aristocratic, with a tomb outside Jerusalem, evidence of his position. "Not many noble are called" (Paul); however, Joseph is described as "rich" (Matt. 27:57); "an honourable counsellor" (Mark 15:43); "good . . . just" (Luke 23:50); "disciple" (John 19:38). In *social* position a counsellor; in *ethical* character generous and just; in *religious* life waiting for the kingdom of God. Was he one of the devout remnant in Israel? How was he drawn to Jesus?

The Present. Now a disciple, but secretly. Was this the summary of his heart condition even as he shrank from the public confession of faith? What fear of his people held him bondage? Was it fear of loss of position or prestige? Would he be put out of the synagogue? Was he proud? Did he fear to risk death? In the council meeting it was Nicodemus who spoke up for Jesus in asking for a fair trial, but Joseph remained silent. Silence can be damning when conscience urges speech in charity and truth.

II. *His Resolve.* The record is clear and plain: "And after this. . . ." We ask, What? The answer is: the cross! What was the dividing line when this man crossed over from fear to faith and from silence to speech? He boldly went in into Pilate, and asked for the body of Jesus" (Mark 15:43, R.V.). Now is the summons to courage. The quiet man becomes eloquent. Remember that he never agreed in the council to the condemnation and crucifixion of Jesus (Luke 23:51). He tried neutrality.

121

The action of Joseph is graphically told. He pays the last rite of devotion to the dead in offering to care for the body of Jesus: "his own new tomb," his own hands — willingly he offers these as evidence of his changed attitude. Actions speak louder than words. The cost of that burial was not alone in those acts but in the public spectacle which drew upon him the slander and criticism of a society which was ready to condemn Jesus. A tombstone doesn't atone for the absence of flowers during the life. But here Joseph is to be commended: for, if the body of Jesus had not been placed in his tomb, it would have been cast out to public burial with criminals. "A garden" suggests a resting place of love and respect. Joseph showed his faith and devotion gradually as he acted in this way. Resolution and decision are costly to some souls, and the roadway to full commitment is never easy.

III. *His Right.* Whatever criticism is levelled against Joseph because we think him a coward or timid, we must not tone down that he is called and known as "a disciple." He was already one even when engaged in the hesitation and the silence of the council meeting. How did he become a disciple? We do not know in detail, but we know the fact that he was one. He *became* a disciple. The secret dealings of God with the soul are hidden from us. Was it at the cross that Joseph came to absolute surrender and devotion to his Lord and Master? Was he one of the crowd that day, hearing the seven words from the cross? Did he see the soldiers and the crowd in their cruelty of spirit? Was he moved by the shrieks of the mob in their blood lust? Was it the calmness and forgiving spirit of the Victor which broke his heart?

Many people of excellent character may be disciples *secretly*. Are there Jews like that today who need confession and committal? One touch and then the heart is aflame. The hesitating can yet be bold and courageous. Confession of discipleship comes through the cross. The disciple finds discipline through the power of that sacrifice. Joseph lost three years of Jesus' companionship and life abundant. We see him beyond the cross and the resurrection in glad confession.

56. The Man Who Wrote a Title

"Pilate wrote a title...."—John 19:19

The title of a book or story is important to convey to the reader a message. A child is given a name even as a title so that the person can be designated apart from others. Sir Walter Scott warns that a man can possess his title yet not receive respect and honor: "High though his titles ... Despite those titles ... the wretch, concentred all in self, ... shall forfeit fair renown, ... and shall go down to the dust unwept, unhonoured, and unsung." Is this true of Pilate?

I. *Historically:* "Pilate wrote...." The Apostles' Creed says "Jesus suffered under Pontius Pilate." What a complex character from the obscure past of the Roman Empire. In a petty post he sat as judge on One who would yet judge the world. He was an obstinate man, cruel, vain, merciless, corrupt, a worldling. He mixed the blood of men in sacrifice. His deeds and gestures reveal him as agnostic in abandoning even the gods of Rome. He knew fear and trouble.

Jesus stood before him three times. He was warned by his wife because of her dream about "that just man." Pilate himself said: "I find no fault in him." An innocent prisoner should be released after fair trial, but Pilate compromises to please the people. He gave sentence as they required. He feared the loss of his position and the patronage of the Caesar. He gave the people a choice between Jesus Barabbas and Jesus the Christ. "Behold the man" was later "Behold your King." Pilate and Herod became friends in a coalition of evil. Pilate washed his hands in water to pretend neutrality. But water could not wash away the stain of blood that day! Custom, convenience, compromise were the words of Pilate's thought, and principle and conviction were trampled under foot.

The tender appeal of Jesus as Pilate spoke much with Him is reflected in the silence of Jesus, who said nothing to Herod or to Caiaphas. Jesus bid for the soul of Pilate then. Pilate's question "What is truth?" indicates that Pilate knew that Jesus was innocent, hence he wrote the title as truth.

II. *Symbolically:* "A title." When Pilate ordered the superscription to be written, someone took the stylus and wrote. The historical act is there for all to ponder. But the fact of history becomes a factor of symbolical significance. "What I have written I have written" is not alone history: it has profound spiritual meaning.

Pilate's life was summed up in that word. In *The Summing Up* by W. Somerset Maugham, a well-known author reveals the wisdom of a lifetime. With an absorbing interest in human nature he has used his writings to portray whatever happened to him in the course of his life. He has taken persons with whom he had slight acquaintance and used them as the foundation of characters in his books. He has been more concerned with the obscure than with the famous.

In this light we can trace the life of Pilate. He was obscure and would not have been known but for his contact with Jesus. Human nature in Pilate manifested its selfishness and sinfulness. Pilate historically becomes a symbol of every man. As he wrote, so we write. As he decided concerning Jesus, so we decide. Each day our thoughts, words, and deeds are being recorded irrevocably and unalterably by an invisible stylus for all time. What is being written now about you? What are you writing? What interpretation of life are you charting for history to read later? What title are we giving to Jesus the Christ? What verdict do we write?

III. *Evangelically:* "Jesus . . . the King." When Pilate wrote that day, little did he think that his words were to become part of the gospel of good news. The claim of Jesus to be King was given prophecy by the title over the cross. The condemned prisoner was the Just One and Saviour: the man Jesus was the King: the cross was the throne of a kingdom.

Written in Hebrew, Latin, and Greek, the message was proclaimed in the languages of religion, government, and culture. All people must know this title experimentally for all areas of life. The title is luminous now in the glow of centuries. What Pilate did we do with our lives and we must do about Jesus finally.

57. Moods of the Soul

"Oh that I had wings like a dove! for then would I fly away, and be at rest."—Psalm 55:6

"Should such a man as I flee?"—Nehemiah 6:11

Most of us carry in our minds a secret picture of ourselves. We think we are a certain kind of person. It may be flattering or distorted. We rate ourselves high or low. By it we tend to live. But there are times when we have changing moods, and that affects the picture. There are two such moods common to all.

I. *The Mood of the Psalmist — to Fly Away.* (The psalm should be read for its background and message.)

This is a natural mood which prevails when relief is sought after strain and toil. The monotony of life erupts, and volcanic action results. For example, the New York bus driver, tired of the routine and drudgery, suddenly disappeared. Three days later he was found sitting under a tree in West Virginia. "Why?" "Well, it was such a lovely day, I didn't feel like wasting it on Route 87." When he returned to work he was somewhat of a hero! Vacation and holidays are necessary respites from the constant routine of life. The pause in the music is for the making of music. Rest brings renewal and revitalizes.

This is the escape idea in literature and amusement. Much in television and other means of amusement ministers to this. Our world around is full of dread and fear in an atomic age. Man seeks to escape if possible. The machine age crushes with its sense of foreboding. But what if the escape is to nothingness? Is there an escape to what is called "religion" but is not necessarily the Christian Faith? There are many examples of attempts at this without true revival.

This is the legitimate cry to fly away. This mood is not sinful or wrong at times. It may come out of the stress of life. Think of the boredom of the privileged, the fear of the insecure, the loneliness of the forgotten and lost, and the wistfulness of the aged and neglected. Even youth has this desire when he sees no future in his upset world. Jonah fled from his responsibility as Elijah did after depression, but some flee in their feeling that life tumbles in upon them and is too much to bear.

II. *The Mood of the Prophet — Not to Flee.* (The story of Nehemiah is background in its thrilling action of rebuilding the city of Jerusalem.)

Nehemiah was threatened by enemies, therefore he will not

125

run away but stand and face them. When there is a task to be done and a commission to be carried out, that is the time to stand. Some sneer, ridicule, taunt, and even threaten life, but Nehemiah will not fly away. Evil reports are circulated, and he is charged with self-seeking, but this will not intimidate him. He will not hide, and he will not run. This reveals the kind of person he was in the strength of faith and courage.

Men will not flee if they are "under orders." Jonah and Elijah are examples of those who gave in easily. Jonah ran from his post of duty and suffered accordingly. He had to retrace his steps and still carry out the commission of God. How much better if he had obeyed at the first. We do not escape our duty by running away. Elijah also lost heart in despondency and depression of spirit. He imagined that evil forces had the upper hand and that he was the only one left to serve Jehovah. He forgot that a Jezebel had her little day and soon the dogs would lick her blood. Discouragement is a weapon of evil to cause some to flee. Think of those in church who have given up their tasks! But a man does not flee when he knows he is "under orders." He stands.

We dare not run away when we think of Jesus. He is the supreme example of One who stood in the evil day: tempted by Satan, deserted by friends, betrayed by one of his apostles, denied by a close friend, forsaken by all his inner group of friends. He did not flee. He accepted the temptation and the cross, despising the shame, and is now set down at the right hand of God. Why? He saw the *joy* before Him.

Are you losing heart and trying to escape? Do not run away. There is a place of strength and power to stand in the hour of testing. Read again the hymn, "In the hour of trial, Jesus plead for me. . . ." Moods of the soul will startle us as they flit by. We can become resolute in faith, strong in courage, and dare to stand and not run.

58. Samson's Riddle

"Out of the eater came forth meat, and out of the strong came forth sweetness."—Judges 14:14

In the biblical writings one of the forms of the popular proverb was the riddle. A riddle was a dark or puzzling saying demanding an answer. In ancient days and at popular festivals an opportunity was given to guess the answer. From the times of Samson and in connection with his wedding feast, this well-known riddle is recorded: "What is sweeter than honey? And what is stronger than a lion?" Enemies and friends failed to guess the answer, and only by unfair means was it found.

Leaving the particular story of Samson and its background, we learn that this riddle has an agelong principle of universal application. It is a key to unlock much that is mysterious and dark. It speaks of the overruling providence of God.

I. *It is the key to the Book of Judges.* The summary of that period was, "every man did that which was right in his own eyes." "There was no king in those days." That was Israel's iron age. Political chaos, religious apostasy, social corruption, moral bankruptcy — these were characteristics of a turbulent and brutish age. Then men were harsh, cruel, and secularized. But in the light of the riddle there was providence. God overruled as sovereign. It was then that out of the darkness and foulness came the beautiful, unsullied, pure character of *Ruth*.

II. *It is the key to the Bible and history.* The law of sin operates, and there is nemesis upon sin. Yet God in His mercy seeks man by a higher law. "Where sin abounded, grace did much more abound" (Rom. 5:20). Grace makes the wrath of man to praise Him. God overruled man's sin. This does not excuse the sinner. What is sown is reaped, and man bears responsibility; but God is able to weave the tangled skein into a pattern of grace and renewal.

Joseph is hated by his brothers and sold to Egypt and supposed dead. There he is tempted to immorality. He loses his position rather than yield to sin, ending in prison and forgotten. Later in that thrilling story his brothers come to him for help, not knowing his identity. The explanation is in the light of this riddle. "Ye thought evil against me, but God meant it for good to save much people alive."

Moses slays an Egyptian in a fit of temper and flees to the desert, where, alone, God disciplines him for 40 years until he is ready to be the national emancipator: forty years thinking he

127

was somebody; forty years realizing he was nobody; forty years experiencing that God was everything. The riddle is the key to his life.

David was guilty of a black crime against a man and a woman. Murder and adultery stained his record. "Against thee, thee only, have I sinned, and done this evil in thy sight"! After repentance, contrition and renewal came: "Have mercy upon me, O God.... Create me a clean heart,... and renew a right spirit within me." He who fell so low rose again to give us the Twenty-third Psalm. The riddle again!

Stephen was a martyr at the start of the church's history. In that persecution hour he was an overcomer in forgiving his enemies, and Saul was converted to become the leader of the church. The wolf became the sheep dog: the enemy became the lover of Christ. Out of Stephen's death came the resurrected life of Paul the apostle. The riddle!

Judas betrayed his Lord, and men crucified the Son of God. That is the darkest crime and the tragedy of tragedies. Truth seemed to be vanquished, and light is blotted out. Yet God took the cross and made it the throne of love's empire. Judgment is there, and hope is born. From such darkness came light; from evil came love; from bondage came liberty. The broken Body became the Bread of life: the outpoured Life becomes the Water of life. In loss is gain. The riddle!

III. *It is the key to the whole of life.* The principle of Samson's riddle is found everywhere. Destroying agencies prepare the way for new life. Geological catastrophes renew the face of the old earth with virgin fields of fertility. The products of decay are the food of new power. The rotting leaves of autumn nourish the flowers and shrubs of spring.

In the clash of arms, the revolutions of men, the tumult of thinkers, and the contentions of convictions are found the birth-pangs of new days. In family life the bitter mesh of sorrow, suffering, or death may come to blight our cherished hopes, but afterwards God overrules to bring forth the sweetness and the strength we need for character. Such outweigh the struggle. From the cross came the Easter victory.

59. Doxologies of the Christian Life

"Blessed be the God and Father of our Lord Jesus Christ...."
—I Peter 1:3, Ephesians 1:3, II Corinthians 1:3, R.V.

Bishop Ken enriched the whole church when he composed the doxology. We sing "Praise God from whom all blessings flow...." Some sing this at the end of a service, others at the beginning, and many at the time of the offering. It is appropriate at any time. The Old Testament had its "hallelujah" — "praise ye Jehovah." The New Testament has its doxologies of "Blessed." In the midst of argument and stern exposition of truth, suddenly the New Testament writers break out in song.

I. The Doxology of *a Recreated Life.* "Blessed be the God and Father of our Lord Jesus Christ, which according to his abundant mercy hath begotten us again unto a lively hope by the resurrection of Jesus Christ from the dead" (I Pet. 1:3).

Here are the unveilings of the splendors of redeeming grace. The vision arouses the song. The heart has its lilt of music.

"According to his mercy...." The grace and love of God are at the heart of Christian experience. Abundance of grace speaks of a pouring out without stint or reservation. Mercy comes to the sinful and undeserving. Pardon is given to the rebel.

"He begat us." Christian vocabulary is unique. Other systems of religion speak of "culture, education, reform, training, evolution." Christianity speaks of rebirth. The other words follow birth. First the seed, the germ, life itself: then growth and increase; not fighting perverted nature, but planting new seed; not purifying external conditions, but giving a new man, an act of the Holy Spirit.

"Unto a living hope." The new life in Christ is linked to that which is future. The future inheritance of the Christian is wrapped up in Christ, whose salvation begins at the cross and continues in his life to be climaxed at His coming again. "At the last day" speaks of future hope. Christ guards us till then. We sing this doxology as we think of the new life in Christ.

II. The Doxology of *a Revalued Life.* "Blessed be the God and Father of our Lord Jesus Christ, who hath blessed us with all spiritual blessings in heavenly places in Christ" (Eph. 1:3).

After recreation comes revaluation. The Christian life is enhanced by a new value being placed upon everything. During

129

sales in the stores we see tickets marked with revised prices and usually "markd down" in value. But not so in the new life in Christ. Then the price or value increases. Paul gives here an inventory of blessings belonging to the Christian:

We are *selected* (vs. 4). Chosen in Christ speaks of election

We are *adopted* (vs. 5), brought into the family of God as children.

We are *accepted* (vs. 6), "in the beloved one" — granted a favor.

We are *redeemed* (vss. 7-8), tasting forgiveness of sins and grace.

We are *enlightened* (vss. 9-10), the mystery of His will made known to us.

We are *enriched* (vss. 11-12), a new inheritance given as heirs.

We are *sealed* (vss. 13-14), the promise and guarantee of glory.

In the Old Testament blessings, material things were involved. In the New Testament, character is seen. The "heavenlies" speak of the eternal and unseen realm. *Sursum corda* — "lift up your hearts."

III. The Doxology of *a Recompensed Life.* "Blessed be God, even the Father of our Lord Jesus Christ, the Father of mercies, and the God of all comfort: who comforteth us in all our tribulation, that we may be able to comfort them which are in any trouble, by the comfort wherewith we ourselves are comforted of God" (II Cor. 1:3, 4).

From recreation and revaluation comes recompense. The new life in Christ results in compensation in this life also.

The Father of mercies tells of compassion and grace. One of the divine attributes is here in abundance. "Like as a father pitieth his children. . . . He will have mercy and abundantly pardon. . . . According to his abundant mercy he saved us. . . ." Think of all the passages which speak of this quality in God.

The God of comfort is the God of *all* comfort. In suffering and sorrow God draws near to assuage grief and bring strength. He feels with and enters into the emotional upset of the heart.

God comforts us that we may comfort others. An unselfish life has begun in Christ. The end of our comforting is the beginning of rendering help to others. The troubles of life are many and grievous to many. Here the Christian assists by sharing with others in their hour of need and helping them to find release from care.

No trouble at first is to be desired, but afterwards it brings its return in stronger character and in the recompense of a richer life in the knowledge of God. We lift up our hearts in thanksgiving for this.

60. Doxologies of the Christian Life

"Now unto him ... be glory...."
—Romans 16:25-27, Ephesians 3:20, Jude 24, 25

The New Testament is interwoven with doxologies of praise and thanks. Ascriptions of praise begin many letters, and writers share their heart's music in memorable words and phrases. We count our many blessings, but more so we sing "Praise God from whom all blessings flow...." All life is to be lived by the Christian with this spirit which acknowledges God to be the giver of all good gifts in Christ.

I. The Doxology of *an Established Life.* "Now *to him that is of power to stablish you* according to my gospel, and the preaching of Jesus Christ, according to the revelation of the mystery, which was kept secret since the world began, but now is made manifest, and by the scriptures of the prophets, according to the commandment of the everlasting God, made known to all nations for the obedience of faith: to God only wise, *be glory* through Jesus Christ for ever. Amen" (Rom. 16:25-27).

Paul was concerned about the converts. Would they stand? John Mark went back for a while. Demas loved the world. Christians in Rome were under fire and persecution. Would they endure in their faith steadfastly?

This section deals with the result of preaching the gospel, wherein obedience by faith brings results. Roots of the oak tree give strength to trunk and branches, so Christians find they are established in faith. God's power is here. God is able.

Read the stories of converts in other lands to see how they stand amid adverse conditions and heathen environment. How do we measure up in our easier circumstances?

II. The Doxology of *an Enriched Life.* "Now *unto him that is able to do exceeding abundantly above all that we ask or think,* according to the power that worketh in us, unto him *be glory* in the church by Christ Jesus throughout all ages, world without end" (Eph. 3:20, 21).

Here are superlatives about abundant life and something far beyond man's imagination. These words follow Paul's prayer that the converts at Ephesus might be enriched by all spiritual blessings. If strengthened with might in the inner life, they would be rich.

Words are interesting when they bring new meanings. Here Paul finds difficulty in expressing the inexpressible.

The heart of this enriched life is that a Christian is handling fabulous wealth. Spiritual reserves and resources are found through the bank of heaven. Note the word "can" is not in the text. God's ability is not dependent upon what we can ask or think. He is able, and He does exercise His power on behalf of His own. What is it that He does? Note Paul's prayer preceding, that Christ's love be reproduced within us. In the enlarged love of the Christian, God's love flows through us in power to the loveless and the unlovely.

III. The Doxology of *an Empowered Life.* "Now *unto him that is able to keep you from falling, and to present you faultless* before the presence of his glory with exceeding joy, to the only wise God our Saviour, *be glory* and majesty, dominion and power, both now and ever. Amen" (Jude 24, 25).

Here is the promise and pledge that the Christian will be kept to the end and beyond this life. To safeguard a deposit in the bank or to keep one from slipping in a treacherous place — this is the thought of Jude. When men threaten with brain-washing or persecution, then the Christian is able to withstand and stand in the evil day. Recall the story of John Hayes, Presbyterian missionary in China, whose story was written in the *Reader's Digest.* Week after week he was subject to the tortures of the Communists. In court he bore witness to his Lord and Saviour and so filled his mind and speech with the living Word of God that they were silenced before him. He was empowered in weakness. He stood in fainting. God enabled him.

The peril in Jude's day was apostasy. Bad religions, false philosophies, competed for the soul of the Christian. Jude asserts that God is able to keep the Christian from falling. Unbelief brings failure of nerve and loss of spiritual morale. When energized by divine power, all the glory belongs to God.

Man is often *willing* to help the needy but is not able to carry through the intention. God is not only willing but *able.* Able to keep, able to present: this is the glorious ability of God in Christ. His wisdom is displayed in it. *Sursum corda* — lift up your hearts and sing the doxology!

61. The Lord We Love

"There is ... one Lord...."—Ephesians 4:5

John Wesley said he must have a whole Christ for his salvation. No apology is needed for the claims made for Christianity. Christianity is Christ received, realized, and reproduced. The Christian experience centers in the Person of Christ. In this day of man's revolt through false philosophies and bad religions, we find Christ is central and incomparable. The final question is always "What think ye of Christ?"

I. He is *unique*. ("I am the way.") His claims include many statements and facts. That He is the true and living way to God is found nowhere else. The New Testament testifies that He is the one Mediator between God and man. He takes the hand of man and joins us to God through His grace. He is the Revealer of God and brings to man the secret knowledge of the divine mystery. Pascal said: "Jesus Christ is the center of everywhere and the object of everything, and he who does not know Him knows nothing of himself and of the order of the Universe."

Uniqueness does not mean something old or from the past. The antique can be duplicated, and the rare can be found again. Christ stands alone as the only Person in His own class and right. His sinlessness marks Him off from the rest of the race. He is both God and man in one Person. As God-man He is pre-eminent. He comes into time not as the product of the race but as the gift of God. His speech and life cannot be compared in character.

II. He is *solitary*. ("I am that I am.") The tremendous claim made by Christ seemed either madness or blasphemy to those who rejected Him. There was something of the unapproachable in Him, as Peter cried, "Depart from me; for I am a sinful man, O Lord." It was the awareness of *another,* even God. At Athens (Acts 17:23) Paul found, among the many altars, one "TO THE UNKNOWN GOD." But the true and living God was not there as an idol. He was found only in the Jesus whom Paul preached alive from the dead.

Jesus cannot be placed in the Hall of Fame or in a Westminster Abbey alongside of the great of this world. No Parthenon contains Him. He will not be listed with the gods of blood, race, and soil which bind modern men in chains. As the fish god Dagon fell from his pedestal before the Ark of the Covenant (I Sam. 5:3), so all other gods and idols must fall before the Christ. "Thou shalt have no other gods before me." Jesus sits at the right hand

133

of God in the majesty of supreme authority. No one else, not even His mother Mary, shares that solitary throne.

III. He is *universal.* ("I am the good shepherd.") As a magnet so Christ draws all without distinction. Lifted up to die the death of the cross and lifted up out of the earth in resurrection power, He now draws people of all races and tongues. He is well named "the Saviour of the world." He came to save people from their sins. As the Son of Man He touches all people in their temptations and trials to bring hope of recovery and salvation.

The one major fact of history in our time is the actual realization that we now have the universal church. For centuries men have worked and prayed for its coming, and it is now in our midst. Through the missionary movement the good news has gone to all nations, and in every land the church has been established. The younger churches are now joined to the older churches, and we sense our oneness and unity in Christ. In world conventions of church and Sunday school or youth the scattered and different people who are now "in Christ" sing the same hymns to their Lord, listen to His Word through the Bible, and all pray "in His Name." Not politics, not nationalism, not language, not armies, but Christ has drawn us together into one fellowship. "There is one flock through the one Shepherd."

IV. He is *final.* ("I am the resurrection, and the life.") The one Lord implies that He is owner of life and the master of all. He who submits to Christ has no longer a will of his own. He learns to accept God's will and Christ's plan. Sovereignty is the dictatorship of love and grace. The mind is given to His guidance, the conscience to His commands, and our hearts to His love.

Christ claims to be "the Alpha and the Omega, the Beginning and the Ending, the First and the Last." His claims may be challenged in our modern age, but His victories are obvious. In the first century the confession of faith was "Jesus is the Lord." That word is the issue of the twentieth century struggle. Humanity is on the march, and the battle is joined. The issue is the Lordship of Christ in every realm. As Saviour He claims all in lordship and supremacy.

62. The Faith We Believe

"One faith...."—Ephesians 4:5

John Wesley said that he must have a whole Bible for his staff. When we think of our Christian faith, we do so in relation to the heritage received through the church. Paul, in I Corinthians 15:1-4, tells that he declared the gospel in terms of what had been received, which he transmitted. We are to "keep in memory" or hold fast to that which has been given. The heritage of truth determines our belief and destiny.

I. A *Biblical* Faith. In world literature the Bible stands supreme as it is translated into the languages and dialects of all people. In our mother tongue the content becomes reality for us. The Moslem religion has its Koran. Hitler had his *Mein Kampf*. Karl Marx had *Das Kapital,* the bible of Communism. The belief or faith given through these books had a basis in the content of writing. So the Christian faith centers in the Bible and Word of God. This brings us face to face with Christ.

When we express our faith, it is in biblical terms. Confessing Christ, we say with Paul, "I know whom I have believed." Testifying to God's love, we say with the psalmist, "The Lord is my shepherd." Convinced of divine providence, we cry, "All things work together for good...." In need of courage and faith we sing, "God is our refuge and strength." When doubt assails we pray, "Though he slay me, yet will I trust in him."

The faith once for all delivered to the saints is that which is bound up with the Bible. How impoverished we would be without this matchless means of relating our faith. By means of the Word of God we find assurance in God's promises and strength for the battle of life. Temptation is overcome by this Word. No wonder Sir Walter Scott cried, "There is but one book, The Bible."

II. A *Redeeming* Faith. In proclaiming this faith, we confront man in his need. A view of man is here in that man has sinned. He is a sinner. Man progresses but to fall again. There is no surety in man's endeavor after the good because of the irrationality and evil in his nature. Today's conflict concerns a view of man, man made in the divine image and yet marred through sin and selfishness.

The so-called superman is now seen to be the godless man. Man boasts of his freedom, but everywhere he is in chains. The Christian faith does not flatter man but reveals man's true state.

A view of Christ as Saviour is also here. The one central fact of

the faith is that God in Christ has redeemed man. The Person of
Christ is the touchstone of new life and salvation. Without Him
man is lost and undone. With Him there is the way to God and
the beginning of being re-made after the divine likeness once lost.
In Christ paradise is regained in newness of life. In sacrifice and
death the Christ brings resurrection and eternal life.

III. A *Singing* Faith. Christianity brings a song. Other faiths
and religions sing in the minor key when they attempt to sing.
The joy and peace which results by faith awakens the heart to
sing. Think of all the hymnbooks of the church and compare
their songs. At the center of faith Christians sing together the
same confession of new life. Compare the oratorios and anthems
which exalt God and Christ. The outstanding musical compositions
are motivated by religious faith.

Two centuries after the death of Bach the meaning of his
chorales was obscure. It was Schweitzer who discovered how they
should be interpreted. His teacher did not understand them. The
well-known student of Bach said, "Many things in the chorales
seem obscure, for they are only explicable by the texts of the Bible
pertaining to them!" Wesley, Watts, and others have set the
church singing because they discovered that faith and our creed
is best expressed in song.

IV. A *Dogmatic* Faith. When the alternatives have been seen in
the light of truth, there is only one place to stand. "Here I
stand," cried Luther. Calvin, Knox, Wesley, Edwards, Huguenots,
Covenanters, Puritans, and Christians of all kinds have come to
this finally. The finality of faith is dogmatic. It does not rest upon
uncertainties but upon rock. "To whom shall we go?" said Peter to
Jesus. "Thou hast the words of eternal life. And we . . . are sure. . . ."

We shun the alternatives of humanism, naturalism, communism,
positivism, atheism, or anything else religious which denies the
crown rights of Jesus Christ. Dogmatic? "He that is not with me
is against me," said Jesus. "I am the way, the truth, and the
life. . . ." We bring our lives into relation to that grand certainty.

63. The Church We Honor

"One body...."—Ephesians 4:4

John Wesley said that he must have the whole church for his fellowship. We need a true conception of the church. Some have a high conception, some low, some Roman, some Protestant. Surprises await us when we examine the New Testament teaching anew. Three metaphors used among others are distinctive.

I. The Church as a *Body*. Its *Unity*. As "the body of Christ" so the church is revealed. This idea is easy to understand when we think of the human body. Here are many members, yet one life. Here are different kinds of members, some seen and some unseen, yet a unity of purpose and use. There is unity amid diversity. The cell life of the human body tells of the miraculous strength of the body. So in the church there are millions of Christian cells, each functioning according to a plan.

According to I Corinthians 12, the body of Christ must recognize that no schism and no jealousy need disrupt the whole. If we accept this working principle of the church, it will save us from heartache. It will also make us sensitive to others who are part of the body of Christ. Who is to judge which member is most important? Our various ministries or activities in the body are not competitive but complementary. Christ is the head of the body, and His life and nature flow through the parts.

Each member needs the other. We belong to a redeemed fellowship. The life given by the head is eternal, the nature imparted is the new nature of the Holy Spirit. We are no longer our own, having been "bought with a price." We have been "called out" from among the nations and are now the covenant people. Our various services as members of the body of the church must be done in love. What happens to others affects us in the unity of the body.

II. The Church as a *Building*. Its *Stability*. Jesus said, "I will build my church" (Matt. 16:18). Since that pledge and promise, the Architect and Builder has been working in every age and throughout the world in this task. The church is stronger and greater than ever. Its members number millions, and it is found in every part of the world. Its universality is an accomplished fact.

Many have been the attacks against the church through persecution, but the church has endured unchanged. Built upon the rock of the deity of Christ as the living Lord of Glory, nothing can shake its foundation. Over against "the gates of hell" — the realm

137

of the unseen — the church wages its battle to bring many captives to glory. We wrestle not with flesh and blood. Our weapons are not carnal but spiritual.

As a building we trace the household of God, the temple of God, the habitation of the Spirit (Eph. 2:19-21). There is a dignity about the church in this light that it is God's building and not man's. We are His workmanship. Empires rise and fall, kingdoms pass, but the church continues the one institution which survives the ages. Upon the foundation God is erecting the superstructure of living stones out of all the nations.

III. The Church as a *Bride*. Its *Purity*. To be "holy and without blame before [Christ] in love" (Eph. 1:4) is the ideal view of the church. In the midst of all criticism and attacks against the church this must be kept in mind as the divine point of view. Christ loved the church and gave Himself for the church. He is like the bridegroom and the church is His bride. He has engaged Himself to her and by the Holy Spirit given the pledge or seal (Eph. 1:13, 14).

The Bridegroom sees a beauty in His bride which is not seen by the world. He has sacrificed to obtain her, and in the cross is the eternal symbol of that great love. Thus the church must ever be distinctive in the world. She must not become part of the world or flirt with the world. She is most influential and arresting in power when she is the church, separate unto God. In God's sight she is without "wrinkle or any such thing"; that is, she is eternally young and beautiful.

Peter speaks of the church as "a chosen generation, a royal priesthood, an holy nation, a peculiar people ... in time past ... not a people, but ... now *the people of God*" (I Pet. 2:9-10). It is this which makes us what we are by God's grace. Therefore we honor the church to which we belong in Christ. Speak a good word for the church.

64. The World We Challenge

"[God] hath made of one blood all nations. . . ."—Acts 17:26

John Wesley said that he must have the whole world for his parish. How big is our world? Is it the community in which we live, or is it the vision of all the nations? Do we measure by microscope or telescope? One of the emerging facts of our day is the unity of the human race. The Creator, "God that made the world and all things therein" (Acts 17:24), is also the Creator of people, and people are the concern of the church. The people of God must be missionary-minded and face our world.

I. This is a world *contracted*. The old dimensions of the old globes and atlases have gone. No longer do we live in isolation from others. Integration and not segregation is the word of the twentieth-century man.

By the conquest of distance we have obliterated the old distinction of the old world and the new world. It is now "one world." Wendell Wilkie traveled around the world in 49 days — 31,000 miles in 160 flying hours — in a memorable day. Now we fly by jet plane in less than two days. The world of our fathers with bullock wagon and sailing vessel has gone.

By miraculous communication we have united the world. Atomic energy, radio, television, radar — these are the magic words of the new age of communication.

By political relationship we have entered a new world. The demands of war, the United Nations idea, the satellite age, the scope of inventions, medical discoveries, science wonders — these wipe out the old separated people of nations. We now live next door to all, and the world is a community and neighborhood.

II. This is a world *open*. This is the biggest political fact which has revolutionized modern thought. What happens in Moscow affects Washington. What is done in the heart of Africa has its repercussions in every land. Our thinking must be world-wide. The world is now open to the missionary and the church as never before. Formerly the few entered other lands as special missionaries and against prejudice. Now the church can go to almost every land, speedily, and every Christian is a missionary no matter what he is doing when he goes to other lands, as tourist or businessman or government employee. Radio and travel ease have opened all lands to the Christian message.

The ferment in other lands among people of diverse cultures and ancient religions has opened the door for a more unprejudiced hearing of the gospel. Former barriers have broken down, and men mingle through sharing the riches of all, whether it be invention, medicines, education, or social change. In that context is the opportunity and open door for the missionary.

III. This is a world *revolting*. Man in revolt is characteristic of our new age. The realism of this is staggering. We should not assume because the world is open to us that everyone is receptive to our message. P. Sorokin, the sociologist of Harvard, reminds us of the change in modern art as the outline of the human figure fades and man is seen in animal nature, not spiritual. "Demoralization, dehumanization, brutalization" are his words to describe what has taken place in pictorial art that belongs to sensate culture. A. Toynbee, in *A Study of History*, speaks of the causes which wreck civilization. These are not acts of God but breakdowns in human nature. He discusses this as "an outbreak of internal discord." In that word is the commentary of the New Testament view that man has sinned and is in revolt.

War, lawlessness, social tensions, and the scientific threat of doom and disaster loom over man as nemesis. This is a lost generation, crowded with neuroses, frustrations, anxiety, a people without hope and without God in the world. Demonic powers of the unseen plague and seduce the minds of men towards evil. The clenched fist of man's defiance against God is seen (Ps. 2:2-3) as a picture of revolt.

We have but *one imperative* for this world. It is the gospel to "go . . . and teach all nations." "The field is the world." God needs servants. Truth needs advocates. "Ye are my witnesses." There is *one Saviour* for *one world*. He has loved and died on the cross. He had compassion on the multitudes, sheep without a shepherd. The harvest truly is ripe. "God so loved the world, that he gave. . . ." This is the world we challenge with Christ and His gospel.

65. Don't Be Discouraged

"I, even I only, am left. . . . Yet I have left me seven thousand in Israel, all the knees which have not bowed to Baal."
—I Kings 19:14, 18

The message of Elijah is vividly portrayed in the historian's record and also in Mendelssohn's oratorio. Whether read or heard in the ministry of song, the result is the same. We are conscious that we touch a life close to our own. Here is a great human, "a man subject to like passions as we are." He is close kin to us in his mood of despondency, and God is near with the encouragement we need.

I. Consider the *background of strength*. Elijah appears as a prophet fearless and bold. Like John the Baptist later, he counted it a small thing to stand before a king when he ministered the word of God continually. Ahab quailed before him and accepted his word. The people recognized him as a man of God. His speech was "Thus saith the Lord." As God's representative he challenged the priests of Baal and mocked them in calm dignity and majestic bearing. He was the vindicator of true religion at Mount Carmel and the one who prayed, "Hear me, Lord." Yet this strong man of courage ran for his life, expecting death. He was discouraged. Why?

II. Think of the *foreground of weakness*. After the strain of that struggle with idolatry and evil, a reaction set in. The prophet who was master of the false prophets and the enemy of heathen godlings is now cowed before the ire of a wicked woman. Jezebel's threat to take his life resulted in his collapse under a juniper tree. Thus it was that he wished he could die, but God came to encourage him by bringing him to Horeb, the Mount of God. There, by a theophany, he was lifted up out of despair. We should like to know why Elijah was so like the weeping willow instead of the sturdy oak in that critical hour? Let us note some of the things he forgot, for thereby lies the way of encouragement.

III. He forgot to take *inspiration from the past*. In the mood of lassitude of spirit, history is a tonic and a corrective. It helps perspective and poise when we see things aright. The solitary incident should not be put out of place and focus. Under the juniper tree there is a place to recall Carmel's mount and the victory of God in that previous encounter with evil.

IV. Elijah was *unaware of physical and mental limitations*. These were real, and faith and courage are easily stampeded when

141

one is tired in body and jaded in mind. A strenuous ministry, the strain of conflict, and the long journey into the wilderness were "too great" for him. Sometimes God's servants need to come apart for rest and renewal.

V. A Man of God *should have known that evil is not omni potent*. This woman, daughter of a king, wife of a king, and mother of a king, might oppose, but the last word is not with Jezebel. It is with God! When the ramifications of sin seem to be impregnable, when temptation is alluring, when there surround us that subtle influence to compromise and sacrifice principle and ideal, *then* is the time to remember that righteousness has not abdicated. Right, not wrong; righteousness, not evil; grace, not sin; God, and not mammon, are omnipotent.

VI. Perhaps Elijah was *upset by the fallacy of the census*. As far as he could count, Elijah thought he was the only one standing for God in the nation. "I, even I only, am left." That is a mood of discouragement into which it is easy to stumble. No crowd rallies, converts are none, assistance from others is non-existent He thought he was alone. Just there is where God comes to remind us that we do not count numerically in the warfare of the spirit Man's strength lies in numbers, but God is pleased to work with the few or the one man who dares to stand alone. Paul was discouraged in Corinth, but God showed him that he was not alone (Acts 18:9-10). God has His witnesses where we do not always see them.

One of the Devil's weapons is discouragement. To those who are lonely, feeling the economic strain, having a moral struggle to be and do the right, or facing a secular world and anti-Christian forces: let us act in the confidence that the God who answers by fire also speaks with the still small voice. He is with us always (Matt. 28:19-20). Through Christ multitudes do not bow the knee to Baal. Lift up your hearts in the encouragement of his presence

66. Pray or Lose Heart

"Men ought always to pray, and not to faint."—Luke 18:1

Life offers us two alternatives: prayer or fainting. The one cancels the other. Our Lord taught the imperative of prayer. Prayer is a necessity, not a luxury.

On the one hand we see men faint, collapse, become discouraged, stop living, lose heart. On the other hand, we find a few who learn to pray and who are reinforced for the struggle. By these alternatives the common life is divided.

I. *Prostration.* This means to give up altogether, to turn coward, to succumb by inner collapse. A city without defenses is open to assault in time of war. A fish out of water struggles in vain. A prayerless man is a denial of his creation and a creature without hope or strength.

Loss of spirit may be attributed to several causes. Physical disabilities disrupt, or suffering warps the outlook. Sensitive souls are baffled by the tensions and trials of life and so despair. Temptation is too much for others, and they give in.

Practical people argue that work and not prayer is needed. To them work is prayer. They scoff at prayer in this kind of world. It seems out of place in an atomic age. Yet they have to admit that in the rush and strain of our complex life men lose heart and faint. (Cf. Matt. 9:36, where Jesus saw men fainting.)

II. *Re-creation.* The alternative to fainting is prayer. This implies the re-creation of spirit and strength. II Corinthians 4:16-18 senses this truth in describing how we "faint not," do not lose heart. The reason is that "the inward man is renewed day by day." The outward presses upon the inward, but the temporal is not allowed to crush the eternal. The things unseen are greater than the seen. This is the secret of transformation.

By prayer the presence and power of God works for us and in us. As science has found the way to break up the atom and electrons, so this spiritual power of God contacts our human need. Our powers are then empowered by God for mighty ends.

Renewal and reinforcement come through prayer. Miracle? Yes, this is an age of the unusual, and we may experience miracles. If we are ready to accept the benefits of the scientific "miracles" of man's achievement, how much more ought we to be ready to relate ourselves to the divine power of an almighty God? God, by His Spirit, re-creates and renews.

III. *Condition.* One of the hindrances to the blessing of this truth lies in our wrong attitudes. One is the mistaken idea of making the act of praying an end in itself. Prayer is a means to an end. It is the engagement of a relationship and a communion. Our life is linked with God. Some are more conscious of their prayers than of the One to whom they pray. Another wrong idea is being conscious of the thing we desire more than the Giver Himself. When need is met we forget God sometimes. The heights of true prayer lie in oneness with the Giver, for prayer is not simply asking for things.

The divine end of prayer is fellowship with God. Cf. Luke 18:9-14, where we see the two attitudes of prayer brought out clearly. One is selfish, and the other is God-glorifying. One is condemned, the other commended. Religious hypocrisy and egotism are seen over against humility and self-abasement. Penitence, not pride, is the condition of prayer.

IV. *Alteration.* As prayer renews, what are the results? A change takes place in the life. Not all prayers are answered, of course. God *denies* some prayers. We may ask amiss, selfishly, thoughtlessly. God can refuse us because He knows we are not ready or it would not be good for us then. God *delays* some prayers. The answer is on the way but not yet. We are impatient and impulsive. God takes time to work out His purpose. We must learn to trust in faith which waits. God *delivers* in some prayers. His answer is there before we call. A moral problem, a fierce temptation, an upset in life — and God is there to help!

Thousands of God's people testify that God answers prayer. "This poor man cried, and the Lord heard him, and saved him out of all his troubles" (Ps. 34:6). The wonder and majesty of it is that God waits upon our weakness! We need not lose heart or give up in life's struggle. We can pray constantly, believingly. We ought!

67. The Paradox of Power

"We preach Christ crucified...the power of God...."
I Corinthians 1:23, 24

If there is anything more than another desired by men, it is power. Our age is a power-conscious age. Power over the forces of nature, power over the minds of men, and the power in and from the secrets of atomic energy spur us on in the pursuit of more power. The strange claim in the text startles in its paradoxical setting. It seems far removed from what men consider effective. To the Christian it holds the dynamic for this life. That which seems to be weak is strong, and that which seems impotent is found to be energizing.

I. The supreme expression of *power* is *moral energy*. Think of the ideas of power found in our world.

The power of *money:* to buy and command a place in this life. Money can enforce the will of some. It crushes if necessary. Competitors can be outwitted. "Money talks." "Every man has his price." So reasons the world spirit.

The Power of *position:* to give social prestige, birth, family, influence — all this sought as most important. Our Lord warned against the worship of Mammon, a false way of power.

The Power of *armaments:* to dominate others. Nations imagine this to be crucial. Millions of dollars and lives are spent in race for supremacy. Peace is not found. Power spells conquest and control.

The Power of *Moral Energy.* Right is might. Morality is mightier than Mammon. Spiritual and moral strength is greater. Truth-telling, honesty, straight-dealing, purity (chaste life) — these are elements which enable and uplift. The *gospel* is the dynamic unto salvation. By it there is power and energy to remake and refashion personality.

II. The supreme expression of *moral energy* is *love*. Love is pre-eminent and superlative. All other virtues and expressions of moral life are gathered up in this. Love crowns and surpasses all. Consider a mother's love for a child, and then ask who can measure the love of God for the world. God's nature and being find outlet in the attribute of love.

Napoleon said that Alexander the Great, Caesar, Charlemagne, and himself built their empires on force, but Jesus founded his on love. He added, "Thou, O Galilean, hast conquered." Love is well described and praised in that matchless hymn of I Corinthians 13.

There love is given the superiority over all other graces. They are but the manifold displays of love itself. This is "Love divine all loves excelling."

III. The supreme expression of *love* is *sacrifice*. Love must give itself in acts. Love is vocal and not silent. Love is active, no passive. History and literature are full of sublime examples. Love overcomes barriers, dares every risk, gives time, strength, and life itself to please the object of devotion. Stephen, stoned, replies by a prayer of forgiveness. Saul is won thereby, for, instead of retalia tion, there was love sacrificing.

When the Roman Empire was overcome, it was challenged, no by force of arms, but by love enduring in martyrdom. The Edic of Milan, A.D. 313, gave freedom of worship to Christians. Thi freedom was won in the arena and at the stake and not on the battlefield. Sacrificial loyalty to their Lord resulted, not in de stroying their enemies, but in slaying the enmity against them and the turning of foes into friends. The love of God in Christ the love of the cross, now poured out through the church.

IV. The supreme expression of *sacrifice* is *death*. Sacrificial living in the self-denials of friends, career, position, home, money or social benefits is noble. But to *die?* Our Lord laid down His life that He might bring us to God. His cross is the apex and crown of His life of self-denial.

As *Paul* writes about power, he is certain that the crucified Christ alone gives genuine power. What did others think?

The *Jews,* with religious disdain, spoke of it as a scandal, a shameful, ignominious, and accursed end to a life.

The *Greeks,* in their quest for ideal man and wisdom, rejected it as foolish and the mutilation of beauty and order.

The *Romans,* with their lust of empire, saw in it nothing but defeat, impotence, and the antithesis of power.

But *to the Christian* this is *the power of God.* David Brainerd's *Journal* tells that the Indians were gripped when he told them about the Crucified. The foolish thing is divine wisdom, and the apparent weak thing is mighty, because He who died *is* the power of God and exercises the authority of God.

68. Prayer as Need

"Bow down thine ear, O Lord, hear me: for I am poor and needy."—Psalm 86:1

The efficacy of prayer is heightened by man's need. No one can be satisfied with less than the eternal. Prayer has many aspects. Intercession, thanksgiving, communion, worship, and adoration are blended in our praying. Here is *petition,* and it is based on *need.* The language of prayer is universal, and we may use this petition.

I. Prayer *Based upon Need:* "I am poor and needy." As prayer is not something of words but of spirit, we may be most eloquent when we plead our need. It is not our power of expression but our weakness which avails with God. We are not received by the wealth of our possessions but by our poverty of spirit. It is the beggar's supplication which commands the Benefactor's supply. Luke's Gospel tells that our Lord promised His Father would not give stones for bread. Hunger of heart finds the responsive heart of God. F. W. Boreham tells the story of a boy in the backwoods of Australia coming to a railway crossing and crying out to the passengers of the train for papers. His sense of need cried out for news of the world at large.

The Lord's Prayer (really the disciples') has in it, "give us day by day our daily bread." Psalm 86 is a mosaic of quotations showing that the language of prayer is the same in all ages. Man boasts of his independence and achievements. He has spanned the globe and blotted out distance. In personality and speech he expresses himself with power. The empires of life seem great. So man thinks he is somebody, until he discovers he must *pray!* Mentally, physically, and morally he relies upon the gifts of nature. Spiritually he must depend upon God. In the measure that we know our *need* and realize our impoverishment we shall pray. The self-sufficient do not pray.

II. Prayer *Expressed by Urgency:* "O Lord, hear me." Sometimes we are aware of much phrasing in prayer but little passion. Our prayers are not at the flood. Formality often quenches the spirit of the heart. But let anyone become desperate in soul agony, and then this note of urgency and importunity creeps in. There is now haste and insistence in petition. The Puritan John Trapp has this comment: "Lest any by former words suspect him to be a merit-monger, he beggeth mercy with instancy and constancy of request."

Why do we pray? Is it merely for something we might receive or for other greater ends? George Meredith said: "Who rises from prayer a better man, his prayer is answered." That is true, and yet it is not the whole truth. The Christian finds the Bible full of promises and invitations about prayer, and these lead him to believe that God awaits our petition as well as our communion. Fatalism has no room for this pleading voice. If our need is real and genuine, we shall not hesitate to use the words of petition and cry out, "hear me." The ejaculatory prayer of Peter, "Lord, save me," was sufficient to bring the saving strength of Christ. Are we desperate in our prayers?

III. Prayer *Awaits Grace:* "Bow down thine ear, O Lord." It is not our cry alone which gives us confidence, but the condescension of God. The throne of glory has become the throne of grace. We may come boldly to find grace in time of need. Our distress is a forcible reason why God hears, for misery is an argument with mercy when it is the sincere expression of the heart. Prayer finally is related to the will and purpose of God for our lives. Here is no caprice, but concern for us; hence grace is the one thing needful.

Scientifically this is true. The light waves are attuned to the eye as sound is to the ear. Our physical need in this way is met by the universe, which contracts and condescends to our need. The whole world of the mysterious universe "bows down." Trapp has the word: "as a careful physician doth to his feeble patient." The doctor must bow down to the need of the weak.

Here is a singular request — that the Lord God should bow down to meet our need. The one plea is that we are poor and needy. And the singular grace of God will answer the request, for the same grace has made the petitioner feel his need.

The New Testament throws much light upon principles of prayer. Our Lord Jesus Christ taught his disciples to pray. At the heart of the teaching is this principle of petition based upon need and sponsored by His mercy and grace. The gospel tells of people *in need* who came to cry out for mercy and help. Jesus did not disappoint them. God will not turn away from us in our need. Are we desperate?

69. What Jesus Would Not Do

*"He could there do no mighty work ... because of their un-
belief."*—Mark 6:5, 6

*"I have yet many things to say unto you, but ye cannot bear
them now."*—John 16:12

*"O Jerusalem, Jerusalem, ... how often would I have gathered
thy children together ..., and ye would not!"*—Matthew 23:37

We have assumed that Jesus could do anything, having all
power and authority. It startles us to read that there were some
things He could not or would not do. Yet Scripture testifies that
He who possessed all authority was straitened and limited in
measure. Even this is evidence of His power — in restraint!

I. *He did not many mighty works* because of *unbelief.* "He
could there do no mighty work ... because of their unbelief"
(Mark 6:5, 6). If the people of that day were astonished at His
teaching and works, He, too, was amazed at their refusal to accept
the evidence of divine power. They recognized His miracles but
refused to admit that His power came from God. They made their
judgment blind. They denied the sequence of the supernatural.
Our Lord did not work miracles to create belief, but he worked
miracles where there was belief.

Modern unbelief denies the supernatural. Glibly accepting
Christian teaching, it, nevertheless, denies the lordship and deity
of Jesus Christ. Many are within the atmosphere of His influence
and blessing, yet are insulated from it. This insulation comes
through prejudice, bigotry, pride, sin, the closing of the mind to
the divine Spirit of God. So the mighty works Jesus would do are
thwarted when men disbelieve.

John Bunyan, in *The Holy War,* describes part of the defense
of the town of Man-Soul by one, Mr. Prejudice, with fifty deaf
men at Ear Gate, opposing Prince Immanuel. Moral conditions
determine the absence of conversions. There are saving exceptions
when there is faith and belief. Unbelief or disbelief is the one
indicted sin of Hebrews 12:1 — the sin which easily besets (and
upsets).

II. *He did not teach* all things because of *unreadiness.* "I have
yet many things to say unto you, but ye cannot bear them now"
(John 16:12). His teaching was conditioned and partial to suit
the receptivity of His disciples. There was finality in Him who
was the Truth, yet he considered the limitations of His own followers. His reticence is matched by our reluctance. He wished to

149

reveal much more to them, but their ears were attuned to other things, and their spirits were dull. The disordered life frightened away the gentle dove of the Holy Spirit, who found no resting place.

It is true now that capacity determines apprehension of that which is revealed. The apostles were in our Lord's school for three years, and yet they did not understand when he told them about the approaching cross and resurrection. There is a progression in revelation and the same in understanding. Later, according to our Lord's promise, the Holy Spirit would teach them further and unfold the meaning. Are we responsive and ready for His teaching? Are we cramped by tradition, shibboleth, and a mind sealed against the entrance of light and illumination? Are we willing to obey as truth is given? What says the Spirit?

III. *He did not save* a city because of *unwillingness.* "O Jerusalem, Jerusalem, how often would I have gathered thy children together ..., and ye would not" (Matt. 23:37). The lament of Jesus over the Holy City is the gesture of the mother-love of God. The emotions of Jesus are significant when thus recorded. Think of the plaintive, weeping note when love is frustrated. This affection is spurned and met by coldness. "How often...." Repeatedly God's overture is made as He seeks the sinner in infinite patience. But what if the human agent refuses the wooing cadences of gospel music?

"How often *would I* . . ., and *ye would not.*" There is the clash of human will with divine will. A.D. 70 came eventually with its terrible and swift destruction of the city which knew not the day of divine visitation. Even Jesus could not save them when they would not be saved. The unwillingness of moral beings unmasks the cruel blight of sin which warps human life.

There are many things Jesus wishes to do, but He is hindered by these too-well-known factors. Yet unbelief may give way to faith; unreadiness to receptivity; and unwillingness to action. At the cross One who refused to save Himself saved others.

It is written, "All power (authority, R.V.) is given unto me ..." (Matt. 28:18). Then why does He not exercise it fully? That is the mystery of the event when "he humbled himself ..." (Phil. 2:8). Thus, while seeking to win men, He may be hindered. The terms of acceptance are still the same: believe, receive, obey.

70. What Is Your Life?

"I press toward the mark...." "That I may win Christ...."
"This one thing I do...."—Philippians 3:14, 8, 13

Every person faces life in one of two ways. Either we are without a definite life-purpose, or we know what God has planned for us. What is the controlling power and motive which regulates life? Many drift and become the flotsam and jetsam of life. A few discover their vocation. Life then is an investment of time, strength, and ability of soul. Given a governing life-purpose, we enter upon the will of God. This has ever been the secret of devoted lives. Paul testifies to this in these words:

I. A Singleness of *Action:* "... forgetting those things which are behind, and reaching forth unto those things which are before, *I press toward the mark* for the prize of the high calling of God in Christ Jesus" (Phil. 3:13, 14).

The man who scatters his energies upon many objects soon loses his energy and his enthusiasm. Paul wrote these words from a Roman prison and near the end of a strenuous life. It was unified in a glorious purpose. Like the athlete, he stretched all his powers to the utmost. He had an eye on the goal. To edit a newspaper the editor must know what to put in the waste basket. Paul knew what to discard.

There was a new valuation upon his life. It began when he met Jesus Christ. The old things passed away. He became a new creation. Laying aside his trust in self-righteousness, traditional religion, boasted heritage, and pharisaical goodness, he embraced the new life in Christ. He cultivated a passion for grace, a longing after holiness, an enthusiasm for Christ. In this new-found activity of spirit he concentrated his energies in the new evaluation of life — no digression, but persistent dedication.

II. A Singleness of *Ambition:* "I count all things but loss for the excellency of the knowledge of Christ Jesus my Lord...*that I may win Christ*" (Phil. 3:8).

A healthy ambition is worth while. It needs to be worthy of the individual and ennobling in its end. Paul was in the grip of a master-passion. This was the chief business of his life. Some pursue money, fame, success, worldly applause, and honor. Here in Paul is an incomparable ambition.

Paul, already a Christian, seeks to win Christ. What did he mean? He did not wish to be a partial Christian. Christ had apprehended him; now he must apprehend that in its deepest

151

meaning. He sought the fulness of Christian experience. He wished to be holy, complete, and balanced under Christ's mastery. As the miner finds a good seam and works to "win" it or exhaust it, so Paul sought to possess the unsearchable riches of Christ. He desired the fabulous wealth of his spiritual birthright. His ambition was God-glorifying and uplifting.

III. A Singleness of *Application:* "I count not myself to have apprehended: but this *one thing I do . . .*" (Phil. 3:13) .

The power of achievement is wrapped up in this word. Browning said, "Who keeps one end in view, Makes all things serve." This does not mean a warped and cramped life. It speaks of selection and discrimination. There are priorities. Paul was busy in tent-making, travelling, organizing, writing, preaching, but in and through these ran this one thing. Everything was contributary to the one end.

Paul was a man of one idea. It may be fashionable to ridicule the man of one idea, but these have left their imprint upon history. It is the single aim and the consecrated application which tells. Nothing could daunt Paul. Nothing could appal him, no prison suppress him, obstacles could not discourage him, the Roman emperor could not muzzle him. Nothing could intimidate him. He lived for one thing.

What are we living for? What is our master-passion? Have we a sense of vocation, a high calling? In the church and in society we need individuals who are abandoned to this high and glorious purpose. Who will live for this one thing that really counts?

Who will consecrate his service to the Christ of God today?
Who will yield, a willing vassal, to His claims and to His sway?
He is worthy, well He proved it, of your highest and your best;
Bend your will, yield your body, do His behest!

This is what life can be at the highest level. This is the secret of the noblest character and the greatest influence. Life must be invested under a master-passion. Let that master-passion be Christ.

71. For or Against?

"All these things are against me."—Genesis 42:36
"All things work together for good. . . ."—Romans 8:28

There are *two attitudes to life*. Jacob's attitude saw the futility of life. Paul's attitude saw the certainty of life. G. K. Chesterton remarked that, when you rent a room, it is important to find out, not about the rent and the cooking only, but what is the landlady's outlook upon life. Some think of life in our world as an occasion of terror and foreboding: others see in it an opportunity to enjoy God's bounty and presence.

I. *Jacob — All these things are against me*. The Jacob saga is full of human interest and pathos.

The Troubles of Life. Jacob had experienced much in his checkered career. *Four funerals* are noted in one chapter (Gen. 35): Deborah (nurse), Rachel (wife), Isaac (father), and Joseph (beloved son) assumed. Thus death plagued him and caused him sorrow. There was *famine* in the land, and this was a grief to him. His *sons Reuben and Judah* stained their lives with impurity and shame. His family knew *dissension* in the hatred shown to Joseph. *His own life* was closing in, and his strength was failing. Did not Jacob say, "Few and evil have the days . . . of my life been . . ."? (Gen. 47:9). The troubles of life are common to all, and no one escapes.

The Tyranny of the Past. This haunted the memory. *His own misdeeds and sins* rose up to stab his memory and prick his conscience. He recalled the days of yesterday, and there was bitterness and shame in his heart. Was there no release from that horror? Jacob was well named *the deceiver* or supplanter. He deceived his father Isaac concerning the blessing of the firstborn. He deceived his brother Esau concerning the birthright. He deceived his father-in-law Laban concerning the bounty.

All these are with us today. We, too, complain and grumble: business is not working out for us aright; some have lost confidence in us; through some circumstance or other we are alone and lonely; ill health dogs our steps; fear pursues us when we think of the uncertain days ahead; plans fail to mature: we feel we are in the grip of hostile forces and an unfriendly universe. Thus despair, futility, suicide, drunkenness, or drugs are sought after by many in their idea of life *against* them.

However, some have risen above their circumstances and made appreciable contributions in music and literature and other arts during such a mood. Handel wrote his oratorio in poverty in a

London garret. Cowper, thwarted in suicide, wrote hymns. Carlyle rewrote his manuscript which had been burned by a careless maid. Gossip preaches when "life tumbles in" at the death of his wife. These things need not be *against* you.

II. *Paul — All things work together for good.* Remarkable words known and memorized to be quoted.

Apparent Contradiction. Many think this cannot be true in view of facts of life. How can evil be good? Study the text for clearer translation. Paraphrase it to be "In everything God works for good." "God makes everything turn out for the best."

Obvious Explanation. The mystery of the text is true in human life to those who meet the conditions of God about it: God works *in* everything; God works *for those* who love Him. The non-Christian cannot see this because it needs faith and trust. God works for *those who are called* according to His purpose and plan. This does not apply to everyone indiscriminately. It is for a select group called the church, who by faith know God and trust Him in His purpose for life.

Practical Application. Paul is claiming that life is touched with meaning and purpose as part of God's plan. Life is not a thing of chance or fatalism.

There are various reactions possible: run away from life, escape; exploit life selfishly; redeem life with meaning. Consider the story of George Matheson, Edinburgh, who lost his sight and consequently his fiancee, and who, in the storm of that experience, wrote "O Love that wilt not let me go. . . ." The line "trace the rainbow in the rain" was not his but the hymn committee's. He wrote, "I *climb* the rainbow. . . ." That is the application of this text when we see all things work together.

"These things" — what are they for Paul? His list in Romans 8:35, 38 and 39 mentions: distress, persecution, famine, nakedness, peril, sword. His reaction is the confident assertion: "I am persuaded that . . . death, life, angels, principalities, powers, things present, things to come, height, depth [none of these things], nor any other creature, shall be able to separate us from the love of God, which is in Christ Jesus our Lord."

The attitude to life is seen in the cross: to man tragedy, but to Christ victory. We assume one of two attitudes — either for or against.

72. God's King and Dictator

"Yet have I set my king upon my holy hill of Zion. I will declare the decree...."—Psalm 2:6, 7

This psalm portrays for us in startling language the present-day war against God. Every age has had examples of men and nations in seeming revolt against divine standards. It has been reserved for our generation to witness total war and universal lawlessness. These are generated by the rise of despots and dictators whose wills are blatantly opposed to the will of God.

I. *The Revolt of the Nations* (vss. 1-3). It is a mystery why finite wills oppose the infinite. The futility is matched by the sovereignty of Almighty God. The picture of the raging nations meditating and scheming through their leaders is graphic and realistic for our day. Human governments are not always on the side of righteousness. Here is a depiction of diplomacy and secrecy plotting rebellion against the moral governorship of the world.

The spirit of anti-God and anti-Christ is noted throughout the world, especially in communistic Russia. Communism is an avowed enemy of Christianity. Definite propaganda is used to fight against God. Bernard Pares, Professor of Russian, London University, in a book on Russia declares that "Communists are more afraid of Religion than of Education." Yet in Russia after many years of persecution the number of Christians is increasing. Other nations are guilty also of denying the sovereignty of God. Moral sanctions break down, and war results.

The psalmist speaks of the vanity and foolishness of those who oppose God. A Pharaoh tried to destroy Israel, but his own daughter was God's instrument to save them through Moses. A Julian, the emperor, sneered at the Christian's "carpenter-master," but his own coffin was being prepared.

II. *The Answer of God* (vss. 4-6). History records instances of God's reply to the spirit of revolt. God is not inactive or indifferent. He sits enthroned and is not earth-bound. The *laughter* of God is terrible. Here is derision and contempt for the puny attempts of man to thwart His will. God is not laughing at the sufferings of men but at their abortive acts of rebellion. Throughout the long era of bloodshed in the world the divine patience is in evidence and, "Vengeance is mine, I will repay," said the Lord. That laughter is our strength that His righteousness prevails.

God's decree is the assurance that "the kingdoms of this world are become the kingdoms of our Lord, and of his Christ." God's anointed Messiah-Son is the only potentate and despot worthy of absolute rulership. The world awaits the day which is certain and sure. Out of the present travail will come the final day of decreed vindication of Jesus Christ.

III. *The Promised Dictator* (vss. 7-9). The character and nature of this One is indicated by the reference to His endless life through resurrection power. Once in time God set His seal upon His Son Jesus Christ, and history will be repeated in that final triumph over all His enemies. The universal dominion promised is not ushered in by evangelization but by personal conquest and subjection of all opposing forces.

Judgment is promised upon those who share in the war against God. The smiting stone of Daniel 2:34 comes to break oppression, and the beneficent reign of God through Christ is symbolized in the straight rod and sceptre of righteousness. A weary, warring, disillusioned world must hail that government as complete and final in its integrity and justice.

IV. *The Gracious Invitation* (vss. 10-12). Meantime, until that day breaks for the nations, God is displaying His grace and patience even as He warns. The gospel is the promise of pardon to rebels. "Be wise now . . . lest. . . ."

This is the golden hour of opportunity to respond to the Redeemer's love. "Kiss the Son" encourages *an act of obedience* which is *through obeisance*. There is blessing for those who "put their trust in him." He who is the Anointed One, the King, the Lord, the Son of God, the Messiah-Saviour, is in grace wooing all men. One day He will be the Judge of all.

This is the picture of God's King and Dictator in the dictatorship of love now in the light of final judgment. The world knows many leaders, kings, emperors, presidents, and dictators, but God's *choice* is His only begotten Son. "All hail the power of Jesus' name. . . ." "Crown Him Lord of all."

73. One Thing Thou Lackest

"One thing thou lackest."—Mark 10:21

We light upon this story with surprise, coming as it does after the incident when Jesus blessed the children. The young man runs to Him to ask the question which must settle life and destiny. He is eager in his quest for the one thing which makes life worth while. Youth seeks a master and desires fulness of life and completeness of expression.

I. *The Qualities of Youth.* We are impressed with the richness of character revealed.

Exemplary in Conduct. "All these things have I observed from my youth" (R.V.). Moral life was good and high in standard, yet simply the truth of a decent life. The Ten Commandments obeyed bring a clean life. Here they were kept in their social aspects, but the youth had failed in one particular. There is a godless goodness. One may have a good life without being Christian.

Spiritually Discerning. "Good Master, what shall I do that I may inherit eternal life?" He connected life with goodness. He was religious enough to see this vital truth. After Jesus' treatment of the children the youth connected goodness with God, a position claimed by Jesus Himself.

High Moral Purpose. "What good thing shall I do?" (Matt. 19:16). This was the eager quest of his heart, the bent of his life. Here is no outward prodigal wasting his substance. He is not derelict. In a lawless and disrupted world today we salute this kind of young man. Morality is worth while although not always Christian.

Courageous. He "ran" to Jesus (R.V.). In the East this was unusual for a man in his position. Convention was defied, and social restrictions were cast aside. He was in earnest. What a sight! There is the courage of the battlefield and the courage of the hospital ward, but moral courage is noble also. The youth was daring much to come to Christ.

Wealth and Position. Here is a young man with all the advantages of wealth and position -- "ruler," "rich," "great possessions." Those in position of authority and power, of wealth and influence, are not always following Jesus. Yet there are some mighty, noble, and great who are called and do follow.

Honest and Sincere. "What lack I yet?" He had faced life's demands and now knew what he desired most. He was ready to confess his need. There was no shirking here and no hypocrisy;

157

yet, when confronted by Jesus in the total commitment, he failed. Sincerity and honesty are not enough to achieve the ideal.

II. *The Attitude of Jesus.* Our Lord was attracted to this young man, hence His comments.

Jesus loved him. Looking into the clear-cut face, he saw the yearning of the heart. He loved him for what he was and for what he might become. When Jesus asked him, "Why callest thou me good? there is none good but one, . . . God," this was not to deny but to claim His deity. The youth recognized goodness incarnate in Jesus and identified that with God. Our Lord loved him for the noble characteristics of his life and the sincerity of his motives. He loved him as he sought the young man's allegiance.

Jesus tested his reality. The claim of Christ cannot be compromised. All must face the same demands of conscience. The challenge of "go . . . sell . . . give . . . come . . . take . . . follow . . ." surprised the youth and disturbed him. He wanted eternal life? Then Jesus told him the terms and conditions. He wished to do something? Then Jesus challenged him to do this. It is sometimes easier to do than to be, to work than to sacrifice.

The youth found that possessions possessed him. He was not really free. Instead of keeping the Ten Commandments, he was unmasked as breaking their spirit and violating the First Commandment. To love God supremely and wholly is the foundation of the moral law, and this he failed to do. He loved self.

III. *The Mistake of the Youth.* The climax of the story is tragic. We are warned as we read, "he went away sorrowful, for he had great possessions." He need not have gone away. Did he return after reflection, later? Who knows? Perhaps. He lacked one thing. That was the self-control of Jesus Christ. He had many things but lacked the one thing which would have given meaning, purpose, direction, and salvation to life. He wanted Jesus, but on his own terms. He might have gone away rejoicing in the final satisfaction of life's quest.

74. One Thing I Know

"One thing I know. . . ."—John 9:25

Here the power of Christ is displayed. A controversy raged between the defenders of the status quo and the man who had received his sight. Jesus had given sight to this poor man who had been blind from birth. The critics did not like the miracle and are contemptuous. As they argue they fail to appreciate that the miracles of Jesus are for moral and beneficent ends. Every miracle is a parable of grace in action. Here is *the value of personal experience* displayed.

I. *An Unanswerable Argument* for the Faith. A convert of this kind confuses the Pharisees, who said, "How did this happen? What did he do to you?" The man's answer was simple and clear. With directness and frankness he said that he knew there had been this change. Men ever seek proof, as science demands evidence. Science is knowledge of facts gained and verified by accurate observation and thinking. This man's changed condition can be verified in thousands of lives.

Conviction is that you know, you are certain. The keynote of this story is conviction, and personal testimony cannot be refuted. The blind sees, and the spiritually blind sees by Christ's power. Some tried to trap this man in speech, but his parents said, "he is of age, let him speak for himself." This is not hearsay but firsthand knowledge; not tradition but truth; not custom but experience. It was personal. He spoke for himself. John Newton in uncertainty sang,

'Tis a point I long to know
Do I love my Lord or no?

How different to be able to sing,

My God, I am thine, what a comfort divine,
What a blessing to know that the Saviour is mine.
In the heavenly Lamb, thrice happy I am,
And my heart it doth dance at the sound of His name.

This is not presumption but faith. When you have passed out of darkness into light, you know the difference.

II. *A Conclusive Argument* for the Faith. The *how* may be shrouded in mystery, but there is no disputing *that* a man "sees." For the first time he sees the world around him, the loved ones of family, the One who gave him sight. "Whereas I was blind, now I see." This is irrefutable.

Consider the variety of men who give this testimony. Multitudes bear witness that Christ has given them spiritual light. Once blinded by sin, they now see, and the eyes of their understanding have been enlightened. They are people in all walks of life. Transformations take place when the drunkard is made sober, the dishonest is made honest, the blasphemer praises God, and the good and religious man is born again.

The character of these converts is such as to bring conviction of the reality of their witness. From the apostle Paul on the Damascus road to modern days: Robert Raikes, who founded the Sunday school; Josephine Butler, who fought to save thousands from the Social Evil; John Howard and Elizabeth Fry, who brought in prison reform. In our churches we have men and women who are living witnesses of the power of Christ to transform their lives. They are among the best people.

III. *A Convincing Argument* for the Faith. This man was convinced that Jesus had the power of God. Do we believe that Christ can work miracles? It is possible to be religious and sincere and yet be spiritually blind. You may know many things and yet be ignorant of the one thing that matters. This man did not have much knowledge of the world in which he lived, but now he knew one thing. What are education, position, success, and pleasure if we lack this one thing? Jesus is known as the Light of the world, and He brought light to the man born blind.

The man gave simple testimony, but it was strong and sure. He kept to the facts. He now walked in the light. He could see. All arguments to the contrary (that it could not happen, that there is no way of examining how this happened, etc.) are all in vain — the man could now see! The man walked in the light.

His witness was convincing because it was clear-cut and definite. It was public for all to know. Critics and friends might doubt and not be able to explain, but he was now enjoying sight. They might try to refute the claims of Christ, but they could not get rid of the man and the miracle in him. Such a man is always a puzzle to those who are still in darkness through sin and are not spiritually enlightened. Do we give the same testimony of the man?

75. One Thing Needful

"One thing is needful...."—Luke 10:42

The Bethany interior is a story of beauty and grace. This was the home where Jesus visited frequently. We are what we are at home. There the true self is revealed. Outside we may appear different, but here we are naturally ourselves. This particular home depicts the average life with its moods. We read that "Jesus loved Martha, and her sister, and Lazarus." The two sisters act in different ways in the presence of Jesus. Mary seems as one who sits idly at the feet of Jesus, while Martha appears as the one busy with the household concerns. When Martha reminds her sister about this, she is told about her own needs in the words of the text.

I. *The common interpretation* is that here is a *contrast* between the two sisters. It has entered our daily speech — we often speak of those who are "the Marthas" and "the Marys." It is supposed that Martha is the worker, practical, busy, and hospitable. In contrast it is suggested that Mary is not a worker but a worshipper, impracticable, perhaps lazy, and contemplative.

This view is helped by the record of Luke 10:38 — "a certain woman named Martha received [Jesus] into her house"; Luke 10:40 — "Martha was cumbered about much serving"; John 11:20 — "Martha, as soon as she heard that Jesus was coming, went and met him...." Then said Martha..., "Lord, if thou hadst been here, my brother had not died"; John 12:2 — "They made him [Jesus] a supper; and Martha served." These references imply a type of character full of action, planning for others.

There is nothing wrong in this. The world needs busy people. Martha was capable in planning and providing, yet she asked Mary to help her in the midst of her much serving.

II. *Another interpretation* is in the *complement* of one life with the other. Both, in this view, were practical women, and each shared the demands of the home with its care. Note the one word, "Mary... *also* sat at Jesus' feet." Mary was not lazy or indolent. Mary, like Martha, took her share of the work, but she also rested and relaxed at the right time. Martha did not take time to rest and meditate. Jesus was saying, "Martha has prepared many dishes, whereas only one is necessary: Mary has chosen the best, the right, dish."

Jesus desired Martha's fellowship, not her food. Mary not only worked but worshipped. Mary *did* as well as thought. Martha *thought less* than she did. When Jesus said that she was troubled

161

about many things and *careful,* He was speaking of a familiar thing. "Take no thought ["be not . . . anxious, R.V.] for the morrow" (Matt. 6:34) . To be free of trouble and worry when we trust is desired.

III. *One thing is needful.* The nourishment of Christ's teaching can be more important than the dishes of the table. Man does not live by bread alone, but by the word of God. Work is right, but worship is necessary. The man of action needs spiritual strength. Jesus said, "Come ye . . . apart . . ., and rest a while." Music must have its pauses for balance and the making of music. The world demands our time and strength for many things, but Jesus said, "Seek ye first the kingdom of God. . . ." The city needs libraries and art galleries as well as ball parks and places of recreation or amusement.

Martha and Mary are not alone in this experience. Peter was like them in his question about John, "What shall this man do?" He was full of care. Jesus told Peter that John was taken care of and there was no need to worry about the future. And John gave us a gospel of light and beauty out of the time spend in meditation.

The church is in the peril of Martha with its machinery and activist programs. Organizations and agencies multiply, but the church needs to learn afresh the need for this one thing in meditation and rest. The church can appoint committees and yet neglect prayer. It can be noisy, fussy, enterprising, but it labors in vain when it spends its time without true worship and power.

Meditation is the lost art today. Soul culture and spiritual development depend upon time spent with the Bible, prayer, worship, meditation. The distinctive thing in Mary's life in comparison to Martha's was *the absence of worry and the presence of worship.* Modern rush and feverish ways of life are no substitute for the Sunday rest and worship and the private hour with God. Peace and poise of spirit are given to those who are like Mary. Martha limited her advance in the Christian life.

76. Amos—Prophet of Righteousness

"The words of Amos...."—Amos 1:1

A rich method of Bible study and sermon communication is the use of a book at one time. Sometimes the book can be given in terms of its central subject, in this case the prophet Amos. Instead of a text or a paragraph, a whole book is given in one sermon. In this way the message of the book is stressed. Leaving the small canvas with its details, the painter seeks to portray the message in broad sweeping strokes on a large canvas. In these nine chapters is the stern word of a strong man.

I *The Man.* We see him as a shepherd, a man of the country. He is neither a prophet nor the son of a prophet. He is what we would term today a *layman*. Rough in dress and speech, he was not trained as a prophet in some school. His training came out of life with its struggle. He lived in the hills and knew the desert with its caravan routes. We are not to think of him as living an isolated life apart from the busy world around. He knew that world to which he ministered. We recognize him to be in the van of those who are like John the Baptist and others of that kind. If at first we are startled by his appearance and his speech, we are grateful that God raised up this man to stab our conscience.

II. *The Mission.* Amos was like the conscience of the nation Israel. He was a voice for God in a day when other religious leaders were but echoes of words long since dead. He brought no soothing words but proclaimed a divine word from on high. It was the voice of judgment rather than of mercy which thundered forth in no uncertain tones. "As summer fruit" is soon gone, so the Lord will speedily bring an end upon the nation of Israel. "A plumbline" is set to reveal the irregularities of moral life. In burning word and metaphor, with telling illustration, by rapier thrust to the conscience, this man did not spare his people. When the shepherd went a-shearing, who could stand before him? He denounced sin, not in the abstract and not in general terms, but each one was pointed out in particular. His mission was not easy and not a popular one, but he carried it through obediently.

III. *The Message.* His words spoke of the truth that God is impartial, therefore the judgment of God must come upon all, including Israel. Privilege brings responsibility. There is an accountability before God whose moral judgment none can escape.

"If Amos came to town today," what would happen? Imagine him in modern dress coming to Times Square, New York, or standing on the Capitol steps, Washington, D. C. Perhaps he can be viewed against the background of every major city of our land and in the world. Supposing he spoke to *America?* Would he be charged with being "un-American"? Think of some things he would mention as calling for drastic action: Sabbath breaking — trading of all kinds, sports and amusements, disregard of public worship by the majority of the people; liquor bills — the increased indulgence reaching into billions of dollars, the consequent debauchery of social life; women's standards (Amos spoke of "the kine," meaning the women of that day. They indulged in drinking, rich food, ivory couches, low moral standards. Compare today's slump in morals) ; greed of gain — exploitation of the poor, eager for the Sabbath to end to begin profit-making, idolatry of the dollar sign; abuses and injustices in civic and social life comparable to those against which the prophet thundered his message.

Thus Amos denounced the sins of the nation he loved. "You only have I known of all the families of the earth: *therefore* I will punish you. . . ." True, God, through Amos, denounced the sins of other nations — which pleased Israel; but He was severe on His own. We today may judge Russia and other nations, but God's prophet speaks against us who are privileged. "Prepare to meet thy God" is for America as well as communistic Russia. Judgment must begin at the house of God (I Pet. 4:17). Our hypocrisies and selfish withholding from God, our refusal to serve except at our convenience: these and much beside condemn us. We sing hymns to drown the cries of injustice and hypocrisy, but the plumbline is set. We need God's righteousness. *The Plumbline reveals our irregularities.*

The message of Amos is *the righteousness of God.* God is no respecter of persons and of nations. All are equally guilty before Him. His chosen people are in the greater condemnation because of their privileges and opportunities. They are held accountable for their actions. The Christian knows of the plumbline of God in the death and resurrection of Christ. God judges. The call is to repent, return, receive.

77. Burden Bearing

"Every man shall bear his own burden."—Galatians 6:5

The text seems contradictory in the light of verse 2. Verses 2 and 5 are complementary. In verse 2 the word is burden or "weight," sometimes excessive. Here it is burden or "pack," something normal. It is used for the pack or load of the soldier or porter. Compare Matt. 11:28, used by our Lord for the burden He lays on His disciples. This verse tells, then, of the regular daily burden laid upon us. Moffatt translates it as "bear your own load of responsibility." Life is full of this.

I. It is *inevitable*. Life as a burden is often mentioned in regular speech. Our personal responsibility for our actions is obvious. No one escapes this. The solidarity of the race is half a truth; the solitariness of the soul is the other half. As a child carries a doll and we early carry parcels, so life has an instinctive measure of acceptance of the loads of life.

II. It is *inscrutable*. Why? we ask. Seers and prophets have pondered this mystery, and no adequate answer has been found outside of revelation. We speak of the providences of life, meaning the unexplained events which dog our pathway. They are outward as well as inward trials. They are unsought, yet we accept them when they are forced on us. Experience teaches us to adjust to the weight and carry the load.

Some are imaginary. They do not have actuality except in the mind or imagination. We have exaggerated notions and imagine that the world is against us. We are like the weeping willow, with hanging head and drooping spirit. Fears fill the mind.

Some are unnecessary. We make them for ourselves to our own hurt. Refusing to face facts, we spoil our tranquility of mind. We ruin the harmony of life when we secretly hug some upsetting spirit in heart. We do not enjoy life in this bondage.

Some are inescapable. Difficulties do exist. The life we live is not easy. The way is rough and arduous for some. Duty, toil, obligation, discipline — these words frighten some. The back is made for the burden we say. But when it is ours, what then?

III. It is *irrevocable*. No one escapes the normal unalterable upsets in life.

Suffering comes. Ill-health, pain, and handicaps are well known. Hospitals and institutions of healing abound to remind us. *Death* is a spectre for every family. Fear makes it a terrible thing. Strong men are cut off, and the unknown brings fear. *Sorrow* is

linked with these. Grief and tears find expression in the hours of
loss. Mental pain is found with sorrow, questions also. *Poverty*
comes. In a world of plenty there are those who do not have the
necessary food and shelter. Unemployment stalks as a shadow.
Doubt will plague the mind. The thinking youth and the skeptical
heart find this a trial and load. Heresy is not always in doubt.
Sin is the final load, and more than a load — a burden or heavy
weight to crush the soul? We must give account to God.

In carrying our own load of responsibility, no one else can share
in the loneliness of the soul. We must choose and relate ourselves
to actual experiences. There are *two attitudes* for us:

We may murmur as did the Israelites in the wilderness when
they had nothing but manna to eat and sought water. They com-
plained against God in that day. Many grumble in our day.

We may learn, as has been suggested. "No chastening [or load
or discipline] ... seemeth to be joyous, but grievous: nevertheless
afterward it yieldeth the peaceable fruit of righteousness unto
them which are exercised thereby" (Heb. 12:11) .

The load carried can contribute to our deveolpment in strength
and enlarged capacity. As muscles are exercised by their repeated
use, so the sinews of faith are strengthened as we carry our own
load of responsibility. A ship with an empty hold may well dread
a storm. When there is a full load, the ship is better prepared for
any tests. Ballast is necessary then. So with the individual who
would march on the highway of life. Let there be a personal pack
to carry and much is gained.

He who carries his own load is not alone. The Burden-Bearer is
always alongside for the emergency. The yoke accepted brings
enlargement and enrichment afterwards. Every man must carry his
own personal load (cf. Psalm 55) . Not in escape but in acceptance
lies the way of compensation.

78. Burden Sharing

"Bear ye one another's burdens, and so fulfil the law of Christ."
—Galatians 6:2

The context is important for interpretation. Verse 5 speaks of carrying the burden alone. That word means "pack," as a soldier's pack on the march. Here in verse 2 it means "weight," that which is heavier than an individual can carry himself. It is an excessive load, an extra, and therefore becomes a handicap when our capacity is limited. In this light, then, we see the wisdom of the injunction that we should share each other's weights or burdens. The spirit of Christ compels us to act seriously in this matter.

I. The *Problem* of Sharing. Of course we do share with each other! Life is so constituted that no one can carry the whole load alone. Thus we assist each other with the heavier responsibilities of our common life. It is stimulating and relieving when another comes alongside to share our burden. This does not mean that we are relieved of it altogether. We are *released* from the full weight but not *relieved* altogether. The other bearer or sharer does not shift the weight to his shoulders alone but only assumes part of the weight.

God would not have anyone seek to be rid of his own load nor have others encourage his idleness and selfishness. We are to do what we can to make others' burdens tolerable and bearable by sympathetic help and support. Perhaps we judge falsely when we look at others. We see them being helped with their weight, and we think they are having an easy time. We little know how much is behind the looks, actions, habits, and speech. A girl who carries her baby brother is not really carrying "a burden": the child is her brother, and that makes a difference in weight! We may not be wanted when we offer to share with others, and that is part of the problem! Like Philip and the eunuch (Acts 8), we do well in going to the person in apparent need, but we must also wait until that person asks us to help.

II. The *Possibilities* of Sharing. These are unlimited. According to our strength, so is our capacity to help others. The spirit makes the difference. We should weep with those that weep and laugh with those who laugh (rejoice with those that rejoice). The various burdens (see "Burden Bearing") — suffering, death, sorrow, poverty, doubt, and sin — are to be shared. How shall the principle be applied?

Doubt. Instead of criticizing the doubter, learn to listen to him.

Faith may rest in some doubting souls. There is a time of doubt and unbelief which leads to certainty of faith; e.g. Dr. R. A. Dale had a time as a student when he had doubts, and some thought him to be heterodox. John A. James heard Dale and invited him to dinner. Instead of angrily demanding that Dale acquiesce in all that he, James, believed as orthodoxy, he discussed the pros and cons as if they had been equals. Young Dale was saved for the Christian ministry then, because the older man shared the burden.

Paul writes in I Corinthians 8:9-13 about *doubtful questions and practices* and urged that the law of love be applied. We are to share the burden of the weaker brother. When the question of "eating and drinking" is involved, then we are to think, not of ourselves, but of the other in love, and so act on his behalf. "Whatsoever is not of faith is sin" discloses the nature of the weight or burden too heavy to bear alone. All sins are weights, but not all burdens are sinful. Yet the legitimate and good may often rob a life of the best things. Lay aside every weight and the sin which easily besets.

Sin is always a burden. This cannot be carried alone. Only God in Christ can bear this for us. Sin is the greatest, most crushing burden of the soul. John Bunyan, in *The Pilgrim's Progress,* has depicted the sinner with the burden on his back, fleeing from the city of destruction. He comes to the cross, and there the burden falls off and rolls into the sepulchre and is seen no more. The Christian message brings the assurance that Christ has carried that load to the tree of death and now we can be free from it. This is what we mean by atonement and forgiveness.

Burdens shared by Christ bring relief, rest, recoverability, strength, sympathy, satisfaction, salvation. Christ came to "carry away our sin," and thus our burdens are laid upon him once and for all. He is the Burden-Bearer. Then we can become burden-sharers for others in need. This is the law of Christ in love.

79. The Lord's Supper

"This do in remembrance of me. . . ."—I Corinthians 11:24

The ritual of the institution of the Communion is given here by the apostle Paul. He had received it of the Lord and so delivered it to the church in Corinth. From the upper room in Jerusalem to the meeting place in a Grecian city is a long way, but there was continuity and oneness of spirit. What is the significance of the Lord's Supper? There are many elements in the commemoration of this observance. Words such as "covenant, ordinance, sacrament, presence" are used by Christians. Here are a few ideas which interpret the service for us.

I. *Historical:* "received of the Lord . . . delivered unto you." Jesus sought to be known and remembered by this action.

In its *institution*. The Lord Himself originated it. The occasion was the night of His betrayal. The Passover feast was being celebrated. He anticipated His cross and suffering. Only disciples were present. Participation was based on experience of faith in Christ. Love prompted the sharing one with another.

In its *instrumentation:* "bread and wine." These were symbols of the Lord's body and blood, one broken, the other shed. Thus He is present in the elements, which are symbols of faith in His death and sacrifice for sin, which is the central fact of the Christian faith.

II. *Memorial:* "this do in remembrance of me." There are other emphases, but here is selected that of remembrance or memorial. Jesus called His disciples "henceforth . . . not servants . . . but friends." It is the privilege of a friend to keep alive the memory of the one loved. In the Passover the idea was that of looking back to the past and remembering. So in the Lord's Supper, which came out of the Passover, the Christian looks back to the sacrifice of Calvary.

This is a memorial and not a mass. This is a supper and not a sacrifice. It is a feast and not a fast. A table and not an altar is at the center. Here no priest stands between man and God, but all disciples gather around a common meeting place with Christ at the center of their faith. All share in the same elements: "Drink ye *all* of it."

The Protestant-evangelical view is that the Lord's Supper or Communion is not a sacrifice repeated. The elements are not changed. The presence of Christ is real to faith. The memorial centers in Christ Himself, His death. No marble slab, no towering cross, no pillar of granite is here, but the simple elements of bread and wine, universal in observance, perpetual in commemoration, sublime in its simplicity. "A table, not a tomb, He willed our gathering place to be."

III. *Prophetical:* "till he come." The fact of the Second Advent is everywhere on the pages of the New Testament. In our Lord's teaching He spoke of that event to come. Here in the final act of remembrance He includes the *hope* of His sure return. The Cross is linked with the Communion and connects with the Coming, bearing witness, not only to the work of the First Advent, but also to the hope of the Second Advent.

It is important to think of this hope in Christ. At the table we look back in faith to the sacrifice of the Cross for redemption. We also look up in love to the priestly ministry of Christ before the throne of God. Then we look on in hope to His coming again. "Every man that hath this hope in him purifieth himself, even as he is pure." Between the Cross and the Coming is set the Communion.

IV. *Evangelical:* "ye shew forth the Lord's death." As often as we observe this feast of Communion, we also proclaim or announce the message of the gospel. "Preaching is truth through personality" (Phillips Brooks). At the Lord's Supper we are preaching and proclaiming the heart of the gospel. Each one sharing in it is a preacher! Here we confess our faith, "I believe." Who listens or sees this? Godward we confess faith before God. Manward we proclaim to onlookers and the world outside that we confess Christ as Saviour and Lord. In this act we are *witnesses* unto Christ (Acts 1:8).

As in the first observance, so we today sing our hymns of praise (cf. Jesus singing the Hallel, Pss. 113-118).

To share in this feast, "let a man examine himself . . ." (vs. 28). The presence of Christ makes the feast. We gather in His name and we gather unto Him. With heart right, life yielded, will obedient, we worship and adore the living Christ, whom we remember in love.

80. On Facing Again the Old Difficulties

"They returned again to Lystra,... Iconium, and Antioch."
—Acts 14:21

To retrace our steps back again to the familiar places and oft traversed pathway may bring joy. This is the mood of Sir Walter Scott's *Lay of the Last Minstrel*. Or the way back may be with humiliation and regret, as in the mood of the Prodigal Son. In this text we trace the mood of *courage* and *faith,* for the servants of God retraced their steps in the face of trial and trouble, persecution and opposition.

I. The *Outward* Journey. A comparison of the experience of Paul and Barnabas suggests:

From Antioch to Antioch in Pisidia. See Acts 13:14 for the latter place, where *a mixed reception* awaited them. They speak in the synagogue, and the whole city is stirred. Some believe the message, but there are certain religious people who reject and persecute, and thus they are *expelled* from the city. In modern times similar situations occur in countries where vested religious interests object to the evangelical gospel.

From Antioch in Pisidia to Iconium. See Acts 14:1-5 for a divided city, where *a mob attacks* them. They are assaulted and despitefully used. Finally they are *stoned,* and they *must flee.*

From Iconium to Lystra. See Acts 14:6-20 for the details of the miracle of healing, the resultant *belief and opposition.* This climaxes in *stoning* and then Paul is *left as dead.* The cure of the cripple so impressed the people and their pagan priest that they sought to burn sacrifices to Barnabas as Zeus (king of the gods), and to Paul as Hermes (messenger of the gods). Only quick action and strong words from Paul saved them from being *worshipped.* Soon after, the same Lystrans hurled stones to kill. Paul recovered, and believers assisted him on his way.

II. The *Return* Journey. The map should be consulted as guide to the location of the places mentioned and the route followed by the missionaries. Paul and Barnabas had established a bridgehead on the enemy's territory, and the toll was high in the price paid.

The first missionary journey was an expedition with an easy way to return to the strategic base of operations. *Antioch from Derbe* was direct and not long. Then why did they choose to retrace their steps *from Derbe,* through Lystra, Iconium, Antioch

171

(Pisidia), Pamphylia, Perga, and Attalia? Why the long road instead of that which was conveniently near at hand? These intrepid men went 20 miles to Lystra, 40 miles to Iconium, 60 miles to Antioch (Pisidia); and then by ship to Antioch. They went out of the way, in difficult, dangerous, impossible journeying. The answer is: the first mile is duty, the second mile is love. *They faced again the old situations with courage.* The reasons can be traced out in this chapter:

First, they *confirmed the faith of disciples.* Second, they *encouraged new Christians in devotion.* Third, they *appointed elder-leaders in each congregation.* In each place it was necessary to instruct, strengthen, guide. A true shepherd thinks of the flock (and the lambs). Paul was not a hireling. Returning to face the stones of Lystra, the threats of Iconium, and the expulsion of Antioch proved the vitality of Christian faith. It is impressive to see this return not as some foolhardy if inadequate cause. There was a cause; and, in devotion to God's will, duty dictated they return that way. The kingdom of God comes through much tribulation.

Paul and Barnabas returned for the sake of the converts. The peril of fanaticism, the threat of stoning again: these did not frighten or intimidate them. Quietly and courageously they went over the same treacherous ground to carry out their mandate for missions. When we estimate the cost of missions, let us not overlook the lives involved. Money is needed, but the financial outlay to spread the gospel around the world is not to be compared with the cost of lives. In every land there are lonely graves where pioneers sacrificed their all.

We learn that the pathway of duty in the will of God is the only safe place in spite of dangers. The open door has many adversaries, but the church still advances through storm and stress. In all walks of life the Christian may have to return to the place of failure and defeat in order to wrest victory and overcome the foe — back to loneliness, misunderstanding, opposition. What a story Paul and Barnabas had to tell when they returned finally to Antioch and told the church all that *God* had done!

81. When Neutrality Is Sin

"Thou stoodest on the other side. . . ."—Obadiah 11

The twenty-one verses of this little book of the prophet deal with the judgment of Edom and the restoration of Israel. It is the shortest of the Old Testament prophecies, but within its brief compass are some arresting words such as are found in this text. They suggest the unenviable position of anyone, nation or individual, standing on the opposite side of the right and just cause by refusing to be committed to the highest and the best under God.

I. *History* furnishes examples of this as the prophet reminds us.

Esau and Jacob were brothers, and the story of their feud is well known. By bartered birthright and profane life the former takes the way of the flesh as against the latter in his way of faith. When Esau has become Edom, a nation, he does violence to Jacob, and in the day of Israel's struggle Edom stands aloof and subsequently becomes one of their enemies. Edom is unbrotherly by neutrality and takes advantage of the spoil. The last of the Edomites was Herod, usurper king in Jerusalem, on the side against the One born to be King.

Other instances in history are familiar. When Armenians were massacred by Turks, there were nations which stood aloof. When little Belgium was in jeopardy in 1914, there were those who took the same attitude. Roger Casement in England and Benedict Arnold in America have names stained by reason of their traitor acts when they "stood on the other side."

II. *The Bible* is no more interesting than when we find in it portraits of those who were guilty of standing aloof. Almost a rogues' gallery can be discerned! Think of Israel flirting with false godlings and being uncertain about the God of Joshua, or halting between two opinions at Mount Carmel before Elijah and found on the other side with Baal worship. Achan was guilty of this when he hid the stuff in his tent and implicated a whole nation under God's judgment. Balaam was proved a weak and false prophet by his intrigue with the other side. When Peter denied his Lord by the fire, he was on the other side. The Parable of the Good Samaritan censures a certain priest and a Levite who passed by on the other side. Joseph of Arimathaea is a good character, but once approbrium stained his fair name because he was a disciple but secretly: he was on the other side. Even the apostle Paul stood aloof when as Saul of Tarsus he consented to the death of Stephen.

173

What shall we say about Annas and Caiaphas, subtle and full of guile? of Pilate, compromising, cowardly, and a time-server? of Herod — "that fox"? of his mistress, whose caprice and lust killed a great and a good man? of Judas, the betrayer of his Master? of Ananias and Sapphira, liars? of Demas, who forsook apostleship for love of the world? All these stood on the other side. What a company!

III. *Individuals* today are the same as yesterday. Human nature has not changed. We are called upon to take our stand and declare ourselves against the vested interests of the drink traffic with its ill-gotten gain and its indulgent living, the gambling fever with its demoralization of life, and many other questions relating to honesty, purity, and right conduct. Then it is that some stand aloof, afraid to be known by any conviction. They watch how the wind blows to steer a safe course without inconvenience. Martin Luther was great because he crowned the hours of crisis by a great decision.

John Bunyan depicts Mr. Pliable in *The Pilgrim's Progress*, after his exit from the Slough of Despond, getting out of the mire on that side which was nearer to his own house. Later some of the neighbors visited him and called him a wise man for coming back, so Pliable sat sneaking among them. At last he got confidence, and he, with them, derided poor Christian, who had gone on the pilgrimage. Thus Pliable stood on the other side.

Some do not admit what they believe. They are afraid to be known as Christians. Neutrality means standing against Christ — on the other side. The final sin which keeps a man from Jesus Christ is the same as Edom's — *pride!* Getting on without God and self-sufficient, kindly disposed toward the church but aloof from any commitment — that is to be aloof and lost. He who decides and commits is saved. He who is neutral, as Pilate washing his hands, is casting his vote against Christ — on the other side.

Where do we stand? On which side are we? It matters.

82. Running Away From God

"Whither shall I flee from thy presence?"—Psalm 139:7

One of the predicaments of modern man is his temptation to seek a way of escape from life. Some seek it in the passing of time through the reading of fiction, some by the illusion created by indulgence in liquor, and others by pleasure which brings frustration. The Old Testament tells of three men who sought to flee. They were running away from God and His will for them.

I. *Jacob* Running Away from God through *the Sin of Deceit* (Gen. 27:43-44). The saga of Jacob is fascinating for its human drama. It reveals much about human nature in the focus on this one man.

Family Deception. Jacob deceives his father, Isaac, and his brother, Esau. Trace what goes on in many families today.

Business Duplicity. Jacob tricks and cheats his father-in-law, Laban (Gen. 30:20). Consider today's sharp practices in business.

Religious Deceit — Hypocrisy. Jacob tried to play with God at the Jabbok and Peniel (Gen. 32:22-32). What an unmasking of religious hypocrisy! God reached Jacob at Bethel (Gen. 28:11) *in sleep on the moor.* Here is the dream and the ladder and the presence of God for Jacob. Victor Hugo, George Eliot, Nathaniel Hawthorne, and William Shakespeare are alike in unmasking the nemesis of sin in human life. They found that in the Bible revelation. Man reaps what he sows in sin.

II. *Elijah* Running Away from God through *Failure in Despondency* (I Kings 19:3). The prophet who stood alone for God in a crooked generation is now:

Despondent under a Juniper Tree ("take away my life..."). The demon of discouragement is still with us and stalks many people.

Quailing at the Threat of Evil, Immoral, Idolatrous Jezebel. How often we fail at the threat of evil, imagining it to be all-powerful!

Mistaken in Judgment ("I, even I only, am life"). He was wrong as men are wrong today in thinking the cause of God retreats.

God reached Elijah in the wilderness in Judea (I Kings 19:5) *in sleep under a tree.* He was asked of God, "Why are you here?" (He was not at the post of duty!) The wind, the earthquake, the fire, and then the still small voice of God brought peace and the lifting up of the heart. We, today, may run when dispirited or lose heart in the midst of work. Let us remember that God is near and ready to help when we are alone.

III. *Jonah* Running Away from God through *Pride of Disobedience* (Jonah 1:3). This story in four chapters is a missionary tale of how God would reach the unevangelized heathen and needs a servant to work.

Disliked *Duty* Given Him Regarding Nineveh. The great city of that day numbered hundreds of thousands, but Jonah disliked them.

Disliked the *Sphere of Service*. His pride and prejudice were stronger than his faith in God, hence his refusal to go.

Disliked the *People* Who Needed God Most. A prophet who changes God's command forfeits the right to lead others.

God reached Jonah in a storm at sea (Jonah 1) *in sleep in a ship*. Florence Nightingale said: "I never said 'No' to God." That was the key to her great life. Jonah said "No" to God at first. What is happening in the church today when men say "No" to God?

Conclusion: Here are three men running away from God as they ran away from life and its responsibilities. Note that God caught up with them in sleep *on a moor, under a tree,* and *in a ship.* The psalmist (139:8-12) tells that no one can escape God anywhere.

Compare "The Hound of Heaven" by Francis Thompson:

> I fled Him, down the nights and down the days;
> I fled Him, down the arches of the years;
> I fled Him, down the labyrinthine ways
>   Of my own mind; and in the midst of tears
> I hid from Him, and under running laughter.
>   Up vistaed slopes, I sped;
>   And shot, precipitated
> Adown Titanic glooms of chasmed fears,
>   From those strong Feet that followed, followed after.
>   But with unhurrying chase,
>   And unperturbed pace,
>   Deliberate speed, majestic instancy,
>   They beat — and a Voice beat
>   More instant than the Feet —
> "All things betray thee, who betrayest Me."

In *contrast* to those who ran, see *Jesus,* who set His face to go to Jerusalem. Unlike Jonah, He did His duty: "A Greater than Jonah is here." Unlike Elijah, He did not fail: "A Greater than Elijah is here." Unlike Jacob, He did not sin: "A Greater than Jacob is here."

Those who run away from life and from God find that God is also there in the sphere to which they go. "Behold, thou art there." God is inescapable; and, in the Holy Spirit, He follows after us

83. By Way of Interpretation

"An interpreter, one among a thousand...."—Job. 33:23

Elihu's words to Job are among the most important in that dramatic epic. In the midst of the problem under study Job is not helped very much by his three friends who counsel him. But once in a while a word stands out of significant worth. Here is one that sends a searchilght of truth over all life.

We find the same idea in John 1:38, 42, 43; John 9:7; and Hebrews 7:2. The Greek word used is *hermēneuō*, from which comes our term "hermeneutics," which is "the science of interpretation." By interpretation we come to understand life's values. The idea is to explain or translate into our understanding.

John Bunyan, in *The Pilgrim's Progress*, has the Pilgrim in an attractive and inviting experience: "Pilgrim went on till he came at the house of the Interpreter, where he knocked over and over; at last one came to the door, and asked who was there. 'Christian, Sir, a traveller.... I would speak with the master of the house.... I was told ... that if I called here you would shew me excellent things, such as would be helpful to me in my journey.' Then said the Interpreter, 'Come in; I will shew thee that which will be profitable to thee.' "

The Holy Spirit is the Interpreter. He is the Guide into all truth. His function is to lead the Christian into all the truth as it is in Jesus Christ, to shew us things to come, and to bring to our remembrance the things concerning Christ. The apostles were promised this by Jesus before the ascension. The ascension brought this fulfilment of the coming of the Spirit to carry out these promises and to continue the work of our Lord in the church and in the world.

In travel abroad there is need of an interpreter because of the differences in language, customs, and culture. When William Carey, India, and Robert Morrison, China, spent their best years as missionaries, they concentrated on the languages and dictionaries. Their legacy lay in grammars, dictionaries, and translations of the Bible for missionaries to use coming after them. They were interpreters. A teacher at school, a mother at home, the linguist in the army — these are interpreters for some. So we find the Holy Spirit our Interpreter as we read and study the Bible. Jesus in the wilderness and Paul in Arabia knew the secrets of interpretation: the latter, "to reveal Christ in me."

What are some of the areas for interpretation? Imagine a church group or congregation seeking light and knowledge. There are seven (among many) subjects demanding attention:

177

I. *What is a Christian?* Discuss the implications of the use of the word for Christian and the three times used in the New Testament for its meaning within the context when first used. See it in relation to all the other names and descriptions given to the followers of Jesus.

II. *What is the church?* Relate the New Testament concepts of this word as used over its development. When did the church begin? Was it at Pentecost or had there been a church before that? (Cf. Old Testament.) What are the marks of the church? What is its root idea? Take nothing for granted here. Study and compare the ideas of "kingdom, people, family, covenant, bride, building, assembly, elect."

III. *Why do men suffer?* An important theme, sure to be discussed by people. Many seek help concerning the mystery. Is suffering because of sin? because of self? because of others? or is there anything beyond these ideas? Why do the innocent suffer? Is that the right question to ask? Why not? Why do they suffer *with God?"*

God is the suffering God. The cross of Jesus must be seen if we are to find light upon the mystery of suffering.

IV. *Why the death of the cross?* Was it as a martyr or an example Jesus died? Was it as a sacrifice on behalf of others? What has sin to do with this? Do the seven words from the cross explain why He died? What benefits come from that strange and mysterious death? How are we related to that death and why?

V. *What is beyond death?* Is death the end of life? Why do we think there is another life beyond? What is its form and nature? What does the New Testament interpret for us in this regard? What do we mean by immortality and the resurrection of the body? What is heaven or hell?

VI. *What is prayer?* Is this a practical way of getting things from God? Or is this an experience of something else? Does God answer prayer? If so, why and how? What change comes to us by prayer — in us?

VII. The church, the preacher, and the teacher are interpreters, but the determining factor of your life is your deduction from their interpretations. What is *your* interpretation?

84. How Do You Judge?

"It is a very small thing that I should be judged of you, or of man's judgment: yea, I judge not mine own self ... but he that judgeth me is the Lord."—I Corinthians 4:3, 4

The Christian life is a judged life. Our Lord said, "Judge not, that ye be not judged." He referred to censorious criticism, sinful prejudice. Paul has something else in mind. He would have us reflect upon the four basic judgments of life.

I. *The Judgment of Self, the Tribunal of Conscience:* "mine own self." Here is self-imposed discipline, not in cloister or cell, not in scourging or whipping. An unhealthy subjectivism is not in view.

The conscience is the basis of our self-scrutiny. Bishop Butler said: "Conscience is that reflective principle with which we judge our acts. Conscience has authority and supremacy but not necessarily power. If it had power it would govern the world. This principle of reflection in every man which distinguishes, passes judgment, and magisterially exerts itself is not merely a judgment *of* fact, but also something judicial: it is a judgment *upon* fact."

Paul could judge himself but refuses to exercise the right: "I know nothing by myself" (vs. 4). "I do not cross-question myself; for, although I am not conscious of having anything against me, that does not clear me" (Moffatt translation). Paul was not aware of guilty knowledge against himself. Failure to be conscious of one's own sins doesn't mean that one is innocent: most prisoners plead "not guilty." No man of himself can estimate his worth and work.

II. *The Judgment of Friends, the Tribunal of the Church:* "judged of you."

Corinth was divided in its leadership and biased views. All life has bias. Faith is bias. We begin life like this. Yet Paul recognized the worth of this seat of judgment, the community of believers. The home has intimate relationships: husband, wife, parents, children, masters, servants; and he writes about these minds. Is it possible to equate aright the value of each other? The church is constantly passing judgment upon its members and the community. This is not censorious judgment but loving discernment in the mind of Christ (2:16).

Consider the story of Toplady, who spoke of John Wesley as "a low and puny tadpole in divinity." "A designing wolf" is the word of Rowland Hill, who thought Wesley "unprincipled as a rock and silly as a jackdaw." Why this difference in judgment?

179

III. *The Judgment of the World, the Tribunal of Public Opinion:* "man's judgment."

In the city of Aberdeen, Scotland, is the motto: "They say, What do they say? Let them say!" *They* in this case stands for the crowd, which is ever judging and criticizing the Christian, to Paul "a very small thing," counting for very little. The crowd judges cruelly, harshly, unkindly, unforgivingly. Let a Christian make a mistake, and his good is forgotten and despised. Paul doesn't deny or despise public opinion, but he denies its competency to pass final judgment on his credentials as a man of God.

Public opinion has arraigned and hanged the innocent, excused the guilty, and compromised in the spirit of the age. Democracy's peril is in levelling off, making everyone alike, obliterating the finer distinctions of moral conduct and righteous standards. Christianity assists the individual to be himself and not a robot in this age of conformity in society and life.

IV. *The Judgment of God, the Trbunal of the Eternal:* the Lord judges — the highest, the truest, the most complete and competent.

Judging *Now* — "he that judgeth me" — presently, every day, continuously, at each, act, in every hour of devotion and worship.

Judgment *to Come* (vs. 5) — a time coming for final judgment: "Judge nothing before the time." At the Second Advent of Christ, in the day of judgment, before the judgment seat of Christ, we shall stand. "The judge standeth before the door" (Jas. 5:9).

Judgment *Revealing:* "bring to light ... make manifest" — the difference between man's day and Christ's day of judgment. The investigation of our inner life is thorough and begins at house of God.

Paul in this context pleads for fidelity, faithfulness on the part of God's people. He didn't regard the judgments of others as comparable to Christ's. An ambassador may attach some importance to the national or local opinion where he is stationed abroad, but he reports home: it is what Washington thinks that matters. *We have to report home* to God, and it is the Judge we face even as we serve Him. The gladiator in the Roman arena didn't mind whether the thumbs of the crowd were up or down (life or death). He looked to the center dais, whereon sat the emperor. Verse 2: it is required, expected, demanded, that a steward in the house be faithful.

85. Martin Luther – Protestant Reformer

"The just shall live by his faith. . . ."—Habakkuk 2:4

On November 10, 1483, the subject of this message was born. In spite of the aspersions cast upon him by those writers who object to his contribution, the place and greatness of Luther is secure in history. We measure him against the background of the ages. Perhaps he will be even greater in the future as time justifies his thesis concerning the liberty of the Christian man in a world threatened by totalitarianism. Thomas Carlyle said that "Luther's experience was one of the greatest moments in modern history."

I. As a *Monk*. View him as a member of the Roman church of the medieval age. In that context we must judge his early years.

Calling. Born at Eisleben, son of a poor miner, he later went to school at Eisenach, Germany. At Erfurt University he studied law. Suddenly he entered a monastery. Why? Doubt makes a monk. Fear filled his mind about the future life, and he sought peace. From childhood he had a picture of God as a merciless Judge. Now he becomes a monk, not to study theology alone, but *to save his soul!* He was exemplary, fasting, scourging himself, reading the Schoolmen, but neglecting the Bible; thus he had no peace.

Crisis. His superior, Staupitz, advised Luther to get the Bible and find faith instead of works. As Luther read, especially the *Letter to the Romans,* the light began to break. After a struggle of two years he found what he sought. As Professor at Wittenberg he proved "difficult" to the authorities so was asked to visit Rome. There in 1511 he had his eyes opend about the papal life. The text of Habakkuk, echoed by Romans 1:17 (Paul), struck home to conscience as he made the pilgrimage. He went to Rome a medieval monk; he returned a protestant believer. He went believing in works for salvation; he returned convinced that salvation was by faith alone.

II. As a *Reformer.*

Luther remained a loyal member of the Roman church at this time. He sought to live and teach by the new faith.

Preacher and teacher. At Wittenberg he taught *experimental theology,* preaching against indulgences. John Tetzel, a leader of Rome, came selling indulgences. Luther protested, and on All Saints Day, November 1, he nailed ninety-five theses on the church door, an academic procedure. Copies were circulated. Luther challenged Tetzel to debate and won. He wrote *Liberty of the Christian Man,* emphasizing *the priesthood of all believers.* He was called to Germany. The pope issued a bull against him, and he was excommunicated, as he did not change his mind. December 10, 1520, he burned the papal bull, and in that fire modern history began for multitudes.

Defender of the faith. At his trial at Diet of Worms, 1521, death threatened him, but he wrote to Spalatin he would "come to Worms if there were as many devils as tiles on houses." He refused to recant in trial and spoke the memorable words: "Here I stand: I can do none else: God help me! Amen." As a prisoner he was protected at Wartburg Castle through his friends, and there he translated the Bible into German. His life and writings were under a ban, but nothing stopped him from writing. The Peasants' War came with its upheaval and tragic years, but Luther went on with his work. Later, as a pastor and married, he wrote and preached for all of Germany to learn the way of evangelical religion. The Roman Mass was abolished largely, and protestant forms of worship appeared. The Bible in the vernacular was circulated, and pastors were trained after Luther's model. The protestant way of religion and faith held sway. Thomas Carlyle said that "Luther was a great man: in intellect, courage, affection, integrity; great as a mountain is great."

III. *As a Christian.* This is the heart and secret of the reformer and protestant. History reveals no kinglier man than the man who was a miner's son. The *Reformation* under Luther was *a revival* of true religion. Worship of God was made an act of the conscience and according to the light of Holy Scripture. No priest now intervened; no indulgences were sold; no works atoned for salvation. Direct access to God was possible. Right of private judgment was upheld. Authority of Scripture was asserted. The soul was justified by faith alone. This evangelical principle was proved to be adequate for the individual without any system. God was Lord of the conscience, and grace prevailed. Protesting against abuses, Luther led men to affirm their faith in Christ as Saviour.

86. Sacrifice and Song

"When the burnt offering began, the song of the Lord began."
—II Chronicles 29:27

This is both a description of historical event in the Old Testament and a principle for all time. In Hezekiah's day the Temple was cleansed and worship renewed. The nation was called back to the central things of faith and devotion (vs. 31), where they were to bring sacrifices and thank offerings as they consecrated themselves to God.

Our gifts are in vain apart from the gift of ourselves. Out of the various offerings of Israel, the burnt offering spoke of the need of perfect dedication. Complete devotion to God is implied in this act. In this light we recognize the principle that song comes after sacrifice.

I. *In Egypt Israel had no song.* There they groaned under taskmasters. Deliverance came through the sacrifice of the Passover and the crossing of the Red Sea: then the song of Miriam and the women took place. "Sing ye to the Lord, for he hath triumphed gloriously." "Then sang Moses and the children of Israel this song unto the Lord" (Exod. 15:1).

II. *In the Land of Promise Israel had no song.* There were periods of declension and backsliding. Then the nation neglected God and broke His commandments. Only when a king like Hezekiah or Josiah led the people back to God in repentance did they find their song. Spiritual declension was rife in the midst of ritual and formalism. The Temple lost its supremacy as the center of worship, and idolatry seduced the nation. Only when the channels of sacrifice and worship were reopened did they find the song of the Lord again.

III. *The Christian church had no song when in decline.* Different periods of church history testify that, when the church was at ease and complacent, the song died away. Only when the church was under persecution and trial has revival come. Preceding the Reformation, there were dark days of no song. When Luther and the Reformation came, the songs of the Lord were heard once more. "A Mighty Fortress Is Our God" is the best known of that period.

Before the eighteenth century and the Evangelical Revival in England there was no song in the churches. Deism and decadence swept the land, and the song of the Lord was heard no more. Then came the Wesleys and Whitefield with the glad tidings of salvation. The message of the Cross was heard again and Christ was exalted.

The "burnt offerings" of John Wesley's preaching resulted in the "song" of Charles Wesley with his over 6,000 hymns. The best known is "Jesus, Lover of My Soul." The Revival set the multitudes to singing.

Paul wrote in prison, and through his sacrifice there came a new song in the night. "Philippians," with its note of *joy,* came from a Roman prison. The fellowship of the sufferings of Christ brought the power of the Resurrection.

IV. *The disciples had no song as they faced the cross.* Knowing the forthcoming death of Jesus brought sorrow and gloom. The song died away. They did not wish this to happen. Then it was that Jesus led them in the Passover feast and the Lord's Supper with its *Hallel* of praises from the Psalms 113-118. "And when they had sung an hymn, they went out unto the mount of Olives" (Matt. 26:30). After the solemn Supper, the sacred Song. After the death of the cross came the resurrection morning with its joy and song. "Lift up your heads, O ye gates..." (Ps. 24). Paul teaches that in the Lord's Supper we are to "keep the feast...." This implies also a song after sacrifice.

V. *Song comes after sacrifice,* music after mercy. When a soul is forgiven and the release to the spirit comes, there is the upsurge of thaksgiving in song. Hezekiah not only sang: he wrote songs of praise. Isaiah 38:20: "The Lord was ready to save me: therefore we will sing my songs to the stringed instruments all the days of our life in the house of the Lord." The hymn book of the Hebrews is unsurpassed in the 150 psalms. They were born in sacrifice, exile, persecution.

Today the Christian can offer *himself* as a burnt offering (Rom. 12:1). Dedication of body includes all powers of soul.

We can offer our *substance* (Neh. 8:10). Gifts to God's work bring a resultant song of joy and gladness.

We can offer our *wills* (Acts 16:25). Whatever our lot, we can learn to trust God and sing songs in the night.

Have we a song? Do we sing from the heart? Is our singing based upon sacrifice?

87. Who Are the Saints?

"To the saints ... at Ephesus ... in Christ...."—Ephesians 1:1
"To the saints ... in Christ ... at Philippi...."—Philippians 1:1
"To the saints ... in Christ ... at Colosse...."—Colossians 1:2

A common belief is that church people will some day become saints. Only when a Christian reaches heaven is there the possibility of achievement. A reading of Romans 1:7 and I Corinthians 1:2 in the King James Version supports this view where the text reads "called *to be* saints." But the words "to be" are in italics and therefore should not be used to find the truth. The Christian is not called *to be* a saint in the future life: he *is called* "saint" now!

I. *The Saints* — "to the saints." Paul's letters are addressed to those who are so named. At the first the followers of Jesus were known as "the people of the way"; then they were nicknamed "Christians." Other terms were used: e.g., "disciples," "brethren," "believers," and, collectively, "the church" or "people of God." "Christian" is used only three times in the New Testament, whereas the word "saints" is found sixty-two times.

The word frightens the modern as though it were too high in attainment for ordinary people. Others rebel against it in their rebound from the thought of being "canonized" and seeming to be different from others and on a pedestal. Because some have used it and talked about it and at the same time have done unholy things, we have passed it by. But we need to recover the meaning and relevance today.

The word simply means that which has been *separated unto God*. We should get rid of the medieval idea of sainthood with its nimbus and dressing up! Every Christian is a saint now in God's sight. He has separated us unto Himself. We are God's workmanship and property. Common life is "sanctified." We see it as God's dwelling place. His Spirit indwells, and we live "under orders." The whole of life becomes "holy" and sacred.

II. *Their Sphere* — "in Rome ... Corinth ... Ephesus ... Philippi ... Colosse." Not in stained glass, not in pictures or frescoes, but in real life we meet the saints. The word "saint" in the singular is not found in the New Testament. We have "saints" because saints live together in community and fellowship, the communion of saints.

In Rome there were saints in Caesar's household. Nero the despot did not know that among his slaves and soldiers were those who would outlive him and change his empire.

In Corinth, the city of commerce and shipping, saints gathered to find the love of Christ. Vice and immorality were overcome in the transforming power of a living Saviour.

In Ephesus the little flock became mightier than the Temple of Diana with its pagan worship and idolatry.

In Philippi the garrison town was invaded by a commando force of people who brought new life and joy.

In Colossae, where the crossroads of nations and people met, the cross was proclaimed with Christ pre-eminent.

The saints were found in all parts of the world because they were commanded to go to the uttermost parts. Today we find saints in all lands and places. Are there any in Moscow, Shanghai, Bombay, San Paulo, Tokyo, and Manila as well as New York, Washington, Toronto, or London? We find them in all walks of life, and we can worship with them in the different meeting places which provide opportunities for fellowship. In market place, business, recreation, music, art, and government as well as in hours of worship we may contact saints working for their Lord.

III. *Their Secret* — "in Christ." These two words are found some 164 times in the New Testament. Saints have the same secret of life and nature. "A man in Christ" describes it.

This is an *experience*. When sin is forgiven, when new life is given, when Christ becomes Master, we are "hid with Christ in God." Paul spoke of those who were "in Christ before me." He regretted his late experience and the wasted years.

This is an *environment*. Place a poker in the fire and soon the fire is in the poker. We live and breathe in air, and the atmosphere and the air is in us also. We are in Christ, and Christ is in us.

The secret finds outlet in wondrous truths. We are justified in Christ, sanctified in Christ, separated in Christ, liberated in Christ, exalted in Christ, joyful in Christ, raised in Christ. We shall be glorified in Christ.

> Christ! I am Christ's! and let the name suffice you,
> Ay, for me too He greatly hath sufficed.
> **Frederic W. H. Myer,** Saint Paul

88. The Potter and the Clay

"He wrought a work on the wheels. And the vessel that he made of clay was marred in the hand of the potter: so he made it again another vessel, as seemed good to the potter to make it."
—Jeremiah 18:3, 4

The prophet was invited to visit the potter's house. There he saw a simple arrangement: two wheels, one above another, connected by a vertical shaft, and a lower wheel worked by the potter's foot. In this way the upper wheel was turned, on which, with his hands, he was shaping a vessel of clay.

I. The *Interpretation*. This occupation reveals God's principle of action with men. The chapter tells of God's dealings with Judah and Judah's choice and end. The potter is God; the clay represents men; the hands are God's; and the wheels are circumstances.

The potter has *power over* the clay. God has power over men. His sovereignty is revealed.

The potter has *a plan for* the clay. God has a plan and purpose for us. A planned life is thus offered to us.

The *clay may resist* the potter. Man may frustrate God's plan. Man's free will is emphasized.

The *potter can remake* the marred clay. God renews life when yielded to His control. Sufficiency of God unfolded.

II. The *Exposition*. In the light of the context we can trace the unfolding:

Nationally. The clay represents Israel, pliable, weak, yielding, becoming brittle and unyielding. The history of Israel corroborates this: in Egypt, in the wilderness, in Palestine, in captivity, a scattered people yet under the molding hand of God; a race of slaves delivered, made a nation, trained, and given a law; a sense of calling and election until "marred" by disobedience and idolatry. (Cf. Rom. 11:15 — "If the casting away of them [Israel] be the reconciling of the world, what shall the receiving of them be, but life from the dead?")

Particularly (vss. 11-17). This refers to Judah. God had to lay them aside a while (vs. 6 — "Cannot I do with you as this potter? . . . As clay is in the potter's hand, so are ye in mine . . ."). There is interaction in this. God doesn't decree the fate of Judah capriciously, but Judah's fatalistic conception of life apart from God, by spurning His way, resulted in hardening until misshapen without beauty or design, she is cast off, a mere semblance of what was in the mind of the potter.

God is the great Artificer of nations as well as of individuals as
is indicated in Isaiah 45:5 spoken of Cyrus, King of Persia — "I
girded thee, though thou hast not known me." Also in Rom.
9:20-21 — "Nay but, O man, who art thou that repliest against
God? Shall the thing formed say to him that formed it, Why hast
thou made me thus? Hath not the potter power over clay; of the
same lump to make one vessel unto honour, and another unto dis-
honour?" Joseph, in Egypt, acknowledged this truth when he said
to his brothers, "So ... it was not you that sent me hither, but
God."

III. The *Application*. In this context we see (1) the sovereignty
of God and (2) the will of man. This is neither fatalism nor
chance. God molds but does not mar life. It is not the fault of the
potter if he finds a kink in the clay, this unyielding substance
which resists. But the potter can remold into a new work, less
honorable than the original design; or, if hopelessly marred, he
can break it and cast it away, then use fresh clay to make a new
vessel. The prophet pleads for the former.

"So he made it again ... as seemed good to the potter." What
he chooses to do, he has a right to do. Unlike clay, man has intelligence and will. What shall the free agent do in relation to the
sovereign will of God? (1) Acknowledge weakness. We have no
power to shape life finally. (2) Acquiesce to the will of God. We
may act and will to be. God is the God of love.

> I worship thee, sweet will of God,
> And all thy ways adore;
> And every day I live, I learn
> To love thee more and more.

When the clay was powerless, no explanation is given about its
marring. The fact stated, the potter doesn't abandon the clay;
he makes it over again, as it seems good to the potter.

"The wheels" refer to circumstances, and these affect our lives.
"The hand of God" refers to providences in which God moves in
mysterious ways.

> He fixed thee mid this dance,
> Of plastic circumstance,
> This present, thou, forsooth, wouldst fain arrest;
> Machinery just meant,
> To give thy soul its bent,
> Try thee and turn thee forth, sufficiently impressed.
> **Robert Browning**

> Have Thine own way, Lord! Have Thine own way!
> Thou are the Potter; I am the clay.
> Mold me and make me after Thy will,
> While I am waiting, yielded and still.
> **Adelaide A. Pollard**

89. Hilarious Giving

"God loveth a cheerful giver."—II Corinthians 9:7

"How shall we raise money?" was a question asked. Quickly the answer came: "Don't raise it: give it!" In that answer is the solution for the needs of the church. There is a theology of the collection. It was not incongruous for Paul to pass from the Alpine heights of resurrection apologetic in I Corinthians 15 to speak in I Corinthians 16: "Now concerning the collection...." Giving is part of the Christian life. We might question the genuineness of a profession if this be absent. God gave, and gives, so we.

I. The *Position* of Giving: "this grace [gift, marg.]" (II Cor. 8:19). When linked to the truth of resurrection, a lofty aspiration is assumed for this act of worship.

Spiritual: "Now concerning the collection..." (I Cor. 16:1-2). No lowering of standards to speak of money in this connection. Much devotion, so-called, is weak at the time of the offering. An acid test of consecration is how we handle money. Is it a spiritual act in how we use it?

Sacred: "first gave their own selves to the Lord" (II Cor. 8:5). Gifts receive value from life-offering. Motive and attitude are revealed in how we give. A sense of stewardship is vital. We do not please men but God. The money of the Christian is dedicated. Is that of the ungodly? Question the appeal to the world for money.

Sacrificial: "grace" (II Cor. 8:7-12). A disposition of the spirit is implied. We are to abound in this grace as well as other Christian virtues. As proof of love to God and in gratitude, we give as we recall His unspeakable Gift.

II. The *Privilege* of Giving: "all" (II Cor. 8:7-8; 9:7). No one has a right to seek exemption from this grace. We should not leave to others what we can do. Whether small or large in man's sight is not the factor to be considered, but whether we are honest with God and do not rob Him. II Corinthians 9:1-4, 12-15, show how some of the poor gave largely because of their faith and thus became strong and rich in spiritual influence. The young should be taught to give as well as the poor.

III. The *Proportion* of Giving: "as God hath prospered him" (I Cor. 16:2). No difficulty is found if we are honest with ourselves and informed from the New Testament.

Personal: "every one of you lay by him in store, as God hath prospered him (I Cor. 16:2). "Every man according as he purposeth in his heart, so let him give; not grudgingly, or of necessity for God loveth a cheerful giver" (II Cor. 9:7). We reap what we sow in giving. No one should miss giving when the love and faith are present.

Systematic: "upon the first day of the week..." (I Cor. 16:2). Every Lord's Day — Resurrection Day — Easter Anniversary — worship day — a day of giving; no haphazard collections, but calculated setting aside a definite amount: not spasmodic giving on the spur of the moment. The "cheerful-hilarious" giver recognizes God's right to all and therefore plans to give. This is not to pay a debt but to provide that no debt be incurred. This delivers from meanness and dishonesty, whether to keep back or to give beyond to keep up appearances.

Adjusted Perpetually: "as God hath prospered" (I Cor. 16:2). This is in the light of *all* belonging to God. He who watches the treasury is no hard taskmaster and will be no man's debtor. Even as we adjust our spending in the light of material needs and changing income, so we should place this first as an act of faith.

No Need of Collections. Paul was business-like. He made plans and arranged for financial affairs upon the basis of high principle to stand the scrutiny of the world. Sacrilege is not only robbing a church building but putting in the offering that which costs nothing. Whether we tithe or no, the New Testament is clear in teaching that we should give God a proportion of income in recognition that all is His. To be honest with our society obligations for income tax, rent, telephone, insurance, light, water, power, and then rob God by careless giving is the way of spiritual impoverishment and bankruptcy. Genuine givers receive the bounty of God.

IV. The *Principle* of Giving: "fellowship" (II Cor. 8:4). A recognition of *stewardship* is one of our clamant needs in the church. Forced, unwilling, niggardly collections are wrong. But hilarious, joyful, communion-like offerings are pleasing to God and blessed to man. Put giving in the full tide of your spiritual life. What does God wish? What is His heart set upon? At Christmas, before we decide our gifts, we ask: "I wonder what he needs? What would please her?" *That* is the genius of giving: it comes out of love. Let us give our gift and, first of all, give ourselves to the Lord. We are in a holy partnership with Jesus Christ through His church to meet the needs of the world.

> We lose what on ourselves we spend,
> We have as treasure without end,
> Whatever to the Lord we lend,
> Who givest all.

Trench

90. The Bored Money Chest

"Jehoiada the priest took a chest, and bored a hole in the lid of it, and set it beside the altar, on the right side as one cometh into the house of the Lord...."—II Kings 12:9

We need to re-think the Biblical basis of giving and stewardship. This Old Testament story is found in the reign of King Jehoash (II Kings 12:1-15). At his request the Temple was to be repaired, but no one took the responsibility. After a delay of twenty-three years (vs. 6) the king urged the priest, Jehoiada, to undertake the task (vs. 7). The money was given by the people, and the workmen dealt faithfully (vs. 15). The whole story may be read as an example of the principles of giving.

I. At the *threshold* of worship is giving. "He took a chest ... on the right side as one cometh into the house of the Lord...."

Worship is the highest act of the soul. The service of the sanctuary finds expression in several acts. Praise is uplifting as we sing. Prayer is a vital part as we adore and intercede. The ordinances find us responsive by means of the symbols of bread, wine, and water. Preaching is also an essential part of worship. The aim of worship is to "present every man perfect in Christ" (Col. 1:28).

A service would be incomplete if we did not give. The offering is not an "extra," but central in spiritual worship. Naturally we must give ourselves first of all, then money as a means of spiritual grace and faith. Giving in this modern world is wrapped up in the use of money. God is the owner of all, and we are stewards.

The placing of the chest on the right side of the altar was symbolic of worship in sincerity and in truth. Nothing is to be casual or careless. Life is to be dedicated. The first act of worship is giving. He who does not learn to give at the threshold knows nothing of the nature of true worship.

II. At the *heart* of worship is giving. He "bored a hole in the lid of the chest...." The priest's act was pointed and appealing. No one could misunderstand the significance of the bored hole! Worship today needs a blood transfusion of that bored hole. This act should be the time of supreme devotion and love. If we hold on to our money until it possesses us, we have not seen that bored hole. Barnabas saw it, but Ananias did not.

When our Lord stood over the treasury in the Temple, He knew what giving meant to each worshipper. When the money was deposited in the chest, man lost control of it, and God took it. What will God do with it? Upon what errand of the kingdom will it go? Money so given has passed out of restricted use into the wider use to spread the gospel and is a symbol of death and resurrection.

"Money talks," they say. It does. It reveals character. Find out what a man thinks of and does with money and you can tell the kind of man he is. By it a Christian serves God. Not the amount a man possesses determines this: the act of devotion, in the little as well as in much, reveals the heart.

III. At the *climax* of worship is giving. He "took a chest ... and set it beside the altar." How suggestive is the association of the money chest with the altar of sacrifice. Judaism had its altar and priestly offering. Christianity has its cross and the giving of true worship. We have no altar in the New Testament and no repeated sacrifice of the cross. But Paul says, "I ... fill up that which is behind of the afflictions of Christ ... for his body's sake, which is the church" (Col. 1:24). Part of that filling up is in giving of life and money to God.

The tragedy of the church is that we have divorced the money chest from the altar. We have separated what God intended to be together. When the sacrifice begins, then the song of the Lord begins also. The minimum is respectable in man's sight, but hilarious giving spells sacrifice. Christians who object to the mention of money have lost sight of this climax of worship.

The lowered morale and spiritual state of the church may be traced to this neglect of giving beside the altar. Having been unfaithful in the unrighteous mammon, we cannot be trusted with the true riches. A dollar bill is acceptable currency in heaven as in the market place. There are spiritual returns (Luke 16:9). The principle of giving is here. Firstfruits are God's. We must settle what to give as a personal affair, but we must learn to give only in the light of this altar of sacrifice. Without that blood mark upon the dollar bill our giving is not what it should be.

We need to be saved from the spirit which separates chest and altar.

91. Harvest Thanksgiving

"What shall I render unto the Lord for all his benefits toward me? I will take the cup of salvation, and call upon the name of the Lord. I will pay my vows unto the Lord now in the presence of all his people. I will offer to thee the sacrifice of thanksgiving, and will call upon the name of the Lord."

—Psalm 116: 12, 13, 14, 17

Thanksgiving Day in America is a holiday of national observance. Of all the days of the year it is welcomed with a large degree of participation. Then families gather together for reunion; then churches are full of worshippers; then a nation stops its busy life to remember and give thanks.

True thanksgiving is not a note: it is a chord. It is not one of many sounds: it is infinite harmony. The question asked by the psalmist is pertinent. Harvest time and autumn is an occasion and opportunity to reflect upon our blessings and benefits so freely given to us by God.

I. *A Recognition of God.* This is the supreme object in thanksgiving. No life is wealthy if God is left out or crowded to the circumference. We are not impoverished if life is God-centered and controlled.

The Pilgrim Fathers, 1620, settling on the New England shore, knew that they had been providentially brought across the ocean by God's guiding hand. They decided to set apart some time for recollection and thanksgiving. Although no annual day was fixed at the beginning, they were the forerunners of our annual day in publicly acknowledging the providence of God toward them. This day has no other holiday comparable to it. It celebrates no battle, no birthday of some great one, no political revolution. This is no pagan holiday as it consecrates the common things of life to God. It is a family day, with home and children, laughter and games, feasting and making merry. Primarily, it is a day of worship toward God.

The Shorter Catechism indicates the relative importance of thanksgiving in the first question: "What is the chief end of man?" to which the answer is: "Man's chief end is to glorify God and to enjoy Him for ever." Not in things but in God is the true end of life. This is the precursor of gratitude.

II. *A Reception of Blessing.* Blessings cannot be numbered. Consider the "blessednesses" of life (Ps. 1). The godly life knows this to be true, and the natural man may well ponder what he has found in the bundle of life. Note the areas of reception by us:

Consider our *national* blessings. Some lands have no liberty or freedom of conscience. Here the Bible is circulated, worship is unmolested, and freedom of speech is ours. We have voting rights and rights of assembly. Furthermore, ours is a land of a bountiful harvest and abundant natural resources.

Think of our *church* blessings. This is the larger family which meets on this day. Public worship with praise, prayer, reading, sermon, and fellowship inspire us. Lives are redeemed and God comes to us in the Saviour Jesus Christ.

Reflect upon our *individual* blessings. "Forget not all his benefits." Sing the doxology. Health, mental powers, moral and spiritual insight, personal and family joys. Even the hard things pay tribute to divine ends of enrichment for us.

III. *A Rendering of Thanks.* But "how?" The psalmist gives answer for us:

"*I will take the cup. . . .*" Was this the drink offering of ancient ritual? Compare the *Hallel,* Psalms 113-118, of which the psalm in which our text is found is part. These psalms were used at the Passover feast, and in that is the "cup of salvation" which celebrated God's redemption of His people. Christ used it and made it the cup of remembrance in the Lord's Supper. Here is personal confession of faith.

"*I will pay my vows. . . .*" Not harsh words but holy words these. "Make me a captive, Lord, And then I shall be free." Have we any hour in life when we registered a vow but have not kept it? The sin of forgetting before God confronts us. Has God asked us for something which we have withheld?

"*I will offer. . . .*" This sacrifice of thanksgiving is not in singing hymns but the dedication of life. Presenting the body to God brings suffering and testing; but, when the burnt offering begins, then the song of the Lord begins also. The dedicated life is the joyful life. Grief is a hermit, but joy is social.

Everything is an occasion for thanksgiving. If a grace or prayer for eating, why not for other things? handling bread, thanks for the Bread of life; drinking water, thanks for the Water of life; receiving heat and light, thanks for the Light of the world; enjoying health, thanks for Him who is our Holiness; reading a book, thanks for the Word of God; enjoying sleep, thanks for the Watcher who neither slumbers nor sleeps! Banish lament: give thanks.

92. Why Suffering?

"Behold, and see if there be any sorrow like unto my sorrow."
—Lamentations 1:12

This is a perennial question. No one has spoken the last word about it. Why not a world without suffering and calamity? Why are we plagued with disease, handicap, and catastrophe? The critic and cynic who sneer against the Christian view of God and the world tell us of defeatism and fatalism through man's suffering. No one desires the reality of a suffering world. The language of Jeremiah, the prophet, has been used to point up the agony of Him who suffered most of all for man's sin. Compare the various relationships of this theme in the light of revelation.

I. *Suffering and Sin.* The Bible points to the connection. In the mystery of pain some are suffering because of their sins (cf. John 5:14, where Jesus told a man just healed, "Sin no more, lest a worse thing come unto thee"). Evil living brings its entail of disease in mind and body. Behind the agony of man lies this mystery of evil. Part of the solidarity of life lies here. We share in it indirectly and, as in this man's life, directly. Think of the human wrecks in our cities through sin. The fevered brow, the haunted look, the defiled imagination, and the broken body are obvious. Living by the sewers and cesspools of life brings the taint of defilement.

II. *Suffering and Self.* Many suffer because of the acts of others. Heredity and ancestry and family are precious words. They tell us that we are what we are through the inheritance given to us. A clean moral life is worth while, and a good inheritance is invaluable. Others who are handicapped in life may trace back to find out that someone sowed their wild oats or violated the laws of God. The innocent reap the sowing of the sinful. Compare John 9:3, where Jesus gives sight to the blind. The question asked, "Master, who did sin, this man, or his parents, that he was born blind?" posed a dilemma. Jesus did not answer yes or no, but, "Neither hath this man sinned, nor his parents. . . ." Some suffering, then, is not due to others. Our Lord did not explain the mystery in detail, but this case is for the manifestation of the power of God. In other words, never mind the mystery: let us remove the disability.

III. *Suffering and the Saviour.* The mystery that the innocent suffer as well as the guilty leads to this revelation through Christ. Beyond the physical and mental there are the spiritual and moral aspects of pain. Into this suffering world Jesus has entered to share it with us. We live in a world of risk, and we are free to choose. Freedom brings responsibility, and we need not imply that God sends this particular meed of suffering to a life by His direct will. We share with others even as Jesus shared with us. Through the overcoming of some handicap by divine aid and skill given to man others are safeguarded and blessed.

> The healing of His seamless dress
> is by our beds of pain;
> We touch Him in life's throng and press,
> and we are whole again.
>
> **Whittier**

IV. *Suffering and Sacrifice.* The spiritual background of our world leads to this. We should not ask, Why do the innocent suffer? We ought to say, Why does anyone suffer *with God?* God suffers, and that is forgotten. Jesus taught that God lost His rest (of creation) through man's sin and suffering. He is restless until man finds rest. He is "touched with the feeling of our infirmities." "The whole creation groans ... in pain ... until now, waiting. ..." "Our light affliction, which is but for a moment. ..." We suffer, then, in a suffering world, with God, waiting for the day of our perfecting.

V. *Suffering and Satisfaction.* Some pain may be penal; some suffering is disciplinary; but God suffers vicariously through His cross in Christ. There you find the sublimest suffering as it is the innocent for the guilty, the sinless for the sinful. The cross is our guide to find light upon the dark mystery of suffering. Through this suffering we find the way of victory and overcoming.

Suffering may produce the beautiful pattern out of a tangled skein. "The sufferings of this present time are not worthy to be compared with the glory which shall be revealed" (Rom. 8:18). The Christian may "know ... the fellowship of his [Christ's] sufferings" (Phil. 3:10). To the non-Christian, pain is an enigma until the cross is seen. The prophet's lament finds fulfilment perfectly in Christ. To see His sorrow transforms ours.

93. What Is Death?

"Death is swallowed up in victory."—I Corinthians 15:54

The dread of death "is a fearful thing" as Shakespeare said. Weeping and sorrow fill the heart of the bereaved when a loved one enters that "valley of the shadow of death." There are those who do not like to think of it, and so they dismiss it in casual speech and joke. Men are afraid to die. To the ungodly there is no hope beyond, and in that crossing of time into eternity there is nothing but darkness and defeat. "The wages of sin is death." People "through fear of death [are] all their lifetime subject to bondage." What is the Bible view of death?

I. *Death is not the end.* To the Christian there is no terminus of life, but the transition to another stage of life. Death releases the spirit from the limitations of the body here. The Old Testament spoke of death as going down to the grave, being gathered unto the fathers. These indicate the passing of the soul into the life beyond, about which little was known and only in part. The New Testament continues the Old Testament revelation with convictions about the life to come. The Buddhist speaks of the snuffing out of a candle and an extinction. The Christian believes in continuance of life. Special words testify to this truth: "decease, departure, exodus, desiring to be clothed upon, absent from the body, gain, earthly house dissolved." These and other words suggest that in death there is an offering of the soul to God.

II. *Death is the final issue.* Here is the climax of life with its struggle and aspirations — all acts, habits, thoughts — the character is fixed by now. In this we exchange the present life for the unseen and eternal.

Camping is a common experience and brings light upon this incidence of death. "We know that if our earthly house of this tabernacle [tent] were dissolved, we have a building [house] of God, an house not made with hands, eternal" (II Cor. 5:1). In camping we live in a tent without much luxury and subject to limitations. In death, then, we lay aside the tent of the mortal to exchange it for a more settled mode of life in a house of God. Here we camp: there we abide. Here we are pilgrims: there we are settled. Death brings that desired issue of life when the mortal is swallowed up of life immortal.

III. *Death is an exodus.* The departure talked about is the way out of limitation into fulness of life. When Israel was led out of

Egypt and out of bondage by a mighty act of God, that is known as The Exodus. The Book of Exodus sings that victory. There was release from slavery and an entrance upon freedom. Shakespeare wrote, "that dread of something after death, that undiscovered country from whose bourn no traveller returns, puzzles the will" *(Hamlet),* but our Lord Jesus Christ *returned* by resurrection. When He spoke of His approaching death, He used the word for decease or exodus.

Death, then, to Christ was an exodus, a victory. To the Christian it is the same. Here are the "heartaches and the thousand natural shocks that flesh is heir to," but through death we are released from them and find an overflowing life beyond. The Promised Land is ours in the glorious state of everlasting life and joy.

IV. *Death is a beginning.* The "valley of the shadow" of the psalmist is not an end but a beginning. Beyond is the sunshine and pasturage. "To die is gain . . . for . . . to depart and to be with Christ . . . is far better" (Phil. 1:21, 23). Paul wrote about his departure, for which he was ready (II Tim. 4:6-8). Some have given a wrong impression about death by putting into hymns the idea of arriving in a harbor, a ship having sailed the seas and hardly able to make port in safety. What a travesty of Christian belief! Paul's word for "departure" is a sailor's word. The ship is *leaving the harbor.* There is the unmooring from the shore, the lifting of the anchor, and the beginning of the voyage.

Death is like that as we sail out of the harbor and on into the boundless ocean of God's love. In death we are released from the many ropes which tie us to the earthly shore. Now we sail on with the Pilot on board. Tennyson caught this in his "Sunset and evening star, and one clear call for me!" The whole hymn should be read and studied for its insight and meaning.

"It is not death to die" for the Christian. "Whosoever liveth and believeth in me shall never die" (John 11:26). Think of Mr. Valiant-for-Truth in Bunyan's *The Pilgrim's Progress,* who said, "I am going to my Father's." When that day came in death, "so he passed over, and all the trumpets sounded for him on the other side."

94. The Life Beyond

"I go to prepare a place for you."—John 14:2

The human heart would like to know about the future. Beyond death there is a future life, so the Christian affirms. We are not snuffed out like a candle. Our God is the God of the living and not of the dead. Some there are who do not share this faith. Like the Sadducees of old, they deny the resurrection. Our conviction is based upon the fact that Jesus Christ arose from the dead, and therefore we must share in the power of that endless life.

I. *The Aspirations of Men.* These assert that there must be continuance beyond death. An instinct within man craves and hopes for something beyond. Whether they are Christian or not, there are those who would hope for immortality.

II. *The Revelation of the Bible.* The many statements and the suggestive symbols and metaphors give a basis for belief. A glorious state is spoken of as the life of those who live in Christ. He has opened the kingdom of heaven to all believers. He has overcome the sharpness of death. Believing this transforms our faith.

III. *The Affirmations of Faith.* Many and varied are the descriptions of that life.

A Prepared Place. This is part of the Father's house (John 14:2). The universe is that house, and within its vast orbit there are many rooms. Earth and time constitute one. Death opens the door into another room beyond. We pass from the limited to the infinite and from the partial to the complete life. The metaphor may also suggest the eastern oasis in the desert. A caravan finds rest and room and refreshment on the journey. There are many of these "mansions" or resting places.

Progress Beyond. We do not experience the fulness of life now. We anticipate further development. When a symphony concert is held, there is a preparatory stage when the musicians tune up. At that time there are many sounds, sometimes producing discord; but, when the conductor appears, there is obedience to his will and the production of music and harmony. This life is the prelude to that afterlife when the full score will bring progress.

Continuity of Life. The law of the conservation of energy illustrates. The really existing things never perish but only change form. Change of body and estate does not change our spiritual life. Life is the crown awaiting those who die in Christ. When Jesus spoke of the patriarchs, he said, "God is not the God of the dead, but of the living" (Matt. 22:32) . The outward form changes and passes, but the spirit abides unchanging and eternal. What we are here by God's grace and product will be the character we take into the next life.

Identity of Personality. The "I" is not lost through this changing experience. Beyond this shadowy scene of time we shall still be the same person in that world beyond. When Jesus appeared after His resurrection from the dead, He was known to hundreds who saw Him and identified Him. The marks of His person were real. He manifested Himself within a body which was still the same and yet had been transformed. We call it a "spiritual body." This present body suits time, and the spiritual body suits eternity. Recognition will follow in that life to come. Spirit will know spirit and spirit will fellowship with spirit "in Christ."

Perfection and Fulness. No life now is satisfied fully. No experience now is free from fault and sin. Here is incompleteness. Beyond, there is the promise of fulness of life and completeness of expression. Prayer and aspiration here will find their answer then. When we think of the frustrated, handicapped, crippled lives now, we believe that God has planned the better life beyond time.

In that greater life "his servants shall serve him" (Rev. 22:3) . Then our service will be that of perfect freedom and unfettered by earthly limitation. In that fuller life we shall "hunger no more, neither thirst any more" (Rev. 7:16) . Capacity given here will find fulness.

As we ponder the many hints, suggestions, metaphors, symbols, and the plain statements of the New Testament, the mind is filled with the glory and the wonder of that immortal life. Then we shall no longer see through the glass darkly (as an enigma) , for then we shall see face to face. The cynic has said that life is a comedy to him who thinks and a tragedy to him who feels. But the Christian answers that life is a victory for him who believes. And that is the conviction which comes from the belief in that life beyond.

95. Christ Became!

"The Word became...."—John 1:14, R.V.

The redemptive ministry of Jesus finds its focus during the Advent season. Passiontide with its cross and resurrection is the climax of that which began now. In this one word "became" is the secret of the Christian faith. Not man's search for God, but God's search for man is stressed. As a searchlight playing on the New Testament, we trace the truth through this Word.

I. He became *flesh* (John 1:14). "Became flesh" describes how the divine nature took into partnership our human nature. In the union of the two is the one unique personality. The mystery of that coming is unfolded as, not the beginning of something new, but that which existed already having new form.

Bethlehem is the center of the story. Here is no ordinary child born through human will or blood. The virtuous life demands a voluntary birth, and this is what is claimed for Jesus. God overshadowed the virgin-mother and the power of the Highest operated in this Holy Child. God took hold of the race to uplift the race in Christ.

II. He became *poor* (II Cor. 8:9). This is one of the startling truths. Poverty suggests need and lack. Some are born without privilege or standing. Christ as Creator became as many of the sons of men. He who was rich became poor. Consider His riches, and then compare His poverty. In His birth He was poor: "no room for them in the inn": the outhouse was His home. He was dependent upon others during His ministry: "The Son of Man hath nowhere to lay his head." Some poor in goods are proud in heart, and some rich in goods are poor in spirit. Jesus' poverty of life is startling as He enriches all.

III. He became *obedient unto death* (Phil. 2:8). He chose to die, willingly and deliberately. The Son of God became the Servant and lived in humility. Deity laid aside its rights. Self-emptying was not of His nature but in limiting His power. The steps of humiliation are set forth in the context. The climax was the death of the cross. In Rev. 1:18, R.S.V. "I died" is a commentary on this thought. The life of Jesus was in the will of God, and the cross was the final expression of that will.

IV. He became *sin* (II Cor. 5:21). His death cannot be understood apart from this fact. He was no martyr dying for a cause. Here is the Sin Offering of the ages. The sinless became sin. He

201

was both Offerer and Offering. He became what He was not, that we, who were not as He was, might become what He is.

The death of the cross, then, is alone and solitary in its light upon sin. The way to God is by sacrifice. In this is the profound mystery of all, that God took upon Himself our sins. By that death-baptism He destroys sin and releases us from its power and thrall.

V. He became *the author of salvation* (Heb. 5:9). In the days of His flesh Jesus learned obedience by the things He suffered. Through this He was able not to sin and was perfected in spiritual and moral worth of character. Salvation comes as a gift of God to those who obey. Obedience is the organ of spiritual illumination. Salvation is not of works, but is given in grace through the Author or Initiator.

> There was none other good enough,
> To pay the price of sin.
> He only could unlock the gate
> Of heaven, and let us in.

VI. He became *the firstfruits of them that slept* (I Cor. 15:20). After the cross comes the resurrection, and after our release from the prison-house of death comes life everlasting. Because Jesus rose from the dead, we have a guarantee of endless life.

Men are in bondage to death through fear, but now, in Christ, that is gone. Sleep is the suggestive picture of those who have died in this faith: the believers will awaken in the morning. I Corinthians 15:51-52 has it that "we shall not all sleep...." Like a harvest to come, Jesus is the firstfruits of that final day.

VII. He became *the head of the corner* (Acts 4:11). The experts were wrong! They rejected Jesus in their limited vision and unbelief. What had Bethlehem and Nazareth to offer? Now the chief corner stone is seen to be indispensable. "The highest place that heaven affords is His by sovereign right."

So Christ became! In these many phases we trace how He worked on our behalf to bring us to God. One day the whole world will acclaim His right and position because of this fact.

The complement is: "as many as received him, to them gave he the right [R.V.] [authority, Greek] *to become* the sons of God, even to them that believe on his name" (John 1:12).

96. Caricature or Copyright?

"Ye are ... the epistle of Christ ministered by us, written not with ink, but with the Spirit of the living God."

—II Corinthians 3:3

Christianity is Christ received, realized, and reproduced. It is not seen as institutional but individual in expression. Two possibilities are always present: *caricature* — the grotesque representation of a person by overemphasis on some characteristic or trait; *copyright* — the exclusive right to copy the original work. This latter is the normal Christian life. Consider these contrasting possibilities.

I. *Conflict or Contentment?* Paul knew these in his experience of the Christian life.

Romans 7:23-24, "I see another law ... warring against the law of my mind, and bringing me into captivity to the law of sin which is in my members. O wretched man that I am! who shall deliver me ...?" "My own behaviour baffles me" (Phillips translation). Here is a conflict of desire, competing interests, moral struggle. This is typical for many Christians. Is this before or after conversion? There is no true freedom of will so long as self is divided. "Reason" pays homage to the ideal, while "flesh" is dominated by the "law of sin." This creates division, impotence, a miserable condition for Paul.

Philippians 4:11-13 (Moffatt translation), "I have been initiated into the secret for all sorts and conditions of life. . . . in him [Christ] . . . I am able for anything." Here is deliverance by Christ: "He," not "it"; "Christ," not "I." Conflict is conteracted by the Spirit. Romans 8 answers Romans 7. Defeat is no longer necessary. A stabilized life follows. In the changing circumstances of Philippians 4:11-13 Paul can live now in poverty or plenty, difficulty or prosperity.

II. *Stunted Growth or Steady Progress?* Christian living depends upon this principle of life.

I Cor. 3:1-2 — "carnal ... babes ... milk." The marks of milk diet indicate childishness, not growing up. Envying, strife, divisions, and partiality reveal this trait. Schism is evidence of it. Following certain teachers and refusing others is carnal-mindedness. Stunted growth comes from this experience in the church.

II Cor. 3:18; 4:1 (Moffatt translation), "We all mirror the glory of the Lord with face unveiled, and so we being transformed into the same likeness as himself, passing from one glory to another

—for this comes of the Lord the Spirit. Hence, as I hold this ministry by God's mercy to me, I never lose heart in it." The open face (not the covered veil as Moses) brings progressive development and growth through the Spirit. We reflect the object of our devotion in worship. The world doesn't demand perfection but sincerity and truth. Christ is the measure of the stature for us.

III. *Husks or Harvest?* Another phase of spiritual experience in this.

John 15:1-8: "beareth not fruit" (vs. 2) ; "cannot bear . . . of itself" (vs. 4) ; "cast forth" (vs. 6) . The opposite is there in "beareth fruit"; bringeth forth much fruit"; "abide, . . . ask what ye will and it shall be done." Like for the prodigal in Luke 15, there can be husks through self-life and self-will in disobedience.

John 12:24: "Except a corn of wheat fall into the ground and die, it abideth alone: but if it die, it bringeth forth much fruit [harvest]." In this striking passage our Lord gives the principle of growth: death to self and sin; losing your life for His sake; pruning and suffering for fruit-bearing and harvest.

IV. *Hypocrisy or Holiness?* Counterfeit Christianity is possible in the light of the genuine. James 4:4, "Ye adulterers and adulteresses, know ye not that the friendship of the world is enmity with God?" What do we mean by "worldliness"? Is this a spirit which besets the Christian life? When and how are we worldly? Does it consist in "Don't go there" and "Don't do that"? What constitutes a secular mind in the church?

I Peter I:15, "As he which hath called you is holy, so be ye holy in all manner of conversation [living, R.V.]." I Thessalonians 5:23, "The very God of peace sanctify you wholly; and I pray God your whole spirit and soul and body be preserved blameless. . . . Faithful is he that calleth you, who also will do it." Does faith rise to this level? Do we live on this plane? I Peter 3:15 speaks of sanctifying Christ as Lord of life. II Peter 1:8-10, "Admonish not to forget the cleansing." These and many other passages teach that the life we now must live be that of holiness (separation unto God), dedication (doing God's will), and living blamelessly in God's sight.

I Corinthians 10:33—11:1 (Moffatt translation) sums up: "Such is my own rule, to satisfy all men in all points, aiming not at my own advantage but at the advantage of the greater number — at their salvation. Copy me, *as I copy Christ.*" (Mimic me.)

The caricature misrepresents: the copyright reproduces. We live within these alternatives as Christians.

97. The Bible–Not Bound

"According to my gospel:...I suffer trouble,...even unto bonds; but the word of God is not bound."—II Timothy 2:8-9

This is a true word, for no person or power can thwart the divine purpose of God through the Bible. In Paul's day he suffered persecution and imprisonment. Then he was bound according to his enemies, yet God overruled to use him even in prison to spread the "good news." The dictatorship of that day sought to curtail the Christian message, but God saw to it that the word of God was unbound.

I. *In the first century* this was true. As in Paul's experience from a prison in Rome, the word of God was freely circulated. The providence that he was a prisoner gave him time and leisure to write to his friends and converts in various cities. These Letters were missionary letters and carried eternal truths.

When Stephen was stoned and Herod killed James and imprisoned Peter (Acts 8:1; 12:1-3), the word of God was not curtailed. When John was exiled to lonely Patmos, it gave him the opportunity of visions of Christ and His kingdom. His book of the Revelation is the answer to those who would stamp out the word of God.

II. *In other periods of history* this continued. We speak of the Dark Ages of the middle centuries before the Reformation. The binding of the Bible and the suppression of the word of God seemed complete and final. But the Renaissance and the Reformation unbound the book! Wyclif, Tyndale, Coverdale, Erasmus, Luther, Calvin, and Knox are names which speak of its unbinding from religious bondage.

In 1538 the royal injunction issued through Chancellor Thomas Cromwell ordered a copy of the Bible to be placed in every English parish church for the use of the common people: "Item, that ye discourage no man pryvely or apertly from the reading or hearing of the same Bible, but shall expresslye provoke, stere, and exhorte every parsone to rede the same, as that whyche ys the verye lively Worde of God...." In an age of romance and adventure, of great achievement, this was the outstanding event to influence the history and character of the English-speaking world. Although chained to a reading desk, the Bible was an unbound book. When Bishop Tonstal of London bought and burned Tyndale's consignments of New Testaments, Tyndale used the money to publish more and better copies.

III. *During the last century* the unbinding continued. Some of the criticism of the Bible has led many to imagine the Bible to be out of date and bound. Although no one was forbidden to read the Bible, in an age of reason and freedom for all, there were those who sought to blanket it by a spurious friendship, a false rationalism, and an unfair criticism, until multitudes looked upon the Bible as in fetters and untrustworthy. But God has unbound the book during recent decades through the science of archaeology.

Among the important discoveries is the Dead Sea Scrolls with their witness to the text of the Bible. The early history of Israel as written in the beginning of the Bible was questioned for a long time as to its veracity. The assumption was that these stories were written much later than the events because the art of writing was supposed to have been later. But in 1888 the Tel Amarna Tablets were found; the Code of Hammurabi in 1902; and later the Lachish Letters: these testify to the historicity of the events in the Bible and that the ancient peoples possessed the art of writing, including Moses.

Leonard Woolley of Oxford unearthed evidences of the Flood in Mesopotamia (Iraq), and Professor Garstang of Liverpool found the site of Jericho to tell of the history of Israel in Joshua's day. By a turn of the spade God unbinds the book. Communist Russia bound the Bible in its atheism, but the British Museum unbinds it by buying from the Communists the Codex Sinaiticus. Dictators may ban the book, but Bible Societies unbind it in millions of copies.

IV. The Bible is unbound *today*. Why? Because it is *divine* — "God-breathed." An eternal quality reposes in its words. It is also *living* — nothing can stop its power to reveal, quicken, and redeem. It also *saves* — the written word reveals God in Christ as the Word of God. What if we *bind* the Book by misuse or disuse? What if we neglect it? We have copies of the Bible: we need only to read and mark and learn from it lest we bind it. God's Spirit unbinds it for the trusting and obedient heart.

98. My Favorite Book

"Thy testimonies are wonderful."—Psalm 119:129

If by my favorite book you mean the book that is oftenest in my hands, the book that most frequently occupies my mind, I can have only one certain answer — the Bible. Like many others brought up within the Christian influence, I have known it, more or less, from my childhood up; but in recent years I have studied it regularly. During that time I must have read it many times and made references to it more than to any other book. Frequently I have read a Gospel or a Letter or a book of a prophet at a sitting. I have found it to be the key to nearly all I have been able to learn about life. The psalmist acclaims what is in mind as personal testimony.

I. Wonderful in *Compilation*. We are surprised at the magnitude of the Bible's greatness and wonder. What is the Bible? How was it formed? It is not one book, but sixty-six books — but sixty-six making a divine library. The late Lord Rosebery said: "Libraries are the cemeteries of dead books." He was referring to much that is on the shelves of public institutions; but the Bible is not described like that. Over a period of some 1,500 years this ancient book developed until its 66 parts were interwoven and accepted by the judgment and conscience of the church as God's final book for man. This book is the costliest we possess and the most valuable. Not alone in money is it valued, but in the life and labor of those who sacrificed to give us this priceless heritage. Well-known figures in history and unknown individuals shared in this task. They are the people "of whom the world was not worthy" (Heb. 11:38). The story of writing, copying, translating, printing, selling, giving, and dying is outstanding. In this is an astounding achievement of faith. God's Spirit is behind the work.

II. Wonderful in *Comparison*. When men of letters and culture compare the Bible with other books, there is this testimony concerning the book of books. The greatest of all translations is the English Bible. It is even more than that: it is the greatest of English books, the first of English classics, the source of the finest influence upon English character and speech. Apart from questions of dogma and theology, the Bible has all the marks of a classic. Its themes are those of perpetual concern in great literature: God, man, or the universe.

In comparison to other books the Bible lasts and endures. Copies, in whole or part, are being distributed by the million and in over

207

1,100 languages and dialects. The Bible also inspires other books and becomes the sourcebook for the finest thought and study of men's minds. A man is not really educated or cultured unless he has some knowledge of the Bible.

III. Wonderful in *Communication.* This is the glory of the Bible. The message or content of the Bible surpasses all others. The impact of it upon the habits and practices of men is significant. Advance in our civilization can be traced to the power of the Bible. When the Bible has been given its place, the people have received an abiding legacy of truth and moral idealism. Freedom and liberty are meaningless words unless they come from the Bible.

Again, the Bible communicates a dynamic quality of moral life and standards. Conversions result from this book. Missionary societies and Bible societies testify to the wonder-working power of the Bible to reach the minds of men everywhere. There is an explosive quality in the Bible, a dynamic of release from sin, and the empowering of the will for righteous living.

The Bible produces results in that God acts through the book. The story of redemption is fully unfolded here. Just as the sun is central to the solar system, so Christ is central in revelation. "In the volume of the book it is written of Me" (Heb. 10:7).

IV. Wonderful in *Certitude.* Nowhere else is there found the note of certainty and assurance for man's spirit. The Bible bears the authentic stamp of the divine. It is the inspired book, and its revelation guarantees its inspiration to be unique. The one thing sure is the vision of God in Christ. When you enjoy the sunshine, you do not doubt the sun. He who has met Jesus Christ knows that this is *God's book.*

This is the book of God and the book of man. Man sees himself in sin, then finds God in grace. Christ honored the Bible of His day and quoted from it out of respect and memory. We do well to follow His example by using this book to the full.

The one thing certain about the Bible is its power to transform us.

99. The Illimitable Things

"Thanks be unto God for his unspeakable gift."
—II Corinthians 9:15

If wonder is the beginning of worship, it is not surprising that the worshipper struggles imperfectly to express the deepest things of the inner life. Language is strained to breaking point to describe spiritual experience. Here is where our guides in the Bible use hyperbole, which concentrates attention on some single feature and exaggerates it. The appeal is to our love of surprise. Statements are made in contrast to our ordinary experience. Several are found in the New Testament in this light.

I. *The world is too small.* "There are also many other things which Jesus did, the which, if they should be written every one, I suppose that even the world itself could not contain the books that should be written" (John 21:25). What a wealth of imagination — "the world . . . the books." Who has ever attemtped to find out the total world's literature? Limit this inquiry to books about the Christian faith and its Founder. Consult the British Museum, London, with its thousands of volumes and the treasures in the Library of Congress, Washington, D.C., as well as the libraries of the world. Specialize in titles about Jesus and a life task begins. Computation is staggering. Or take the output of the Bible societies since 1808 with their printing of Scriptures in over one thousand languages and dialects and the millions of copies circulated. The reason is the fragmentariness of the records of our Lord's life and ministry. Four brief extracts, sketches, tracts, are all we have; yet these are sufficient for salvation and life. John adds this word in the Fourth Gospel because the Life of lives is exhaustless, unfinished, because Christ is alive and working now. We add the witness of the church in all ages since. Who is able to write or complete that greatest of all lives or tell its influence? We deal with the *Eternal.*

II. *The time is too short.* "And what shall I more say? for the time would fail me to tell of . . . [those] . . . of whom the world was not worthy" (Heb. 11:32). Here is no story of a Mr. Sloth or Mr. Sluggard, but a Mr. Valiant-for-Truth, Mr. Greatheart, and Mr. Faithful. The honor roll of heroes and heroines of faith is selective and not complete. It is from a past age and yet leaves room for all ages. The outer garment of reputation is laid aside for the inner garb of character. These are the people who count in the making of history: those who walked with God (Enoch); some dead, yet speaking (Abel); those who go out not knowing where (Abraham): but all in faith. Faith is seen as the principle of life and action. We are surrounded by a vast array of witnesses who bear testimony to the power that shapes the destiny of men and nations. If this story could be pieced together as a whole and in mosaic, the assembled would find that time was all too short to tell the story of God's mighty acts in saving and redeeming mankind. We deal with the *boundless.*

III. *Language is too straitened.* "Eye hath not seen, nor ear heard, neither have entered into the heart of man, the things which God hath prepared for them that love him. But God hath revealed them unto us by his Spirit" (I Cor. 2:9-10).

The New Testament traffics in ideas which are eternal and spiritual. Human speech is limited to express the glories of total Christian experience. What God has begun here will one day be brought to perfection and fulness. Finite communication is one of the difficulties of speech, whether by radio, television, writing, or preaching: so Paul found as he struggled to translate the divine message in the first century. Bible translations are an attempt to get back to the original language used in order to find the best modern word to communicate the eternal truth. Often translators paraphrase instead of translate!

Notice some of the ways in which Paul endeavored to remint old words and ideas and how new words in his day were the vehicle of truth. Expressing the inexpressible is never an easy task, as these show: "The love of Christ . . . passeth knowledge" (Eph. 3:19). Think of the length, breadth, height, and depth of love transcending human love (vs. 18). "The peace of God which passeth all understanding" (Phil 4:7). God's peace is beyond man's understanding, superior in rank and excellence. "The unsearchable riches of Christ" (Eph. 3:8). Here is fathomless wealth untraced out by God, illimitable treasure.

Christ is not exhausted by our interpretations of Him or by any one group or age. He is *of the ages.* One day we shall know, but now we know the *Illimitable is true.*

> Oh could I tell ye surely would believe it!
> Oh could I only say what I have seen!
> How should I tell or how can ye receive it,
> How, till he bringeth you where I have been?
>   **Frederic W. H. Myers,** Saint Paul

100. Seeing the Unseen

"Open his eyes, that he may see."—II Kings 6:17

Elisha's young servant was perplexed, fearful, and questioning. It was a time of crisis and conflict. The answer of the prophet gave evidence of an assurance in the reality of the Unseen. To see the unseen hosts of God when in danger is a strength for endurance and courage.

I. *The Things Seen.* These are the temporal and transient, the earthly, material things. They relate to the whole of human life, in terms of armies, difficulties, trouble, sorrow, trial, fears, half-heartedness, dangers. The young man saw these things in the surrounding host of the Syrian army, but then he didn't see everything! "How shall we do?" He saw the danger but not deliverance. He saw armies but not angels. He saw the difficulties of human resources but not the opportunity of divine reserves. He could calculate, but his arithmetic was not within the dimensions of heavenly reckoning.

II. *The Prayer of Elisha.* Elisha did not attempt to encourage the youth by some new strategy. He had recourse to prayer, the evidence that he was a true prophet. Elisha saw the armies also, just like his servant, but he saw much more, and he knew much more: he knew what to do.

God's way of replenishing the diminishing power of His servant was not by an increase of material or earthly powers but by the vision of the eternal and the unseen. There was no change in God but in His servant. In nature the powers of electricity, coal, radium, radio, and atomic energy were always there for ages of time, but man had not found them.

Elisha did not pray for an army to come: the *unseen host* was there already. The manifestation, not the presence, of the angels was the miracle. Many things present now are hidden from us because we are not ready for the opened eyes. There is a wise and beneficent hiding by God. There is more in the universe than sea and sky; more in suffering than pain and sting; more in the Bible than chapters and verses; more in the church than singing and preaching.

The prayer to "open the young man's eyes" is vital. It was like the experience of Hagar when the word came, "Thou God. seest me." Job also cried, "Now mine eyes see Thee." When Latimer and Ridley went to the stake in England, Ridley said to Latimer, "Play the man: we shall this day light a torch. . . ." Tyndale also prayed, "Open the King of England's eyes." The answer came in 1611 with the translation of the King James Version of the Bible, destined to be the English Classic and the book for millions.

III. *The Answer to Prayer.* The young man sees the unseen. God's hosts are invisible, silent, but not unreal. No noise is heard in the awareness of their presence. Surrounding Elisha and his servant, they shared God's protecting power. No unreality here as one spirit with us is the promise of a host. Cf. Hebrews 12:1, R.S.V., "surrounded by . . . a cloud of witnesses." We believe that the redeemed are not dead but alive and active even as Moses and Elijah were with Christ on the Mount of Transfiguration. Our Lord appeared in the upper room.

The church today is not alone in its militant struggle. We are surrounded by the unseen hosts of the invisible and triumphant church. As we worship we are with not only those whom we see: we are joined with the unseen church in worship. The whole church is one. Often a Christian faints and loses heart as he forgets this. Missionaries fail when dispirited. An army without spirit is defeated before the engagement. The army of Syria was mighty, but the unseen host of God smote it with blindness. In 1588 the Armada of Spain swept upon England to enforce Romanism and defeat Protestantism, but the unseen host of God smote it with storm and wind. Napoleon marched to conquer all of Europe, but the unseen host of God smote his men with snow and cold. God's armies are silent but powerful.

IV. *The Universal Need to Pray.* This prayer especially is for our day. The world says, "Seeing is believing." The gospel says, "Believing is seeing." This redeems the ordinary, glorifies the commonplace, and brings hope and courage to endure. Fear goes, and faith sings in triumph. "They that are with us are more than they that are with them." The statesman Elisha need not fear to do the right. The businessman can be honest. The youth can dare to stand for purity and right.

The opened eyes relate to the Bible, the church, the Christ. *He* is "the Master light of all our seeing." As Captain of the Lord's Host, there is spiritual convoy in temptation and conflict, the hosts of fire and light.

101. Christmas – Message and Miracle

"I bring you good tidings."—Luke 2:10
"This shall be a sign unto you."—Luke 2:12

The art of keeping Christmas is to live in the light of our Saviour's advent. What a difference if He had not come! All our joys and privileges can be traced to His coming among men. Bethlehem is not merely a town in Palestine but:

> The place where God was homeless,
> And all men at home.

Christianity is bounded by Bethlehem and Calvary. At the beginning there was the cry of a Babe in a crib: at the end there was the cry of a Man on a cross. Christmas is without meaning unless we understand this relationship. The insidious peril of our time is that we leave Christ out of Christmas. We give our gifts and receive them, but do we give place for God's gift of a Saviour?

Charles Dickens said: "I will honor Christmas in my heart and try to keep it all the year. I will live in the past, the present, and the future. The spirits of all three shall strive within me. I will not rub out the lessons that they teach me." Let us seek to "rub in" some of the abiding truths revealed at Christmas.

I. *Message:* "I bring you good tidings of great joy, which shall be to all people. For unto you is born this day in the city of David a Saviour, which is Christ the Lord" (Luke 2:10-11).

The wonder and glory of this season bursts upon us, as it did long ago, with excitement and glory. At the time of Jesus' birth in the quietness of the outhouse of the inn, Mary and Joseph were aware of the divine presence overshadowing them. Rightly we sing the German carol, "Stille Nacht," or "Holy Night." There was a stillness and holy quietness there.

But outside all was different according to the Gospel accounts. The *shepherds* in the field were aroused and startled by the glory of God which shone upon them, and they were filled with fear and awe. An *angel* messenger communicated to them the message of Christ's coming. At the same time *a choir* of heaven sang the first Christmas song and carol in praise to God for what had happened. With that background of ravishing music the shepherds hurried to Bethlehem to see for themselves what had transpired. Haste, excitement, movement, drama – all are here.

The *message,* then, is clear. The gospel is centered in this event and word. *Joy* to the world was announced. Good tidings were *for all people.* God's *Saviour* had come, and He was the Anointed of God and the only *Lord* of life. What a message to transform life and destiny! Each word and phrase is pregnant with meaning and message.

II. *Miracle:* "This shall be a sign unto you" (Luke 2:12). The sense of the miraculous is present. This is most reasonable and right when we know the Person and the deeds of the One who makes superlative claims. The unusual life postulates a unique birth. It was natural and voluntary, but it was also above-the-natural and virgin. The virtue and power of that supreme Life demands an unusual entrance upon time which speaks of pre-existence. This is the testimony of the New Testament. The fact of Christ requires the factor of miracle or wonder or sign. This is the claim of Christmas. Our hymns and carols (recall them by name and line) are empty and void if we lose this sense of wonder through the miracle of Bethlehem. The angelic word stressed the fact that the coming of Jesus was a "sign."

What Luke writes is confirmed by John in the Gospel of his name (1:14, R.V. — "The Word became flesh, and dwelt among us"). Christmas cannot be understood apart from this miracle of miracles. Here the glory of God displays itself in a human life. God Himself has entered into our life. The glory flashes and flames across the ages in grace and truth. As the divine Wisdom or Reason, as the Mind and Spirit behind all that is known, this Person is the Key to unlock the mysteries of life and eternity.

All truth finds its focus in Christ. He claimed to be *the Truth.* As the Truth He rebukes our pride, our prejudice, our passions. He separates even as He would save in grace. Truth divides even as grace draws. Truth winnows even as grace woos. Truth scorches our sin even as grace mellows. Truth tells of the Star, pointing to the incarnation; and grace tells of the cross, pointing to our redemption. Grace and truth are one in this Child born at Bethlehem.

The sign at Christmas was the Babe in weakness. God came, not in pomp and might, but in lowliness and humility. His wisdom and way are not as men.

> I know not how that Bethlehem's Babe
> Could in the Godhead be;
> I only know the Manger Child
> Has brought God's life to me.
>
> **H. W. Farrington**

102. Christmas –
Mystery and Mercy

"Great is the mystery of godliness."—I Timothy 3:16
"Through the tender mercy of our God."—Luke 1:78

Preaching at Christmas is inspiring to both preacher and hearer. The simplicity of the message and the note of expectancy abound. Divine proclamation is allied to matchless music and incomparable song. With such a background the gospel is not difficult to proclaim. All a preacher needs to do is to open his heart and mind and pour out what has been stored up for years through meditation and experience. Yet this is the time to stress also the wonder and glory and the mystery and mercy of God.

I. *Mystery:* "Great is the mystery of godliness: God was manifest in the flesh" (I Tim. 3:16). Here is the supreme mystery of the ages. Without a sense of mystery we are never awed and thus we do not engage in the highest acts of true worship. The advent of Jesus is different from the birth of any other child. A deep and abiding mystery overshadows His coming. It is veiled in humility and yet shrouded in glory. Neither the discoveries of nature nor the gropings of the mind could probe this strange birth. Its secrets are the disclosure of revelation. The profound influence and power exerted by Jesus Christ throughout the centuries cannot be explained by natural causes. Mystery surrounds the first Christmas. God conceals Himself even as He reveals. He veils His secret ways even as He sets forth His grace.

> I cannot tell why He whom angels worship
> Should set His love upon the sons of men,
> Or why as Shepherd He should seek the wanderers
> And bring them back, I know not how or when.
> But this I know, that He was born of Mary,
> When Bethlehem's stable was His only home,
> And that at Nazareth He lived and labored,
> And so the Saviour, Saviour of the world is come.

So W. Y. Fullerton portrayed this truth in a poem destined to take its place among the abiding hymns of Christmastide.

No one can understand the significance of Christmas until we see the mystery of Christ's coming as the coming of *God* into human life to redeem us. That God chose this way and means to demonstrate His concern and love' for sinning man is the hidden secret of the ages before Christmas and has become the mystery of the ages since. "God was in Christ." Thus we should emphasize the *Holy* Christmas rather than the Happy or Merry Christmas, for joy issues from the holy. The central figure at Bethlehem is not Joseph or Mary or the shepherds or the angels or the wise men, but the Holy Child. The angelic salutation to the mother of Jesus was, "The Holy Ghost shall come upon thee, and the power of the Highest shall overshadow thee: therefore also that *holy* thing which shall be born of thee shall be called the Son of God" (Luke 1:35).

II. *Mercy:* "The tender mercy of our God; whereby the day-spring from on high hath visited us" (Luke 1:78). Associated with message, miracle, and mystery is mercy. This is one of our needs in a world of hatred, cruelty, lust, and tyranny. God is not a despot but "the God and Father of our Lord Jesus Christ" (Eph. 1:3). That is why we know Christmas to be the birthday of God's *mercy* to sinning people. Christ came to remove our sins. As *Saviour* He saves and redeems; He forgives and pardons. Christmas is the time to proclaim the gospel. That old English word came from the root signifying "God spelling out." He spelled out His love and mercy, and thus the gospel is good news indeed!

> I cannot tell how patiently He suffered
>   When with His peace He graced this place of tears,
> Or how upon the Cross His heart was broken,
>   The crown of pain to three and thirty years.
> But this I know, He heals the broken-hearted,
>   And stays their sins and calms their lurking fear,
> And lifts the burden from the heavy-laden,
>   And so the Saviour, Saviour of the world is here.

In a lawless world there is no peace for nations or individuals until we welcome the Saviour. It is not enough to sing "Peace on earth and good will to men" until first of all we become men of good will. Good will comes when we bow to God's will. His will is holy. It is the will displayed in the Christ of Bethlehem as the only Saviour of men. He came to do God's will, and in it was the choice of the cross. The cross deals with our sin, which disrupts life and brings trouble and misery. There at the cross we see the full meaning of the message of Christmas. There *mercy* is poured out to all who have sinned. That is God's Christmas gift to the children of men. Stress, then, again the eternal mystery and proclaim the mercy of God.

103. Why the Long Road?

"And it came to pass, when Pharoah had let the people go, that God led them not through the way of the land of the Philistines, although that was near; ... but God led the people about, through the way of the wilderness of the Red sea...."
—Exodus 13:17, 18

At the end of a journey or at the beginning of one we are prone to estimate the length of it and sometimes wonder why it is so long. The end of the year or the beginning of a new year are times when this mood is upon us. Providence is the name we give to that which is mysterious and unknown, believing that God is in it when the road of life is long and difficult. Like the Israelites, we learn much from mixed experiences of life.

I. *The Way of God's Guidance.* That God led them is evidence that His guidance was not only offered and promised but carried through under certain conditions. It suggests that in life there is a plan and a purpose. That He did not lead them by the way of the Philistines indicates that they were not ready to meet the exacting demands of that way. In spite of delay and apparent hindrance of the circuitous route, this route brought enrichment and new strength. The short cut was barred, and the long road opened out possibilities of education and training to meet the future. The shortest way is not necessarily the nearest to the goal. This is true in education and evident in life.

The measure of a life is not in the years lived but in the crises met and overcome. The destination and the end of the road are more important than the mileage covered.

Delay and disappointment are not always denials of God's love. Barriers may prove to be benedictions and hindrances helps.

Small nations which have struggled with their limitations often exert power for world influence beyond their size.

Thomas Carlyle suffered poverty in youth but testified that its pressure gave him moral sinews of steel.

An obstacle race will bring out in the runner that "extra" grit and stamina. Storms are the training for sailors to master the sea. The cross is the way to the crown.

John Bunyan knew the long road in prison for twelve years, but then he wrote the immortal books. The church has advanced by failure, opposition, tears, sacrifice, delays, and patient discipline. The Philistines may bar the way which seems the quickest way, but one day their champion Goliath will be slain by a stripling David.

II. *The Will of God's Providence.* Behind this is the miracle of divine surprises. In Egypt the Israelites were slaves, without order and an easy prey to the fighting Philistines. They were not ready for the Promised Land. They required a leader, a law, and a lesson in trusting God. The change of route was important, but the change in themselves was more so.

In the long road there was the bitterness of Marah, the disappointment of Rephidim, the sweetness of Elim, and the revelation of Sinai. By these "many mansions" or "resting places" they came to a new outlook upon God and life. Manna is preferred to the fleshpots of Egypt. The wilderness strips of pride, self-sufficiency, and self-glory. Instead of the haphazard going of a horde of slaves, undisciplined, unregulated, Israel went up to their new home "harnessed" and orderly as an army in their new-found strength.

God's providence for life is supreme. To find out God's will through the long road of testing and training is worth while. Paul entered Asia with the gospel, but God led him by the long road in Europe and the writings of the prison. David Livingstone sought to go to China, but God led him by the long road and Africa. Adoniram Judson endeavored to enter India, but God led him by the long road and Burma.

Thus we learn that the best way is not always the shortest. It is not by uncontrolled speed but by safe driving that we progress. Our Lord's life was that of the long road. Thirty years in silence prepared for three and a half years' public ministry. God took the long road in revealing His mind and will through the Bible. Over fifteen hundred years and through many different writers under the control of His Spirit He gave the word of truth to the world.

What do we find on the long road? That depends upon our attitude, either of faith or faithlessness. One certainty is the witness on the road of the pillar of cloud by day and the pillar of fire by night. Harry Lauder sang, "When I come to the end of the road. . . ." A greater, Our Lord, promised that, on the long road, "lo, I am with you alway."

104. Time and Eternity

"He [God] hath made every thing beautiful in his time: also He hath set the world in their heart."—Ecclesiastes 3:11

The end of the year is an occasion for retrospect and recollection. Custom has so ordered our lives that we are given to reflection and resolution. More important, however, than the hackneyed good wishes in leaving the old for the new is to ponder the wise man's words of the text. More people give thought and energy to time and to eternity lest they be thought "other-worldly." But actually we are living in the light of eternity. These two words sum up the contrasting ways and views of life.

I. *Contrast?* In the circle of time we are near the chaplet of eternity. Man's mortality is swallowed up in immortality. From December to January is a short step, but our outlook is affected by the contrast. The last month and the end of the year is linked with the first month and the beginning of the new year. We compare the tried and known way behind and the unknown pathway ahead. The two come startlingly close together. Men build houses and dig graves. Time speaks of the sorrows and insecurities of life, eternity tells of a new song and a hope. In this life there are meetings and good byes, change and decay; beyond, reunions and eternal beginnings.

II. *Complement?* We may think of these as a necessity one to another. One without the other is incomplete. Life here is probation and schooling; hereafter is completion and fulfilment. Time strips away the limitations of life, and eternity clothes us with the garments of destiny. Seed sown is garnered in harvest. Under the winter snow there is seeming death but actually the promise of resurrection life. "To every thing there is a season, and a time to every purpose under the heaven." Days, weeks, months, years, the seasons follow regularly. The generations rise and pass away in the rhythm of God's order.

III. *Crowning?* Many fail because they lack direction; they do not know their goal. Men pursue the passing things and search for idols without finding the lasting and the permanent. Eternity must crown time if there is to be meaning and purpose to all our strivings and hopes.

The weekly magazine *Time* gives a digest of this mortal life in the subjects of the Index: Army, Art, Books, Business, Cinema, Education, Letters, Medicine, Milestones, Miscellany, Music,

People, Press, Radio, Religion, Science, Theatre. These are the interests of time. The race is one: what of the goal eternity?

IV. *Certainty?* Is eternity given to promise what we miss in time? Some live for time and deny the promise of eternity. Some are unsure and disbelieve in an after life. No one has a lease on time. "Ye ... say, to day ... we will go into such a city ... buy ... sell ... get gain: whereas ye know not what shall be on the morrow. For what is your life? ... a vapor, that ... vanisheth...." (Ja. 4:13-14). Compare the man who built his barns and said, "Soul, thou hast much goods laid up for many years; take thine ease ..." (Luke 12:16-21).

Time seems near and eternity remote to some. But a Shakespeare in *Hamlet* spoke of "that sleep of death ... that dread of something after death...." Jesus returned from that "undiscovered country" and gave us the promise of everlasting life: "I am the resurrection, and the life; he that believeth in me, though he were dead, yet shall he live" (John 11:25). See also Revelation 1:18.

V. *Crux?* The Christian gospel speaks of life now in time, and urges preparation for the life to come in eternity. The Gospels tell of two states after death, one of bliss and the other of loss. How many give thought to the life beyond? With life and time so brief, we ought to think seriously of eternity. What preparation is made for that other state? Men make their wills for time, but few write one for eternity. The final audit is coming, and it will matter then what we have done with God's Son in this time. Life will be judged. Jesus is the final Arbiter of destiny. His cross and resurrection indicate that. He sifts and separates even as He saves. He speaks of the separation of tares from wheat and the foolish from the wise; and of a great gulf fixed. Time is matched by eternity. God has set this capacity and knowledge in our hearts, the sense of mystery, the awareness of the infinite and the beyond. Where will you spend eternity is an agelong question.

INDEX

Topical

Textual Index

Date Due

DEC 14 '73			
SEP 13 '78			
F			
SEP 14 '77			
DEC 13 '77			
OCT 3 78			
FEB 25 '80			